Edward Winslow's English Origins

Liam Donnelly

Volume One: The Road to Kempsey

Published May 2022

ISBN 978-0-9576913-4-6

First Edition, First Impression May 2022

Edited, designed and prepared for printing by the author.

Preface

Governor Edward Winslow, a significant figure of US history, was baptised in Droitwich, Worcestershire before his schooling in Worcester and a printing apprenticeship in London.

Unhappy with the prevailing political and religious *status quo,* Edward left England in 1617 to join the English Separatist church in Leiden, Holland where he swiftly rose to prominence. By June 1620, along with fellow signatories Samuel Fuller, William Bradford, Isaac Allerton and William Brewster, Edward established terms for the Pilgrims' expedition to North America, eventually making landfall in Plymouth Massachusetts in November the same year. The *Mayflower Compact* was immediately signed on arrival, defining the settlers' terms of governance within a framework of allegiance to the English Crown, and its fundamental significance was spelt out in 1920 by Massachusetts Governor and later US President, Calvin Coolidge:

> They drew up a form of government which has been designated as the first real constitution of modern times. It was democratic, an acknowledgment of liberty under law and order and the giving to each person the right to participate in the government, while they promised to be obedient to the laws.

Edward Winslow has rightly earned a place of pre-eminence and renown among the founding fathers of the United States. He stands as one of the leaders of the proto-governance of the USA. A prominent intermediary between the settlers and the English authorities, Winslow served three terms as Governor, and by 1643 had become one of the commissioners of the *United Colonies of New England.* Working for *Lord Protector* Oliver Cromwell in 1646, Edward Winslow was destined never to see his Plymouth Colony community again; leading a British expedition to the West Indies in 1654, Edward Winslow died of sickness, and was buried at sea.

Genealogists have struggled for perhaps two centuries to trace Edward's English origins. In the 1870s US historian David Holton was expressing optimism that soon *enough material would be assembled to reach consensus,* but by 1985 Gene Stratton grimly observed that not even the identity of Edward Winslow's grandfather could be determined with certainty.

Maybe it is not so bleak. Re-examination of extant historical records for this study has revealed the scale of a previously unquantified problem:

Preface

fundamental flaws and significant omissions have blighted objective appraisal of the Winslows' history. Accordingly, the first two chapters of this work attempt to set the record straight by addressing these errors and omissions, while introducing new and important Winslow material of which Holton was probably unaware. Chapter 3 explores the timelines for individual Winslow family members to ensure that each is correctly identified from within the primary reference materials. Chapter 4 combines this data with secondary and other circumstantial evidence to explain how and why Winslow family members had reached Kempsey by 1432, and what had attracted them there.

The Winslow history uncovered by this research is surprising. The family operated in royal circles as well as in the judiciary and the City of London gilds, and were prominent landholders. Because of his meritorious service, one Winslow received a royal pardon for a homicide; another was visited by the king's physician after a calamitous episode with his sword; another, excommunicated by the archbishop of Canterbury, simply bypassed both the archbishop and his King, and took his case direct to the Pope. What is even more extraordinary from the findings of the research conducted is confirmation the prominent place that the Winslow family occupied in the social network of medieval England, much evidence for which is covered in this volume. Further evidence to be presented in Volume 2 will establish the post-1250 familial descent beyond 1432 and provide new details of the family charts.

The original plan had always been to cover the entire narrative to 1660 in a single volume; but elapse of time has dictated otherwise. So far the research undertaken has lasted fifteen years; and some further corroboration of evidence will be necessary before Volume 2 appears. Publication at this stage will facilitate critical appraisal and review ahead of the publication of the rest of the base data. My particular thanks in this regard are extended to Craig Failor and his team of Judy Quinn and Kathy Myers from the Winslow Heritage Society, all of whom have been especially supportive.

Others who have offered support and encouragement for publication of this book include the late Dr Tim Ryder, Classical scholar and historian. Several academic Institutions have provided access resources, notably Cambridge University Library and the Bodleian Rare Manuscripts team at Oxford, along with Cambridge Antiquarian Society, Buckinghamshire Archaeological Society and Buckinghamshire Record Society. My thanks to them all, and especially to Jan Chivé for her endless patience.

The principal purpose of this reappraisal is to create a valid baseline over which the entire Winslow narrative can be reconstructed, and to stimulate

Preface

further debate about the origins of one of the important figures in American History. All feedback, questions and suggestions are most welcome, and should be emailed to the author: winslowgov@icloud.com

All communications will be acknowledged. Errors, omissions or confusions in this book are entirely my own responsibility. I have no personal agenda in the underlying Winslow narrative nor any familial association with the Winslow family itself other than through the name of my house, and hence the fascination in establishing an impartial historical narrative about this family of international importance. The next volume is already in production.

Liam Donnelly
Wincelow Hall

May 2022

Acknowledgement from the Winslow Heritage Society

Decerptus Floreo

"Although Cut Off, I Flourish" shares the thought that while the Winslow families in America have been cut off from those abroad, all Winslows continue to flourish. As an inclusive society, the Winslow Heritage Society welcomes descendants from all countries. While our society's primary attention has concentrated on Winslow families who settled in America, Liam Donnelly's book brings us back to our English legacy in great detail and discovery. His research has expanded our scope of knowledge and presents us with extraordinary Winslow ancestry.

www.winslowheritagesociety.org

Preface

Abbreviations

The following abbreviations are used in the footnotes:

Abbreviation	Title
Cal. Close	Calendar of the Close Rolls preserved in the Public Record Office (1892-1963)
Cal. Inq. Misc.	Calendar of Inquisitions Miscellaneous (Chancery) preserved in the Public Record Office (H.M.S.O. 1916-68)
Cal. Inq. p.m.	Calendar of Inquisitions post mortem preserved in the Public Record Office (H.M.S.O. 1904-88)
Cal. Pat.	Calendar of the Patent Rolls preserved in the Public Record Office (H.M.S.O. 1891-1986)
Cat. Anct. D.	Descriptive Catalogue of Ancient Deeds in the Public Record Office (H.M.S.O. 1890-1915)
D.N.B.	Dictionary of National Biography
Ex. e Rot. Fin. (Rec. Com.)	*Excerpta e Rotulis Finium in Turri Londinensi asservati*, Henry III, 1216-72 (Record Commission, 1835-6)
Feud. Aids	Inquisitions and Assessments relating to Feudal Aids preserved in the Public Record Office (H.M.S.O. 1899-1920)
Hist. Parl.	The History of Parliament (History of Parliament Trust, 1964-)
N.R.A.	National Register of Archives
P.C.C.	Prerogative Court of Canterbury
P.R.O.	Public Record Office
P.R.S.	Pipe Roll Society
V.C.H.	Victoria County History

Table of Contents

Table of Unique Winslow Suffixes

SUFFIX	INDIVIDUAL	SUFFIX RATIONALE
Bercarius	Robert Winslow c. 1270	Described as *Bercarius*, found in Oxfordshire
Barrowden	Richard Winslow, active 1290s	Located in Barrowden, Rutland
Patriarch	William Winslow, active 1284-1313	Resident near Winslow, Buckinghamshire
Muster	Walter Winslow, active 1322-46	Holton discloses his call to muster, 1322
Wodyam	Walter Winslow, active 1332-1350	Possible family nickname
Cellarer	William Winslow, active 1326- 1400	Monk of St. Albans
Galfrid	Geoffrey Winslow, active 1327	Alternative spelling of Geoffrey
Handmills	Richard Winslow c. 1330	Participant in St. Albans handmills case
Maunciple	John Winslow c.1330 – c.1400	Mary Crouchman's husband, maunciple
Hunsdon	John Winslow, active 1352-83	Later a resident of Hunsdon
Kimpton	Walter Winslow, 1368	Located in Kimpton, Herts
Candlewick	William Winslow, active 1370-1400	Lived in Candlewick St., City of London
Chesham	John Winslow, active 1392-1423	Lived in Chesham Bois, Bucks
Hostytter	John Winslow, 1365	Termed *Hostytter* in Cordwainer Ward
Pavilioner	William Winslow, active 1381-1414	Pavilioner to King Richard II
Chaplain	William Winslow, active 1397-1414	Termed *Chaplain* in public records
Armiger	William Winslow, active 1389-1415	Termed *Armiger* in his 1415 Will
Clacton	Richard Winslow, 1375-1415	Vicar in Clacton
Kensington	Edmund Winslow, 1411-1417	Activity in Kensington
Salop	John Winslow 1419-24	Inheritance included Shropshire *(Salop)*
Soton	John Winslow 1415, perhaps to 1447	Located in Southampton *(Soton)*
Junior	John Winslow, 1423	Son of John Winslow *Chesham*
Saddler	Thomas Winslow, active 1400-22	Saddler by trade
Alnwick	Thomas Winslow, active 1437-61	Agnes Poure's son, killed in siege of Alnwick

Edward Winslow's English Origins

1 Traditional View Reconsidered

1.1 Continuing Absence of Consensus

David-Parsons Holton's book *Winslow Memorial: Family Records of the Winslows and their Descendants in America,* published in 1877, put forward theories about the English origins and ancestral roots of Governor Edward Winslow.[1] Instead of concluding the debate, Holton's work has stimulated historians to extend their research.

Holton mentions correspondence between Isaac Winslow and Francis Thompson dated 4 March 1845 where Thompson rejects the proposal that the Winslows originated from Denmark.[2] Holton responds by proposing his own version of the Winslow family chart based on primary and secondary sources available to him:[3]

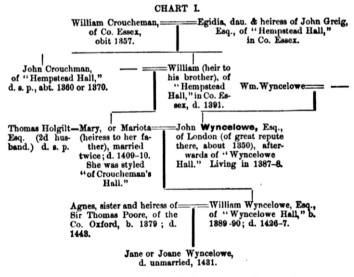

Figure 1-1 Holton's Winslow Family Chart centred on Hempstead

---

[1] Holton, David-Parsons, *Winslow Memorial: Family Records of the Winslows and their Descendants in America,* New York, 1877
[2] Holton, intro. p. 5
[3] Holton, intro. p. 6

Edward Winslow's English Origins

Holton acknowledges difficulties faced by researchers in establishing the Winslow family's true origins, but his confidence remains abundant:[4]

> As Edward Winslow, the principal leader of the pilgrims, was a person of note in England, and extremely well connected, it is much to be regretted that so few papers concerning his family were preserved; for, no doubt, he could have given a regular account of the family, had not the religious fanaticism of the day been a bar to it. But we must content ourselves with taking advantage of all information which may be obtained in carefully examining the immense mass of various records which exists in this country, either in public establishments, or in the hands of private individuals; and I have very little doubt by time and patience this connecting link between the families I have alluded to will finally crown our labours.

While Holton is correct in recognising the *immense mass of various records*, thorough interpretation of the material available demands time and patience, and research to date has not yet achieved the desired level of consensus. As for the *various records*, some materials used in his research are no longer accessible. Holton introduces this passage about Walter Winslow dating from 1322:[5]

> In further illustration, I will here give you the copy of an ancient written preserved among the Parliamentary record, viz. Anno 1322 – Walter de Wynslaive [sic], Esquire (Gentleman at Arms) returned by the sheriff, pursuant to writ, tested at Bishopsthrope [sic], 20 June, 15 Edward 2d [1322], as summoned from the County of Buckingham to perform Military Service in person against the Scotts – to muster at New Castle upon the Tyne on the eve of St. James the Apostle, 24th July, 16th Edward II.

The Introduction to a new 2005 edition of the Parliamentary Rolls notes that original documentation has survived for only eight of the twenty-six assemblies between 1307 and November 1325, meaning that records are missing for six parliaments from May 1322 to November 1325, the period covered by Holton's reference.[6]

But that does not necessarily invalidate Holton's statement, nor imply its inauthenticity or spuriousness. Gwendolyn Beaufoy echoes the summons to *Walter de Wynslaive* in her book about her ancient family when she talks in the 1930s of a similar instruction issued to her *Beaufeu* family ancestor *Richard de Bella Fago*:[7]

> 1322. Richard was returned by the sheriff pursuant to Writ tested at Bishop's Thorp, June 20, as summoned from Co. Oxford to perform military service in person against the Scots. Muster at Newcastle upon Tyne on the eve of Saint James the Apostle 24th of July, 16 Edward II.

Beaufoy's independent citation using the same phrase *to perform military service in person against the Scots* corroborates the likelihood that Holton's quotation is

---

[4] Holton intro. p. 9
[5] Holton intro. p. 8
[6] Parliament Rolls of Medieval England, Woodbridge, 2005, introduction.
[7] Gwendolyn Beaufoy, Leaves From a Beech Tree, Basil Blackwell, Oxford, 1930 p. 26

Edward Winslow's English Origins

authentic. Like Walter Winslow from Buckinghamshire, Richard Beaufeu from Oxford has been summoned to war from his home county. The Beaufoy family, variously *Beaufeu, Beaufitz, Bella Fago, Beaufu, Beaufoy* or *Beaufiz* probably originated from *Beaufour*, a small village in Calvados, Normandy,[8] and would advance by the early 1300s to become members of the *Trailbaston* judiciary under Edward I, as did the Poure family. Walter Winslow's surname suggests that he does not originate from Normandy. It is also important to remember in both cases that no such summons to the King's wars was ever issued to persons of insignificance. The Beaufeu family would also become kinsmen of the Winslows.

The details of Walter Winslow's summons allow us to assume that Buckinghamshire was his home county, and we can therefore make the informed guess that his surname or *byname* probably derives from the Buckinghamshire town of *Winslow*. The town name *Winslow* developed from the Anglo-Saxon *Wineslauue* back in the eighth century, became *Weneslai* by the time of the Conquest, and *Wineslawe* or *Wynselowe* by the thirteenth.[9] These circumstantial details provide valuable clues to pinpoint Walter's origins.

Unfortunately for researchers, the county of Buckinghamshire was not the only source of the *Winslow* surname; because in medieval times other English towns had names sounding similar to *Weneslai*. Modern-day *Wensley* in Yorkshire is one of these, more famous these days for its *Wensleydale* cheese and located two hundred miles away from Buckinghamshire. Holton's *mass of various records* has to be sifted thoroughly if we want to establish indisputably that the intended Winslow family is being identified.

As we will see shortly in an episode at *Topcliffe*, there is plenty of scope for confusion. The scale of the problem here can be understood by inspecting the index of historian Brandon Fradd's recent book about the Winslows of Kempsey[10] which discloses no fewer than twenty-two variant spellings of the *Winslow* surname contained in the local court records just for one single manor, and presumably for a single family. For now the only conclusion we can draw is that the surname *Winslow* at that time was unfamiliar to those parts of Worcestershire.

Before we embark on the quest for the origins of Edward Winslow we must be sure that we have the means to identify the family members correctly. Holton was addressing this problem when he was rejecting Denmark as a place from which they originated, and drew up his Winslow family chart presented above in Figure 1-1 based on the best evidence available to him at the time. But what Holton did not appreciate was that much of the historical research on the Winslow family heritage

---

[8] See L. V. Delisle, *Orderici Vitalis Historiae Ecclesiasticae*, ed. A. Le Prévost, Paris, 1838-55
[9] So Parishes: Winslow, V.C.H. of Buckingham, vol. 3, ed. William Page, London, 1925, p. 465
[10] Brandon Fradd, *Winslow Families of Worcestershire 1400-1700*, Newbury Street Press, Boston 2009, p.321

Edward Winslow's English Origins

conducted by previous historians was substantially inaccurate, and the scale of this inaccuracy is easy to demonstrate.

Eliminate the Inconsistencies

> *...we must content ourselves with taking advantage of all information which may be obtained in carefully examining the immense mass of various records which exists in this country..*

If we check the dates and connections contained in Holton's chart in figure 1.1 and compare them with the original primary historical records, we soon discover that much of Holton's data is factually incorrect. There are many reasons why; and details of the discrepancies will emerge later in this chapter. But that is only one element of a bigger problem. New and incorrect narratives have evolved through incorporation of earlier inaccuracies, compounding the general disorder.

The extent to which the integrity of the Winslow historical tradition has been compromised is easily demonstrated by comparing three interpretations of events from modern sources with a version revalidated from the primary medieval records. The basis of these corrections is set out later in this chapter. For this exercise we will compare 1877 Holton's version of the Winslow tradition with two other versions, one earlier and one later. The earlier historian selected is Thomas Wright whose work was published in 1831;[11] the more recent source selected is the *Victoria County History* or *V.C.H.* covering Cambridgeshire and the Isle of Ely, published in 1982.[12]

All three sources are addressing many of the same historical facts or events. Wright was documenting important families in towns and villages of Essex for his *History of Essex. V.C.H.* covers the Cambridgeshire town of Trumpington, home to the Winslow and Crouchman families included by Holton in his chart in figure 1.1.

All three versions should reflect the primary source data, but inspection establishes that plainly they do not. The inconsistencies are marked in red below.

Comparative Analysis

DETAIL	ACTUAL	WRIGHT	HOLTON	V.C.H.
Year of Publication:		*1831*	*1877*	*1982*
Sir William Crouchman death	1351	1358	1357	1349
Crouchman false generation inserted	No	No	No	Yes
John Crouchman death	1367	1368	*c. 1360-70*	1367
William Crouchman death	1371	1391	1391	1371
John Winslow father	John	Unstated	William	Unstated
John Winslow profession	Several	Unstated	Unstated	Grocer

---

[11] Wright, Thomas, *History of Essex*, 2 vols., Geo. Virtue, London, 1831
[12] *V.C.H. History of the County of Cambridge & Isle of Ely*, vol. 8, ed. A P M Wright, London, 1982

DETAIL	ACTUAL	WRIGHT	HOLTON	V.C.H.
John Winslow death	1399-1400	Unstated	Unstated	1406
Mariota's first husband's forename	John	Thomas	John	John
Mariota Winslow death	1406	1409	1409-10	By 1420
Agnes Winslow maiden name	Tibbay	Unstated	Poure	Unstated
Son William Winslow death	1415	1419	1426-7	1419
Elizabeth Huntingdon to Mariota	Aunt	Unstated	Unstated	Sister
Joan Winslow death	1426	1431	1431	1426

Figure 1-2 Winslow Source Data Comparison

As we will find out shortly, the biggest single source of divergence arises through confusing dates of *inquests* with dates of *death*. Several inquests ran on for years; and in one extreme case, for decades. A reworking of Holton's Winslow family chart incorporating the changes is provided at the end of this chapter.

Alternative Theories of the Winslow Origins

One historian holding an opinion about the origin of the Winslows different from many historians is Brandon Fradd. He published his book about the Winslows of Kempsey in 2009. Working in collaboration with Marshall K. Kirk and Kenneth Smallbone, Fradd has documented the activities of generations of a family with the surname *Winslow* in the town of Kempsey from the early 1430 onwards. In Fradd's view these people were the proto-family of Governor Edward Winslow.

Kempsey is a town in Worcestershire, and Fradd is able to prove that generations of Winslows were living there continuously since at least 1432. Fradd's divergence from other historians like Holton arises over one fundamental point: in Fradd's view the locality around Worcestershire was the exclusive place of origin for the Kempsey Winslows, and as a family unit these Winslows were unrelated by blood to any other Winslows elsewhere in England.

Though his pioneering work, Fradd and his colleagues have significantly expanded the body of extant information about the Winslows by publishing a commentary on an invaluable and hitherto inaccessible collection of new primary source materials, the *Kempsey Manorial Court Records*.[13] The surviving Kempsey Manor records open in 1408 and do not run consecutively.[14] The first two periods of coverage run from 1408 to 1411, and from 1417 through 1422, but no references to any Winslows are contained in those sections.[15] After another gap from 1422 to October 1432, we find a *Henry Wynslowe* in the records whose name continues to appear in court records up to 1448. The sequence of Winslow family court attendance continues after *Henry Wynslowe*.

---

[13] Fradd, see especially chapter 5
[14] So Fradd, pp. 61-105
[15] So Fradd, p. 61

Edward Winslow's English Origins

Under typical manor court rules, a representative from each resident family was obliged to attend the medieval manor court in person. We can speculate from the gap in the Manor records that the Winslows began settling in Kempsey sometime between 1422 and 1432. Fradd places the Worcestershire Winslow family origins somewhere adjacent to Kempsey, and he suggests *Winslow* in Shropshire, some twenty miles away. This is further considered below.

Fradd's views about the Kempsey Winslows's origins align with some subsequent authors. In her book *The Mayflower Generation* published in 2017, Rebecca Fraser opens with a chapter entitled *Droitwich*, the Worcestershire town where Governor Winslow was baptised in 1595. Fraser notes that for several hundred years the Winslows had been living in Worcestershire as *yeoman farmers*, and she does not speculate on other possible origins. She also notes that the Winslows in the early 1600s were proud to describe themselves as *Yeomen*, a term that she interprets as meaning *middle class*.[16]

Fraser dismisses talk of possible aristocratic origins for the Winslows as a product of the class-ridden nineteenth century, although she mentions a seventeenth-century Worcestershire document suggesting that Kenelm Winslow may have been a man of considerable estate.[17]

Stephen Tomkins's 2020 publication *The Journey of the Mayflower* deals with the entrenchment and intensification of religious dissent from the time of Queen Mary in 1553 up to the time of the Mayflower's departure in 1620. Tomkins focuses more on the culture of dissent rather than the genealogy of individual dissenters. Accordingly, he limits his comments about Governor Winslow's family and upbringing in Droitwich to the observation that Edward Winslow was *the son of a prosperous saltmaker*.[18]

While Fradd's study indicates that the Winslows probably emerged into local prominence after 1432, he does not explore their initial motivation nor incentive to move there, nor offers evidence about their lives before Kempsey. The validity of Fradd's theory will be considered in the light of other evidence; what is indisputable is Fradd's achievement in establishing when the Winslows first appear in Worcestershire, and in documenting their subsequent activities.

1.2   Re-alignment

Winslows and Crouchmans

Figure 1-2 has highlighted the scale of disagreement among historians on points of detail relating to the Winslows, and this section aims to correct some of those

---

[16] Rebecca Fraser, The Mayflower Generation, Chatto & Windus, London, 2017 pp. 3-4
[17] Fraser, p. 4
[18] Steven Tomkins, The Journey to the Mayflower, Pegasus Books, New York, 2020, p. 310

errors, particularly relating to the Crouchman and Winslow families. Later chapters introduce supplementary material presumably unavailable to previous historians like Holton.

We will look at four Crouchman family members identified here as Sir William Crouchman C1, his elder son and heir John Crouchman C2, John's heir William Crouchman C3, and Sir William's second son and eventual heir William Crouchman C4. William C4 was father of the Mariota who married John Winslow in 1375.

There is also a paradox to resolve. Why was Sir William Crouchman C1 succeeded by two sons, when his will specifically mentioned a single son and heir? How did Mariota's marriage come about? We need to check out the Crouchman lineage.

Corrections to Holton's Family Chart

NAME	CORRECTIONS / CLARIFICATIONS
William Crouchman C1	Sir William, of Cambridgeshire, not Essex; died 1351, not 1357.
Egidia Grigge	Sir William's second wife born 1322-3. Parents: John & Margaret Grigge.
John Crouchman C2	Elder son of Sir William & Egidia, died a minor, 1367.
William Crouchman C3	Son of John C2; born 1362, died c. 1367, passed over for inheritance.
William Crouchman C4	Mariota's father, younger brother of C2, born 1351, died 1371, not 1391.
Wm. Wyncelowe	Not the father of John Winslow of Hempstead.
John Wyncelowe	Did not originate in London. Born c. 1330, died c. 1400.
Mariota Crouchman	Born 1366-7, daughter of William C4, d. 1406, not 1409-10, nor c. 1420.
Thomas Holgill	Royal official, Mariota's second husband, he had remarried by 1411.
William Wynselowe	John and Mariota's son born 1387, died August 1415, not 1426-7.
Agnes	Wife of the above, daughter of Sir John Tibbay, not of Sir Thomas Poure.
Joan Wynselowe	Daughter of Agnes Tibbay and William Winslow. Died 1426, not 1431.

Figure 1-3 Amendments to Holton's Winslow Family Chart

Sir William Crouchman, C1

Birth date uncertain, possibly around 1280. Died 20 June 1351.

The unforeseen consequences of Sir William's death in 1351 would prove to be considerable. The reason for including such a level of detail about the Crouchmans becomes apparent later.

Holton correctly recognises *Mariota* or *Mary* Crouchman, granddaughter of this Sir William Crouchman C1, as John Winslow's wife. The first issue to address is that the identity of John Winslow's father was *John* and not *William*, something to be confirmed in Chapter 3. Sir William Crouchman's profession was as a member of the judiciary closely associated with the De Vere family, Earls of Oxford.

Identifying the year in which Sir William Crouchman C1 died has been challenging. V.C.H. uniquely proposes that Sir William Crouchman died in 1349 and was succeeded by an otherwise unknown William Crouchman who died in 1351,

Edward Winslow's English Origins

interposing an extra generation. There are many subsequent reported inquests on Sir William C1 which have compounded the confusion. One was held several days after Sir William's death,[19] and another in 1352, and further references to Sir William's death continued for decades.[20] Finally in 1422 an inquest clarifies matters by addressing Sir William as *senior*. Here is the relevant extract:[21]

> William Croucheman senior died on 20 June 1351..

There is copious contemporary information about Sir William Crouchman C1. The earliest reference to him located for this work is found in 1302 relating to Thriplow village in Cambridgeshire where the entitlement to a quarter share of a knight's fee for *William Crouchman* is confirmed:[22]

> 1302. William Crocheman ¼ fee in Tripplelawe held of the Bishop of Ely.

Perhaps this entry was referring to his father William; or perhaps instead it marked attainment of majority for William Crouchman C1, implying a birth date around 1280, projecting an age of around 70 years at his death in 1351: a not unreasonable speculation to which we will return. The next such entry dates from 1346:

> 1346. William Crocheman 1/4 fee in Tripplelawe held of the Bishop of Ely, previously the property of William Crocheman.[23]

Perhaps the purpose of this entry is reconfirmation of Sir William's land tenure. The entry cannot have been a transfer to Egidia's child William, because William C3 was not yet born. Maybe the reference *previously the property of William Crocheman* may relate to William the late father of Sir William. There is no evidence to substantiate either theory, so the 1302 entry is assumed to be referring to William Crouchman C1.

We know that William Crouchman C1 operated in the judiciary because he was reported as having been ejected from office of coroner in the county town of Cambridge adjacent to Trumpington on 11 November 1311, and the earlier speculation about his birth date around 1280 would place him in his early thirties by 1311, again not an unreasonable assumption as we discover later:[24]

> To the sheriff of Cambridge. Order to cause a coroner for that county to be elected in place of William Crocheman, whom the king has amoved for insufficient qualification.

Notwithstanding this reversal, William Crouchman would enjoy a successful subsequent career in civil and judicial administration, and his early loss of responsibility may have reflected inexperience rather than incompetence. Meanwhile, a reference from 1314 to someone called John Cayly mentions a

---

[19] Cal. Inq. p.m. Edward iii, vol. 10, entry 144, p.133-34.
[20] So for example Cal. Inq. p.m., Edward iii, vol. 10, 1352-60, pp. 133-4
[21] Cal. Inq. p.m. 1422, 21-907: William Wyncelawe, C 138/62/14 mm. 1-2
[22] Feud. Aids, vol. 1, p. 147
[23] Feud. Aids, vol. 1, p. 166
[24] Cal. Close, Edward ii, vol. 1, 1307-1313, pp. 381

Edward Winslow's English Origins

Trumpington landholding gifted by William Crouchman,[25] as clarified in a report dated April 1314 addressed to *John Abel, escheator this side Trent*.[26]

Accusations of misfeasance levelled at William Crouchman and his then wife Anne place him in Trumpington in 1315, although it is unclear whether he was yet a resident. We will find out later that William C1 would eventually lease Trumpington Manor from the Beaufeu family in 1327. The Archbishop of Canterbury mentioned is Simon Mepeham, predecessor of the John de Stratford with whom Walter Winslow would later become acquainted:[27]

> ....complaint by John de Barenton that William Crocheman of Trumpeton, and Anne his wife, broke certain chests of his at Trumpeton, co. Cambridge, and carried away his goods. By K. on the information of the Archbishop of Canterbury.

1332 is a busy year for William Crouchman visiting Santiago as a pilgrim, and with Walter and Nicholas Crouchman, presumably blood relatives, acting as his attorneys.[28]

> March 24. Westminster. William Crocheman, going on pilgrimage to Santiago, has letters nominating Nicholas Crocheman and Walter Crocheman his attorneys in England..

Around this time William had married Egidia, John Grigge's nine-year-old daughter and heir, so we can deduce that William's former wife Anne had passed away. December 1332 marks the death of John Grigge accompanied by controversy more fully reported later. John Grigge's father held Hempstead in 1303.[29]

By March 1336 William Crouchman has received a knighthood.[30] Meanwhile Sir William has been engaged by John de Vere, Earl of Oxford with an extensive estate spread throughout England. Sir William is acting as a trusted advisor to this senior member of the English nobility, also his feudal overlord in Hempstead.

By December 1338 Crouchman joins a commission for raising troops headed by De Vere together with another leading noblemen, Humphrey de Bohun, Earl of Hereford and Essex,[31] prompted by events in May 1337 where the French King Philip VI has decided to bring Gascony back under French control, displacing and dispossessing Edward III, and thereby triggering the Hundred Years War.

December 1340 sees Sir William promoted higher up the judiciary. He and de Vere are commissioned to examine possible extortions in Kent, Sussex, Southampton and Wilts. In January 1341 William Crouchman is appointed as a justice for Sussex where he is working with *Thomas de Brewose*,[32] a name to remember for later. In

---

[25] *Cal. Inq. p.m., Edward ii, vol. 5, 1307-27, p. 253*
[26] *Cal. Close, Edward ii, vol. 2, 1313-1318, p. 53*
[27] *Cal. Pat., Edward ii, vol. 2, 1313-1317, p. 417*
[28] *Cal. Pat., Edward iii, vol. 2, 1330-34, p. 259*
[29] *Feudal Aids AD1284-1431. Vol. ii, Essex, 1303 p.147*
[30] *Cal. Pat., Edward iii vol. 3, 1334-38, p. 233*
[31] *Cal. Pat., Edward iii, vol. 4, 1338-40, p. 141*
[32] *Cal. Close, Edward iii, vol. 6, 1341-43, p. 204*

Edward Winslow's English Origins

February 1341 William Crouchman and the Earl are appointed to examine felonies in Kent.[33] Further commissions in March follow for the county of Essex,[34] and by July 1341 William Crouchman is working on new assignments directly for John de Vere,[35] before returning to Sussex in October to hold hearings about apparent *oppressions by ministers of the king*.[36]

The busy schedule continues. By Michaelmas 1341 William Crouchman is granted privileges in the Earl's estate in Downham near Chelmsford, some thirty five miles due south of Hempstead, presumably signalling the Earl's satisfaction for good service rendered.[37] 1342 finds William Crouchman working some twenty miles further east of Hempstead in Lavenham on an enquiry about damage to the Earl of Oxford's property.[38] After the minor setback early in his career as an aspiring coroner, Sir William Crouchman has now emerged as an established public justice, and personal administrator for one of England's premier Earls.

William Crouchman and his wife Egidia are both mentioned in an entry from the Feet of Fines in 1344 concerning transfer of properties and more than one thousand acres of land straddling several North Essex villages, an extensive estate that includes Hempstead and the adjacent Helion's Bumpstead and Little Radwinter.[39] The transferees are Walter Crouchman and a Master William Warde of Trumpington. We saw earlier that Walter Crouchman, presumably a relative, was acting as Sir William's attorney on his trip abroad to Santiago, so the same Walter is probably representing Sir William here. Although Sir William is addressed here as *chevalier*, such recognition is not routinely applied to all the subsequent contemporary references.

Walter Crouchman is mentioned again in 1347 following an allegation of assault in Steeple Bumpstead, the village four miles east of Hempstead,[40] and maybe Walter's presence indicates that he is also deputising in some capacity during Sir William's frequent absences away from his home and estate in Hempstead.

An entry from 1345 refers to Sir William's successful repayment of a significantly large loan of £400 owed to *Stephen de Cavendissh*, citizen of London.[41] The same year Sir William is given a commission of *oyer et terminer* concerning a complaint over an alleged assault,[42] and in August that same year he files a complaint of his own about loss of assets from his estate in Trumpington,[43] suggesting that while Sir

---

[33] *Cal. Pat., Edward iii, vol. 5, 1340-43, p. 204*
[34] *Cal. Pat., Edward iii, vol. 5, 1340-43, p. 209*
[35] *Cal. Pat., Edward iii, vol. 5, 1340-43, p. 254*
[36] *Cal. Pat., Edward iii, vol. 5, 1340-43, p. 320*
[37] *Feet of Fines, Essex, Edward iii, vol. 3, 1326-1422, entry 571, p. 60*
[38] *Cal. Pat., Edward iii, vol. 5, 1340-43, p. 552*
[39] *Feet of Fines, Essex, Edward iii, vol. 3, 1326-1422, entry 692, p. 72*
[40] *Cal. Pat., Edward iii, vol. 7, 1345-48, p. 460*
[41] *Cal. Close, Edward iii, vol. 7, 1343-46, p. 581*
[42] *Cal. Pat., Edward iii, vol. 7, 1343-45, p. 573*
[43] *Cal. Pat., Edward iii, vol. 7, 1343-45, p. 582*

William and Egidia continue to use Crouchmans Hall in Hempstead, their increasingly affluent lifestyle has allowed them to maintain alternative residences elsewhere.

An entry from 12 June 1346 records Sir William and John de Vere Earl of Oxford indebted to Stephen de Cavendissh for the very large sum of £654, *to be levied, in default of payment, of their lands and chattels in co. Essex.* An addendum sets out favourable settlement terms that reduce total liability by nearly £300, although the reasons for such apparent generosity are not disclosed.[44]

January 1347 records Sir William's appointment to a royal commission to Chelmsford in the company of established justices *Richard de Kelleshull, John de Sutton, William de Notton* and *John de la Rokele*.[45] This was the Rokely who in 1353 was to suffer the same misfortune of demotion from his role as a coroner as had befallen Sir William some forty years earlier.[46] And like Sir William Crouchman before them, Kelleshull, Sutton and Notton will advance to knighthoods later in their careers.

The final extant public reference to Sir William dates from 22 Jun 1347. He is acting as a witness for the marriage of the son of his neighbour, Sir William de Langham of Hempstead Hall, located only a mile or so from Crouchman's own manor.[47] This corrects another error in Holton's chart: Hempstead Hall was never home to the Crouchman sons, nor to Egidia Grigge.

> *Witnesses: Sir John de Roos, Sir William Crocheman, knights, John de Helyon, John de Neuport, Henry de la Launde, Nicholas Latre. Dated at Hemsted on Friday the feast of St. Alban, 21 Edward III [June 22, 1347]*

No further professional commissions are accepted after this, so Sir William is probably enjoying a comfortable retirement following an extended and successful career in civil administration up to his eventual death in 1351:[48]

> *William Crocheman died about Whitsunday, 25 Edward III [1351], leaving one son and heir, a minor.*

Subsequent evidence will prove that Sir William is survived by two sons, so why *one son and heir, a minor*? We must work out when Egidia Grigge's children were born.

The Grigges were evidently a prosperous family before they appear in the records for Hempstead, but little can be established about their connections. The *Grigge* name is found elsewhere in East Anglia, such as a *Herveus Grigge* described as being from the seaport of *Jernemue* or Yarmouth, listed among campaigners under Henry II in May 1230 preparing an invasion to Normandy to recover lands lost by King John

---

[44] *Cal. Close, Edward iii, vol. 8, 1346-49, p. 85*
[45] *Cal. Pat., Edward iii: vol. 7, 1345-48, p. 239*
[46] *Cal. Close, Edward iii: vol. 9, 1349-54, p. 533*
[47] *Cal. Close, Edward iii, vol. 8, 1346-1349, p. 296*
[48] *Cal. Inq. p.m., Edward iii, vol. 10, 1351, 1352-60, pp. 133-4 entry 133*

Edward Winslow's English Origins

some thirty years earlier.[49] The offer of protection addressed to *these people who have come with their boats as far as Portsmouth, and crossed the sea* suggests that Harvey Grigge may also have operated in shipping and trade, perhaps the source of family prosperity. John Grigge from Hempstead clearly has an appetite for property transfers because the Feet of Fines for Essex records a transfer in 1329:[50]

> 60. Mich. Hugh Mareschal and Ellen his wife, pl. by John de Fynchyngfeld [Finchingfield] in her place John Grygge, def. 1 messuage, 40 acres of land, 2 acres of meadow, 1 acre of pasture and 8d. rent in Hamstede and Great Samford Pl. and the heirs of their bodies to hold of the chief lords, with remainder to the right heirs of Hugh.

Just as his property portfolio is growing, so John Grigge dies abruptly.[51]

> JOHN GRIGGE or GREGGE of Hamstede, Writ, 13 December, 6 Edward III. Inq. taken ex officio 13 December, 6 Edward III. [Writ issued December 1332]

> Bomstedehelyoun. [Helions Bumpstead in Essex] 1a. land, held of John son and heir of Henry de Helyoun, a minor and in the king's wardship, by knight's service and by scutage when it runs.

> The marriage of Giles (Egidia) his daughter and heir, aged 9 years, belongs to the king by reason of the said acre of land and the minority of the said Giles, who is eloigned (elongata) from the king's wardship, &c., by Margaret sometime the wife of John Grigge, and others unknown, and is married to William Crocheman, within the king's seisin and against the prohibition of the king's escheators, as is said.

> Hamstede, Finchingfeld and Sampford. Three messuages and 700a. land, held jointly by the said John Grigge and Margaret his wife, but of whom is unknown at present.

> ESSEX. Inq. taken at Chelmenesford [Chelmsford, Essex] on Wednesday before St. Gregory the Pope, 7 Edward III. The said John Gregge held no lands or tenements in his demesne as of fee in the county, except those which he held jointly with Margaret his wife, by fine levied in the king's court.

As already noted, William Crouchman C1 had departed on a pilgrimage to the tomb of the James the Apostle in Santiago de Compostela in Galicia around March 24th 1332,[52] an undertaking typically promising *plenary indulgence*, full remission of his mortal sins.[53] John Grigge's death was not announced until December. With access to the wealth from a prospective father-in-law's inheritance, William Crouchman had every reason to thank the Almighty. Maybe he took Egidia with him.

We have established that Sir William Crouchman's death occurred in 1351. His inquest three days after his reported death omits his title and his wife's name, and does not even disclose the name of his heir, but simply states: [54]

---

[49] *Cal. Pat., Henry iii, vol. 2, 1225-32, p. 372*
[50] *Feet of Fines, Essex, Edward iii, vol. 3, 1326-1422, entry 60, p. 6*
[51] *Cal. Inq. p.m., Edward III, vol. 7, File 31, entry 404, p. 302*
[52] *Cal. Pat., , Edward iii, vol. 2, 1330-34, p. 259*
[53] *So Kent, William, Indulgences. The Catholic Encyclopedia vol. 7, New York, Robert Appleton Company, 1910*
[54] *Cal. Inq. p.m., Edward iii, vol. 10, 1351, pp. 133-4*

Inq. taken at Great Sampford, Thursday the eve of the Nativity of St. John the Baptist, 27 Edward III.

Great Sampford. 154a. 1r. arable, 4a. meadow, 1a. pasture, 3 ½a. wood and 18d. rent held of Joan, daughter and heir of William de Welle, as of the manor of Great Sampford, in the king's custody by the death of William de Welle and the minority of the said Joan, by knight's service and by service of rendering 35s. 10d. at the said manor, which rent was reckoned in the extent of the manor made after the death of William Welle and delivered to Guy de Bryen who has the custody of the manor, which is held of the king in chief.

William Crocheman died about Whitsunday, 25 Edward III, leaving one son and heir, a minor.

Sir William C1 had married Egidia by 1332 when she was aged nine, and we know from later inquests that he had two sons and a daughter with Egidia – John C2, William C4, and Elizabeth Crouchman. Sequence of succession following Sir William's death is imperfectly communicated through numerous inquests, but eventually Sir William's estate passes to his great-grandson William Winslow, son of Mariota and John Winslow once William has attained his age of majority:[55]

WILLIAM CROUCHEMAN, Writ 18 April 1410. ESSEX. Inquisition. Great Sampford. 8 Nov.

He held 153 a. arable, 4 a. meadow, 1 a. pasture, 3½a. wood and 8d. rent in Great Sampford in his demesne as of fee of Joan, daughter and heir of William Welles, a minor in the ward of Edward III, service unknown, annual value 10s.9d.

He died on 20 June 1351. William Wyncelawe, son of Mary wife of John Wyncelawe and daughter of William his son, is next heir, aged 21 years on 1 Nov. 1409.

A follow-up inquest is held in March and July 1422, seventy years after the death of Sir William C1 where, as already noted, he is described as *senior*. By now his great-grandson William Winslow is dead, and his successor will be William's daughter Joan Winslow:[56]

WILLIAM WYNCELAWE Writ, devenerunt, 12 March 1422, ordering enquiry into what lands and tenements came into the hand of Edward III and remain in the hand of the present king by reason of the death of William Croucheman senior and the minority of his kinsman and heir William Wyncelawe, of whom and by what service they were held, and their value. William Wyncelawe was the son of Mary widow of John Wyncelawe and daughter of William Croucheman son of William Croucheman senior, whose heir William Wyncelawe was, and who held of Joan, daughter and heir of William Welles, a minor in the wardship of Edward III.Essex. Inquisition. Saffron Walden. 28 July. Jurors: ...

No lands or tenements came into the hand of Edward III by reason of the death of William Croucheman or the minority of William Wyncelawe.

William Croucheman senior died on 20 June 1351 and because of the minority of his son and heir William the land came into the king's hand. When Joan came of age the same year she and her husband Henry Coggeshale entered the manor but before they were put into

---

[55] *Cal. Inq. p.m. Henry iv, entry 19/742++*
[56] *Cal. Inq. p.m. 1422, 21-907: William Wyncelawe, C 138/62/14 mm. 1-2*

Edward Winslow's English Origins

possession the younger William Croucheman died and the lands descended to the younger William's daughter and heir Mary. On Mary's death they passed to her son and heir William Wyncelawe, and then to William's daughter Joan, who survives and was aged 8 years on 11 June 1421.

Joan Winslow, Sir William's surviving great-great granddaughter aged 8 years in 1421 has succeeded to the Crouchman / Winslow estate.

John Crouchman C2

From evidence presented at his inquest, John Crouchman C2, elder son of Sir William Crouchman C1, was born around 1346 when Egidia was aged around 23 years. That refutes the possibility that John was a son of Sir William C1 and his first wife Anne whose death must have predated 1332, the year when William C1 married Egidia. John died a minor in 1367. Holton suggests that John died sometime between 1360 and 1370 and the text of John's inquest is as follows:[57]

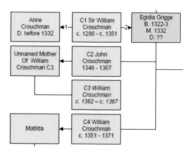

Figure 1-4 Descent of John Crouchman C2

JOHN SON AND HEIR OF WILLIAM CROCHEMAN.

Writ after the death of the said John, who has died a minor in the king's wardship. 18 November, 41 Edward III [Note: this 18 Nov 1367 is the date of the writ, not the date of John's death, which was March 1367 as per below.]

Inq. (indented) taken at Samford, Wednesday the morrow of the Conversion of St. Paul, 42 Edward III [Jan 25].. Samford. The said John, whose father held of the heir of William de Welle, a minor in the king's wardship, by knight's service, died while a minor in the king's wardship. He held no lands &c. of the king in chief on the day of his death, but he held 153a. arable, 4a. meadow, 1a. pasture, 4½a. wood and 18d. rent in Samford of Henry de Kokeshale and Joan his wife, daughter and heir of William de Welle aforesaid, as of the right of the said Joan, by service of 35s. 10d. yearly. He died on the feast of the Annunciation last [25 March 1367]. William his son, aged 5 years and more, is his heir.

Although John Crouchman C2 died a minor, he had already fathered William Crouchman C3, confirmed from the above inquest as aged more than 5 years in November 1367, so pointing to a date of conception around 1361-2 when John C2 would have been aged around 15 years. The inquest on Sir William Crouchman C1 stated that he left a single son and heir, suggesting that Egidia was expecting baby William Crouchman C4 when Sir William died, allowing us to speculate that William Crouchman C4 was born perhaps a couple of months later in summer / autumn 1351. If earlier speculation is correct, Sir William would have been in his seventies.

---

[57] Cal. Inq. p.m. Edward iii, vol. 12, file 198, p. 174

We also know that William Crouchman C4 died shortly after 15 August 1371. Here is an extract from the inquest that also mentions that he was still a minor, and from the additional evidence that Sir William was succeeded by a single son and heir we can be confident that the birth of William C4 must have post-dated the death of his father:

> The said William brother of John died on Tuesday after the Assumption, 45 Edward III

Despite resolving the issue of his birthdate, we still have issues with the text of his 1367 inquest which contains the obvious misstatement highlighted below in red.[58] For maximum clarity, the Crouchman explanatory personal suffixes C1 to C4 have been inserted into the original text. The original error was significant enough to require subsequent correction in the official public record.[59]

> William [C4] brother and heir of John [C2] son and heir of William Crocheman [C1], a minor
>
> Writ of devenerunt concerning the lands which came into the hands of Edward III by reason of the death of the said William Crocheman, [C4] and by reason of the minority of the said William [C4] brother of John [C2]. 4 November, 15 Richard II [4 Nov 1391].
>
> Inq. taken at Hemstede, Thursday after St. Lucy, 15 Richard II.
>
> The said William [C4] brother of John [C2] held in his demesne as of fee on the day of his death the under-mentioned lands &c.; and they remain in the king's hands since his death.
>
> ...153 a. arable, 4 a. meadow, 1 a. pasture, 4½a. wood and 18d. rent of assise, held of Joan daughter and heir of William de Walle, then a minor in the king's wardship. They are worth 10s. yearly after payment of 35s. 10d. rent of assise belonging to the manor of Samford.
>
> The said William [C4] brother of John [C2] died on Tuesday after the Assumption, 45 Edward III [sometime in the week following 15 August 1371]. Mariot [Mary] daughter of William son of John, aged 26 years and more, is his heir.

Here the phrase *son of John* above is incorrect, and should read *William brother of John*. The son of John is William C3; Mariota's father is William C4, son of Sir William C1. William C3 was born around 1361-2, and Mariota was born around 1365-6, placing William C3 a young boy aged around 5 years when Mariota was born. As someone barely out of his infancy, William C3 can never have been Mariota's biological father.

For these reasons a correction was issued in the Close Rolls addressed to the Escheator of Essex dated January 1393 revising this earlier misstatement.[60] This time the name *Mariota* is replaced with *Mary*:

> Mary, being daughter of the said William [C4] brother of John [C2].

The earlier reference from 1392 gave Mary's age as 26 or more, indicating a year of birth around 1365-6 when her father William C4, born in summer or autumn 1351, was barely a teenager. Although William C4 died in mid-August 1371, this

---

[58] *Cal. Inq. p.m. Richard ii, vol. 16, file 69, entry 1105*
[59] *Cal. Inq. p.m. Richard ii, vol. 16, file 69, entry 1105*
[60] *Cal. Close, Richard ii, vol. 5, 1392-1306, p. 45*

inquest took place as late as 1391, possibly prompted by a desire to establish an indisputable right of succession both for Mariota and for her husband John Winslow, but also to protect the interests of her infant son William Winslow, born recently when the couple were living in Norfolk, as explained later.

One additional question not even raised in the proceedings is why William C3 was never acknowledged as heir after the death of his father John C2. We can only assume that William C3 had probably died before an inquest could be convened.

The eventual successors to the Hempstead estate were the descendants of Sir William's daughter Elizabeth Crouchman, married into the established Huntingdon family based in Sawston village in Cambridgeshire some four miles south east of Trumpington. Elizabeth was thus Mariota's aunt, not her sister.

The sequence of events about Sir William outlined above partially explains why so many errors have developed in the Winslows' early historical tradition; the truth emerges with clarity only when all the parts of the evidence have been collated and studied. And that is not the end of it.

Mariota / Mary Crouchman, Wife of John Winslow

On the death of her father William C4 in 1371, Mariota Crouchman was aged only five years or so. She was eventually confirmed as beneficiary of her father's estate at the inquest held after she was in her mid-twenties in 1391.

A binding agreement over the future of the Crouchman inheritance had initially been reached in May 1375 whereby the Crouchman estate would revert to Elizabeth's line with the Huntingdons if Mariota did not attain a specified age and have a family of her own, or if Mariota's line subsequently died out.[61] The estate mentioned in the agreement covered not only *the manor of Trumpyngton and all lands therein sometime of William Crocheman knight*, but also *the reversion of lands held in dower* as well as *the manors of Hampstede, Fynchyngfeld, Samford, Bumpstede, Asshedon and Radewynter, with the reversion of all lands etc. therein.*[62] The estate was considerable, and we will speculate later about why John Winslow had been selected or approved as Mariota's future husband, and the prevailing circumstances.

Assuming William Winslow was born in Norfolk in November 1387, Mariota was aged around twenty-one years when she became a mother, and about thirty-three when her first husband John Winslow died around 1400. We know that John Winslow was still alive in April 1397 because of the royal protection order extended ahead of his expedition to Ireland,[63] and his readiness to re-join the campaign in April 1399 is also reported.[64] No reliable evidence has been found to indicate that

---

[61] *Cal. Close, Edward iii, vol. 14, 1374-7, p. 223*
[62] *Cal. Close, Edward iii, vol. 14, 1374-7, p. 116*
[63] *Cal. Pat., Richard ii, vol. 5, 1391-6, p. 506*
[64] *Cal. Pat., Richard ii, vol. 6, 1399-9, p. 524*

he was still alive after 1399, and no record of his death has been located. Mariota subsequently married Thomas Holgyll and died on February 25 1406, leaving her son William Winslow an orphan aged around 17 years.

Evidence to support these assertions appears later, but first we must deal with another puzzle. An entry from the Essex Feet of Fines dated autumn (Michaelmas term) of 1405 deals with a property transaction close by Hempstead involving *John Wyncelowe and Mary his wife,* implying that John is still alive:[65]

> *97. Mich. John Kent of Thaxstede and William atte Fan of Thaxstede, pl. John Wyncelowe and Mary his wife, def. I messuage, 200 acres of land, 10 acres of meadow and 3s rent in Asshedon, Steventon and Berkelowe. Def. quitclaimed to pl. and the heirs of John. Cons. 100 marks.*

We know that Mariota was married to Thomas Holgyll when she died in February 1406. It is possible but highly improbable that John Winslow was still alive in 1405. That would have given Mary only about four months to lose and bury a husband, to have a respectful time of mourning, to become betrothed and to remarry, and eventually herself to die, all in an unrealistically compressed timeframe. More likely, the Feet of Fines announcement as late as autumn 1405 probably reflects administrative delays compounded by other issues relating to John's death.

Legal wardship of Mariota's son William passed to her second husband, Thomas Holgill. We learn from one source that William's date of birth was November 1 1387 based on an enquiry calling for evidence of proof of age. The reference to *John Wyncelawe of Oxford* below remains puzzling:[66]

> *WILLIAM WYNCELAWE Writ for proof of age of William Wyncelawe son and heir of Mary wife of Thomas Holgyll and formerly wife of John Wyncelawe of Oxford. He is in the ward of Thomas Holgyll who should be informed. 8 Dec. 1410.*

> *NORFOLK. Proof of age. Watton. 5 Jan. 1411…. Peter de Holkham, aged 50 years and more, says that William is aged 21 years and more since 1 Nov. last, because he was born at Cranworth in Norfolk on 1 Nov. 1387 and baptised in the church there. He was in the church and saw the baptism. The other jurors confirm the date for the reasons given…*

William Winslow was not evidently residing with his stepfather given the statement that Thomas Holgyll *should be informed* about the proof of age. Confirmation of the date of death for William's mother Mary appears in the *Calendar of Inquisitions Post Mortem.* Note that while the writ is dated 1410, Mariota's date of death is clearly given as 25 February 1406, correcting another misstatement in Holton's chart:[67]

> *MARY WIFE OF THOMAS HOLGYLL. Writ 18 April 1410.*

> *ESSEX. Inquisition. Great Sampford. 8 Nov.*

---

[65] *Feet of Fines for Essex, vol. 3, Essex Society For Archaeology And History, 2017, entry 97, p. 242*
[66] *Cal. Inq. p.m., Henry iv, vol. 19, 1411, C 137/84, no. 48, entry 898*
[67] *Cal. Inq. p.m., Henry iv, vol. 19, entry C 137/76, no. 4, entry 673*

Edward Winslow's English Origins

She held in her demesne as of fee: Hempstead, 1 tenement, of the earl of Oxford, a minor in the king's ward, service unknown, annual value 2s. Great Sampford, a capital messuage called 'Wodehall', of the same by knight service, annual value 6s. 8d.

She died on 25 Feb. 1406. Thomas Holgyll has held and taken the profits since her death by the king's grant [enrolment not found]. William Wyncelawe, her son by her former husband John Wyncelawe, is next heir. He was 21 on 1 Nov. 1409.

The earlier confirmation that William was born in 1387 is contradicted by the reference above, implying instead that he was born in 1388. It is unclear how long Mary and Holgyll had been married before her death aged about 39 years in 1406, but we know that by May 6 1412 Thomas Holgyll had a new wife called Elizabeth.[68]

Next to pass away was William Winslow, son of John Winslow and Mariota. His will written in London on 6 July 1415 and reproduced in the Appendix describes the young twenty-something William proudly embarking in the company of his king on a military campaign to France. Sadly William died of disease only six weeks later at the end of August shortly after arriving in France, and missed the battle of Agincourt on October 25 1415. The text of his will corrects another anomaly in Holton's chart, as follows.[69]

Firstly, William's 1415 will names his executors: wife *Agnes* and *Thomas de Tibbay*. Thomas is William's brother-in-law. William's late father-in-law, Sir John de Tibbay, had been murdered in the City of London the previous summer, and perhaps William's will was finalised as William passed through London *en route* to France on 6 July 1415. William dies seven weeks after signing off this will and leaves bequests for the fabric of *Hempstede Church*, suggesting that he still lived and worshiped in the village, and to his wife *a bed of red and white worsted*. He begs wife Agnes to support his uncle Richard Winslow.

The important correction here for Holton's narrative is that William's wife and widow is not *Agnes Poure*, but *Agnes Winslow, née Tibbay*. She is styled *Agnes Wynsley* in her will from 1443, and requests to be buried in the same church as her father in Newgate alongside her mother. Her mother's will of 1426 identifies her daughter as *Agnes Wynslaw* and notes that by now William's executor Thomas *clerk* is dead:[70]

1426. Joan de Tybbay. To be buried at the Friars Minors. Bequeathed two nobles to be distributed amongst the Friars on the day of her burial. Mentions her sons, Thomas—clerk, deceased—and John de Tybbay, and her daughter, Agnes Wynslaw.

An inquest in Radwinter in 1419 states that William's young daughter Joan was six years old on the feast of St. Barnabas *last*,[71] meaning that she was barely old

---

[68] *Cal. Close, Henry iv, vol. 4, 1409-13, pp. 334-5*
[69] *Marche Quire number 34; see appendix 6.1 below*
[70] *Wills relating to Grey Friars, London: 1374-1430, ed. C L Kingsford, Manchester, 1922, p. 91.*
[71] *Chancery IPM, 7 Henry v, 1419-20, no. 43*

enough to have known her father before he went off to war in 1415. The Patent Rolls from 1420 report that William Kynwolmershhe, the King's deputy Treasurer, is promoting an orderly transition of the family estate in her favour:[72]

> *Commission, by mainprise of John Leventhorpe of the county of Hertford the younger and Robert Myrfyn of the county of Kent, to John Leventhorpe, esquire, of the keeping of a capital messuage called 'Wodehalle' in Great Sampford and a tenement in Hempstede late of Mary late the wife of Thomas Holgill, deceased... now in the king's hands, to hold during the minority of Joan the daughter and heiress of William, with her marriage without disparagement and so from heir to heir, paying £40 in hand for the keeping and marriage if they be adjudged to the king, finding a competent maintenance for the heir, maintaining all houses, enclosures and buildings and supporting all other charges. By bill of William Kynwolmersshe, deputy treasurer.*

Joan died aged barely in her teens on St Margaret's day, 20 July 1426, and the subsequent descent of the family estate, now extended by inclusion of Wood Hall, followed directives agreed on Mariota's betrothal in 1375 more than half a century previously. In the writ from 3 August 1426, Joan is described as a minor in the King's custody.[73]

> *Inquisition taken Friday after the Nativity of the Virgin [Sept 8] 5 Henry VI at Walden, co. Essex. A tenement called Wodehall in Fynchyngfeld and Great Sampford and a tenement called Crouchemans in Hampstede, all in co. Essex, a wood called Spaigneswode in Fynchynfeld (containing 30 acres whereof the owners can fell yearly 2 acres)......*

> *...the premises came into the hands of the present king by reason of the minority of Joan, daughter and heir of the said William, who also lately died a minor. ...Joan died on the feast of St Margaret last past. Walter Huntyngdon is her kinsman and heir since she died without issue. He is the son of John Huntyngdon, son of Elizabeth, sister of William father of the said Mary, and is aged 24 years.*

The lineal descent from John Winslow, husband of Mariota Crouchman, has now died out. According to the terms of their 1375 marriage settlement, *Walter Huntyngdon* has inherited through his grandmother Elizabeth Crouchman, sister of William Crouchman C4, Mariota's father. Mariota had been Joan's grandmother on the paternal side, and Elizabeth therefore a great-great-Aunt to Mary's granddaughter Joan Winslow, and thus Elizabeth Crouchman was not Mariota Crouchman's sister as some researchers have maintained.

Winslow Forename Ambiguity

This brief review of the Crouchmans has highlighted the evident difficulties in identifying family members who share forenames, and the greater clarity achievable by using the suffixes *C1* to *C4*. A similar principle is applied when the main Winslow family is studied. Chapter 3 identifies nearly thirty Winslow males

---

[72] *Cal. Pat., Henry v, vol. 2. 1416-22, p. 254*
[73] *Cal. Inq. Misc., 5 Henry vi, no. 7 File 27.*

Edward Winslow's English Origins

up to 1420, sharing only eight forenames between them. More than three quarters are named *John, William* or *Thomas,* accounting for twenty of the total*:*

John	William	Thomas	Walter	Richard	Edmund	Galfrid	Robert
10	7	3	2	2	1	1	1

Figure 1-5 Distribution of Winslow Forenames

Chapter 3 carries the evidence located in the medieval record for each of these Winslows identified. Some of the separate entries turn out to be references to the same person in Chapter 3 once the distinction between individuals is clarified. Three of the group, each named John, are not necessarily connected to the Buckinghamshire Winslow branch at all; one of these, *John Wynslou,* is not even found in England. To mitigate the risk of misidentification, each family member descending from Buckinghamshire has been allocated a unique suffix. This highlights a secondary problem that does not apply to the Crouchmans.

Unlike the Crouchmans, the *Winslow* surname is derived from place names and so far two sources have been identified, one in Buckinghamshire and one in Yorkshire. Families in separate counties at opposite ends of England apart are unlikely to be related by blood, a theory supported by evidence to be presented in Chapter 2. To trace the origins of Edward Winslow unambiguously we must identify and eliminate unrelated parties from consideration. So before we address the repeated forenames, we must understand the principles of *bynames* and ensure we are correctly identifying the various Winslows located in the historical record.

1.3   Medieval Bynames

Prior to the Norman Conquest, the majority of Anglo-Saxon landowners were recognised by a single forename without a surname. The Essex Domesday record lists 88 landowners, predominantly immigrants from Normandy, whose names include *Robert Malet, Tihel le Breton and Eudo the Steward.*[74] Of the 88 names, 11 individuals have no second name, and with names like *Sasselin, Modwin, Ilbod, Hagebern, Gundwin* and *Stanhard* their origin is unmistakably Anglo Saxon, to a modern ear sounding more Wagnerian than Anglo-French.

Gradually the use of a single name identifier gave way to adoption of the Norman habit of combining a forename with a second identifier, and native Anglo Saxons began to employ *bynames,* the equivalent of a surname derived from an attribute. It is an easy concept to explain through examples.

A name like *Sasselin* have been sufficient to identify the bearer in a home location, but someone away from home needing more precise identification required something extra. The adoption of a *byname* established the identity of the

---

[74] *Domesday Book, Essex, John Morris ed., Phillimore 1983, introduction, section 1a, entry 72*

individual with greater precision. The extended name could be applied to contexts like property acquisition to evidence exclusive right of tenure. So for two Johns living in the same town, the adoption of locational bynames like *Attewood* and *Townsend* – by the wood, on the edge of town – enhanced the precision of identification within the home territory.

Possessive bynames are another type. So John Richards might be Richard's son, John. Other bynames might be based on appearance, such as the suffix *Longshanks* applied to King Edward 1 in acknowledgement of his unusually tall stature.

Some bynames were presumably intended to be humorous, in the style of a nickname. The Essex Domesday record cited above included one such name for a prospective Lothario with the byname *God-Save-Ladies* to accompany his forename, Roger.

Buckinghamshire Bynames

The most important type of byname was applied to those with status within a hometown, or who frequently travelled away from it. This was the *geographical* byname based on the hometown's name. So *William* from *Wynselowe* in Buckinghamshire could become *William de Wynselowe;* someone of this name appears in 1302-3 in the town of Swanbourne in Buckinghamshire geographically located some two miles away from Winslow, vindicating the validity of the theory.

Winslow Homonyms in Yorkshire

Unfortunately for historians trying to identify family origins, medieval England contained towns whose bynames bore strong resemblance to each other, two of which were *Wenslai* in Buckinghamshire and *Wensley* in Yorkshire. Difficulties arise when medieval transcribers of official documents fail to be meticulously consistent in their transcriptions; we could speculate that if a particular surname sounded wholly unfamiliar, then a clerk attempting transcription might adopt a variant resembling something previously encountered.

An example of this practice is found with the Yorkshire Winslows. The origin of their surname was *Wensley*, and the confusion arising from the name can be evidenced through an episode from 1327 recorded in *Toppeclyve*, modern-day Topcliffe, situated twenty miles away from the City of York.[75] Several parties are cited in the legal action brought against them all by *Henry de Percy* for trespass. The co-accused include *John de Wynselawe* and *Thomas de Wynselawe*, along with *William de Bayhouse, Thomas de Bayhouse, Robert de Stokesley, Begwynus Beleson, John de*

Figure 1-6 Location of Topcliffe

---

[75] *Cal. Pat., Edward ii, vol. 5, 1324-7, p. 138*

Popelton and *Adam de Popelton*. The charge against them is that they *broke his park at Toppeclyve, co. York, hunted therein and carried away deer.*

The bynames and background for each member of this group will be checked in turn to identify their possible place of origin, and the information so derived will be applied to their co-accused, the *Thomas* and *John* sharing the byname *de Wynselawe.*

- o The *Bayhouse* surname may have originally derived from *Bayeux* in Normandy, but there is a reference to a *John de Bayhous of Helperby* from November 1319 acknowledging that *he owes to Roger de Seleby of York 20 marks; to be levied, in default of payment, of his lands and chattels in co. York.* The references to *Helperby* and *Selby* place the family name in Yorkshire.[76] *Helperby* is only some 15 miles northwest of York, and Selby is in North Yorkshire. A further reference from 1359 to a *Robert de Bayhous, knight*[77] places him as a justice acting in Lincolnshire, the county opposite Yorkshire across the River Humber estuary.
- o Robert de Stokesley's byname presumably is from *Stokesley*, a place on the edge of the North York Moors.
- o The Popletons presumably originate from the village of that name some three miles north of York.
- o The Belesons are mentioned in 1319[78] in connection with the gaol of Beverley, situated in the East Riding some forty miles east and slightly south of York.
- o Topcliffe, the site of the alleged offence, is 25 miles from Wensley village, 5 miles from Helperby, 27 miles from Stokesley, and 21 miles from York, a convenient central point for joint assembly and participation in their day's sport. Wensley is a long way from the South of England, being 215 miles north of London and 180 miles north of Winslow in Buckinghamshire.

On the balance of probability these two people called *Thomas* and *John Wynselawe* in the official records are probably Yorkshiremen enjoying a day out with local friends. Their proximity to Wensley suggests strongly that their surnames originate from Yorkshire, making it unlikely that these *de Wynselawes* are blood relatives of the Buckinghamshire Winslows.

Disambiguation of the Winslow byname for the early medieval period can be painstaking work, and studying the context of the reference as demonstrated with the *Topcliffe* example can be helpful, but not conclusive. As time progressed and bynames became both more recognised and more uniform, so spelling conventions developed, and greater consistency applied to the transcription of their names: Buckinghamshire Winslow bynames typically started *Wyns-* or *Wynce-* and ended with *-lowe*, while Yorkshire versions started *Wens-* and ended with *-lawe*.

---

[76] *Cal. Close, Edward ii, vol. 8, 1318-23, 1319, p. 215*
[77] *Cal. Close, Edward iii, vol. 10, 1354-60, p. 543*
[78] *Parliament Rolls, Edward ii, May 1319, SC 9/22*

Unfortunately for historians, these spelling conventions were not rigidly applied. *Thomas* and *John de Wynselawe* cited above carry hybrid names not fully conforming with either convention, just as both references in the 1410 and 1411 inquests about John Winslow of Hempstead are addressed to *John Wyncelawe*. An extreme case occurs when William Winslow the King's Pavilioner has his rights to previous privileges reaffirmed after the overthrow of King Richard II in 1399. The official record variously identifies him as *Wynselowe, Wenslawe* and *Wyncelowe*, despite self-evidently relating to the same prominent individual.

An even more extreme example applies to Henry Winslow at his regular Kempsey court attendances between 1432 and 1448. Five variants of his byname are recorded: *Wynslowe, Wynneslow, Wyndeslow, Wynneslowe* and *Wynselowe*, all approximate homonyms of *Winslow,* but again indisputably referring to the same person,[79] and reinforcing the argument that the Winslows were outsiders to Kempsey. We have already noted the index to Fradd's work on the Winslows of Kempsey listing more than twenty Winslow name variants, all apparently references to the same blood relatives.

A different problem is encountered when we find a *Winslow* name elsewhere in a place otherwise unconnected with a known Winslow location. *Robert de Winslow* with the additional byname *bercarius* is found in *Sideham* or Sydenham, Oxfordshire around 1285.[80]

Another *Winslow,* again without obvious locational association, is *Richard de Wynslawe* found in the 1296 Rutland Subsidy Roll for the town of Barrowden where he has a taxable worth of 2s 4½d.[81] It is noteworthy that this *Richard* is evidently wealthy enough to be taxed at all. Like *Robert de Winslow,* Richard's location in this part of rural England offers no immediate clue to his origins. Rutland has no adjacent location with a name resembling *Winslow.*[82] Barrowden is 150 miles away from Wensley in Yorkshire, 55 miles away Buckinghamshire and 90 miles away from Worcestershire.

So far we have found only two places in England whose names have demonstrably generated *Winslow* bynames: *Winslow* in Buckinghamshire and *Wensley* in Yorkshire, both disyllabic words. A further search was launched to identify possible *Winslow* name variants in public records between 1200 and 1300. The Close Rolls between 1234 and 1302 offered only one approximation to a two-syllable *Winslow* homonym: *Wenley*[83] located in Norfolk, immediately rejected as an insufficiently close match. All the rest are trisyllabic. Does that make any difference? The objective is to create a personal identifier incapable of confusion with anyone else's

---

[79] So Cal. Pat., Henry iv, vol. 1,1399-1401, p. 111
[80] Cat. Anct. D., vol. 6, ed. H C Maxwell Lyte (London, 1915), entry C. 5663, p. 251
[81] Postles, Rutland Lay Subsidy based on P.R.O. E179/165/1 , Leicester University, undated
[82] Only five town names in Rutland start with W: Wardley, Edith Weston, Whissendine, Whitwell and Wing
[83] Cal. Close, July 1271, Henry iii, 1268-1272, p. 421

Edward Winslow's English Origins

name, so logically the byname would derive unambiguously from the place of origin. Here is the Close Roll list of near-homonyms:

YEARS	PLACES FROM CLOSE ROLLS
1234-1237	Wendeslaghedal (presumably modern-day Wensleydale)
1237-1268	None
1268-1272	Wenleye, Norfolk
1272-1279	Wyntereslewe (modern-day Winterslow, co. Wilts)
1279-1288	Wendelesworth (modern-day Wandsworth, London)
1288-1296	Wyndeleshore (modern-day Windsor, Berks)
1296-1302	Wendesle (Wensley), Wedenesleye (both South Derbyshire)

Figure 1-7 Winslow homophones 1235-1302 from the Close Rolls

For the Patent Rolls, the search was extended to include both people and place names over the date range of 1216 to 1301. Again, no close homophonic names were identified.

YEARS	PLACES AND PEOPLE FROM ROLLS PATENT
1216-66	None
1266-72	De Wyncele, De Wincele Kings Sergeants, Nicholas & Nicholas
1272-81	*Winceby*, modern-day Whitby; Wyncele, Nicholas, Serjeant, re Jersey, Channel Isles
1281-92	Wyntelowe, person re Ireland
1292-1301	Wyntreslawe , Winterslow Wilts

Figure 1-8 Winslow homophones 1275-1300 from the Rolls Patent

The search was further extended to check indices of medieval public manuscripts available in Cambridge University Library, such as Pipe Rolls and Fine Rolls, and over a similar timeline. Search criteria were further extended to any names starting *Win-* and *Wyn-, Wen-, Wend-, Wind-* and *Wynd-,* plus or minus letter *H* following the initial *W*. The indices of the manuscripts studied disclosed no further matches for *Wynslowe* or *Wynslawe*.

The next test started with the list of English place names produced by Lewis in 1848 which was checked to find obvious matches to *Winslow* or *Wenslow*,[84] a relatively unscientific approach due to natural evolution of place names between the 1290s and 1848. We had already established that Yorkshire and Buckinghamshire were known sources, and Wiltshire, Herefordshire and Derbyshire disclosed some additional candidates:

PREFIX	LOCATIONS FOR BYNAMES	COUNTY
WEN-	Wensley and Snitterton	Derbyshire
	Wensley (Holy Trinity)	Leyburn, N. Yorkshire
WIN-	Winslow	Buckinghamshire

---

[84] *A Topographical Dictionary of England, ed. Samuel Lewis, London, 1848*

Edward Winslow's English Origins

PREFIX	LOCATIONS FOR BYNAMES	COUNTY
	Winslow	Herefordshire
	Winsley	Wiltshire
	Hartwith, with Winsley	W. Yorkshire
	Winterslow	Wiltshire

Figure 1-9 English Towns as possible Homonyms of the Wynslawe name in 1848

Of the ten references found for *Winslow*, nine related to the immediate vicinity of the Buckinghamshire town, and one was for the *Winslow* adjacent to Bromyard in Herefordshire, described in 1848 as a township of 484 inhabitants. The search was widened to include place names prefixed by *Wen-* or *Win-*after finding that by 1848 place names starting *Wyn* had evidently gone out of fashion.

For the two Wiltshire towns *Winterslow* and *Winsley,* the 1332 Wiltshire Tax List includes trisyllabic *Wynterslewe*[85] and *Wimeslegh,*[86] but no persons were found with a name similar to *Winslow* that might have evolved from the area.

Wensley in Derbyshire is presumed to be the source of the local byname *Wensley* or *Wendeslegh* found there, the most famous of whom was probably *Sir Thomas Wensley,* described in the *History of Parliament* as originating from *an old and distinguished family* that had been resident in Wensley from the early 13th century, strong evidence of yet another leading family's adoption and monopolisation of their town name for their surname.[87] Sir Thomas, a staunch supporter of the Lancastrian cause, enjoyed patronage from both John of Gaunt and Henry Bolingbroke, latterly King Henry IV. Sir Thomas died in the battle of Shrewsbury in 1406.

Figure 1-10 Wensley Derbyshire

Derbyshire also offers plenty of people called *Wynnesley.* *William Wynnesley* is acting as mainpernor in the county in 1390,[88] *Thomas Wynnesley* appears in a court case,[89] and *William Wynnesley* of Herefordshire in mentioned in connection with a trespass by 1397.[90] A reference from 1400 mentions William *Wynnesley* of *Wynnesley co. Hereforde,*[91] and in 1423 we find a *Richard Wynnesley* of *Wynnesley, co. Hereford, gentilman,* in connection with a debt.[92]

---

[85] *Wiltshire Tax List of 1332, ed. D. A. Crowley, Wiltshire Record Society, Trowbridge 1989, p. 113*
[86] *Crowley, p. 121*
[87] *History of Parliament, 1386-1421, Roskell, J. S. vol. 4, p. 807, also online*
[88] *Cal. Close, Richard ii, vol. 4, 1389-1392, p. 150*
[89] *Cal. Close, , Richard ii, vol. 5, 1392-1396, p. 172*
[90] *Cal. Close, Richard ii, vol. 6, 1396-1399, p. 82*
[91] *Cal. Close, Henry iv, vol. 1, 1399-1402, p. 110*
[92] *Cal. Pat., Henry vi, vol. 1 1422-29, p. 145*

Edward Winslow's English Origins

Although no evidence has been found to suggest that the name *Wensley* ever mutated into anything like *Winslow* in medieval times, one modern editorial transcription of an entry in the Feet of Fines for a hearing held at Westminster in 1488 relating to a Shropshire and Worcestershire property transaction in *Wynnesley* has transliterated the medieval place name into *Winslow* without apparent justification. Similarly the medieval name *Roland Wynnesley* has been transcribed in the same source into *Roland Winslow*. Such a controversial editorial decision is at odds with the evidence provided above about the retention of the *Wynnesley* surname root in that context.

Herefordshire offers two places that might have generated a Winslow byname. One is *Wynnesley*, and there is no apparent local evidence that the name *Wynnesley* ever mutated into *Winslow*, presumably because it is trisyllabic.[93] The other potential source of the Winslow surname unsurprisingly is the small hamlet of *Winslow* near Bromyard which Fradd proposes as the exclusive origin of the Worcestershire Winslows' surname. The difficulty with Fradd's hypothesis is the absence of medieval evidence to indicate that the surname *Winslow* had ever been in use around the immediate geographical location of Bromyard prior to

Figure 1-11 Wynnesley, Herefordshire

1432 when the Winslow family first appear in Kempsey. Such absence of evidence does not disprove Fradd's theory, but equally there is no tangible evidence to prove that it is right. Fradd categorically rejects G Andrews Moriarty's view that the Winslows in Worcester shared ancestry with other Winslows in England because he finds Moriarty's evidence *unconvincing,* but without articulating the reason for his objection.[94]

Reference to an otherwise unknown *Joan Winslow* is found in the context of Herefordshire is in 1419 and relating to properties spanning several counties inherited through her late husband, and equally unknown John Winslow.[95] The circumstances of this inheritance will be covered in volume 2.

To summarise, only two candidates have been identified as sources for the Winslow byname in Yorkshire and Buckinghamshire. Fradd suggests Winslow in Bromyard as another potential source location, but so far no clear evidence has been found to support his hypothesis. Fradd's option is not rejected outright either, and will be reconsidered in the light of other evidence later.

---

[93] *Feet of Fines, CP 25/1/291/64, number 84*
[94] *See The Wynslowe Family, G. Andrews Moriarty, Miscellanea Genealogica et Heraldica, 5th series, 6, 1926-8*
[95] *Feet of Fines, CP 25/1/291/64, number 84*

1.4   Unique Suffixes

Holton's Winslow family chart incorrectly links *William Winslow*, son of Mariota and John Winslow of Hempstead, with *William Winslow*, husband of Agnes Poure. The two share the same name but are patently different individuals. A third *William Winslow*, formerly King's Pavilioner, died around the same time between 1414-5. The risk of misidentification is obvious.

Earlier we adopted unique suffixes to differentiate the Crouchmans. Now we will apply a similarly simple system to the Winslows so that individual family members can be distinguished easily. The three William Winslows above become:

William Winslow Chaplain – *Agnes Poure's husband, a Wiltshire chaplain and lawyer.*

William Winslow Pavilioner – *King Richard II's Pavilioner.*

William Winslow Armiger – *son of John Winslow Maunciple, styled Armiger in his will.*

One early reference to John Winslow husband of *Mariota* describes him as a *Maunciple,* someone who manages acquisition and safekeeping of food in an institution like a monastery; hence John Winslow's suffix *Maunciple.* This reference is found in the next chapter.

The list of suffixes in use and applied to the Winslow appears ahead of Chapter 1 on page vi above.

Edward Winslow's English Origins

1.5   Reworking Holton's Winslow Family Chart

Using the prime source information presented and reassessed in this chapter, Holton's version of the Winslow family chart can be redrawn as shown below.

Chapters 2 and 3 will supply further detail allowing this initial chart to be extended accordingly. Suffixes *Maunciple, Bailiff* and *Armiger* have been applied.

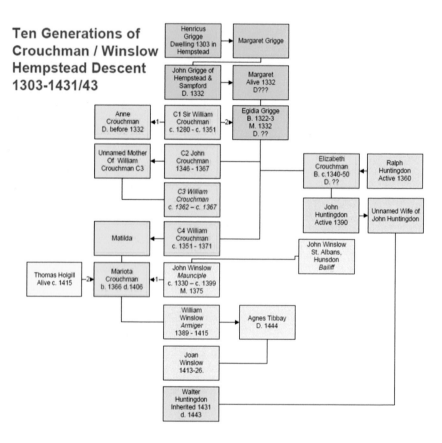

Chart 1-12 Preliminary Reworking of Holton's Winslow Family Chart centred on Hempstead

2   Some Additional Evidence

So far both Buckinghamshire and Yorkshire have been identified as definite sources of the Winslow byname in medieval times. Winslow in Shropshire has also been suggested, but no direct evidence has been found so far to support its inclusion. At this stage nothing is ruled out. The previous chapter has also disclosed a *Robert* and a *Richard* Winslow from the counties of Oxfordshire and Rutland respectively, but so far their places of origin in the thirteenth century cannot be determined with certainty from the context.

This chapter explores two additional sources of primary evidence about the Buckinghamshire Winslows possibly unfamiliar to some researchers. Both are the product of relatively recent publications. *Gesta* is the first of these, a history of the Abbey of St. Albans that controlled the town of Winslow in Buckinghamshire. The second is publication for the first time of the Winslow Manor Court Books or *WMCB*, the journal of the proceedings of the Abbot's court in Winslow analogous to the Kempsey Manor Court Books edited by Fradd. In contrast, the edition of *Gesta*, published in Holton's lifetime in the late 1860s, contains margin notes in English, but most of its text remains untranslated from its original Latin, interspersed with some occasional French.

Both works connect to some of the Winslow family members already identified through Holton. Walter Winslow *Muster* appears in WMCB as a landowner whose family enjoy a unique local status. John Winslow known here as *Maunciple* appears in both works as something of a controversial figure. Both *Gesta* and *WMCB* contain references to other members of the wider Buckinghamshire Winslow family with sufficient detail to allow Holton's Winslow family chart to be extended significantly, and a revised family chart appears at the end of this chapter.

2.1   *Gesta Abbatum Monasterii Sancti Albani*

Translated into English, the full title of this work means *the Acts of the Abbots of the Monastery of St. Albans*, a compilation assembled by chronicler Thomas Walsingham from a number of sources including materials from Matthew Paris who died in 1259. Walsingham died in 1422. Abbreviated here to *Gesta,* the work contain numerous references to contemporary events impacting the medieval

Edward Winslow's English Origins

Winslow family. Henry Riley oversaw publication of the *Gesta* in 1867-9 as three volumes, and explains the publication's origin in his introduction to Volume 1:[1]

> *The Cottonian Manuscript Claudius E. iv., which supplies the text of the Gesta Abbatum Mon. Sancti Albani, printed in these volumes, is a compilation, to all appearance, of the last ten years of the fourteenth century. The manuscript, a large folio, was evidently written, under the supervision of Thomas Walsingham, in the Scriptorium, or copying-room, of St. Alban's.[2]*

Structurally the *Gesta* form a single block of continuous text compiled by different writers documenting events in the lives of successive Abbots. Riley suggests that the first section to 1255 was largely the work of Matthew Paris, and that Paris probably collated the second section to 1308, with the remainder running through to 1401.[3]

Winslow in Buckinghamshire has a long history. The V.C.H. for County of Buckingham reports that Offa, the devout Christian King of the Mercians, determined to establish the Benedictine monastery of St. Albans during a visit to his Winslow Manor. After its foundation in 793 he endowed it with an estate comprising Winslow, Granborough and Little Horwood.[4] Legal documentation evidencing Offa's gift was apparently assembled in a cartulary previously held at the Abbey, some original components of which are now incomplete and dispersed.[5] King Offa is better known for reportedly commissioning *Offa's Dyke*, a massive earthwork excavated to establish a boundary between England and Wales. To put Offa's gift into a broader perspective of historical events, it is worth reflecting that the year 793 AD is closer to the Nativity of Christ than it is to the departure of the Mayflower in 1620.

The *Gesta* narrative opens with a fanciful sequence of miracles, apparitions and divine phenomena associated with King Offa's original bequest. What follows is a *mise en scène* detailing persistent mismanagement interspersed with legal disputes and friction. Rushbrook Williams judges the *Gesta* narrative largely fanciful, driven by the community's overriding economic objective of maintaining solvency and allied to a desire to fight off competing claims from other abbeys, while depicting the Abbey as a venerable institution of antiquity with entitlements stretching far back into antiquity:[6]

> *It seems plain that the St Albans brethren of the 13th century, with a very intelligible desire to make their unique position among English monasteries date from the earliest days, put forward the theory that privileges and exemptions which, from the point of fact, had been*

---

[1] *Gesta Abbatum Monasterii Sancti Albani, Thomas Walsingham and others, ed. H. T. Riley, 3 vols., 1867-9, vol. 1, intro. p. xi*

[2] *Gesta, vol. 1, intro., without page number reference, but effectively p. ix*

[3] *Gesta, vol. 1, intro., pp. x-xii*

[4] *See V.C.H. for County of Buckingham: vol. 3, ed. William Page, London, 1925, esp. pp. 465-470*

[5] *Anglo-Saxon England, vol. 22, ed. Lapidge, Godden, Keynes, CUP, 2007, pp. 258-63*

[6] *History of the Abbey of St. Alban, Rushbrook Williams, Longmans Green, London 1917, Introductory p. 15*

acquired one by one, were merely a renewal of those which the house had possessed from the earliest years of its existence. In support of the theory they fabricated documentary evidence with much naiveté and little compunction..

In his 1908 history of St. Albans,[7] Page notes a sharp increase in disputes between the Abbey and the town from the time of Abbot Roger Norton between 1260 and 1291, the root cause of which was invariably poor economic management. Rushbrook Williams reports on the relative strength and resilience of the local economy despite the Abbey's interventions:[8]

The importance and the wealth of the town steadily grew; during the troubles of 1265 it was so strong as to be nicknamed "Little London", and so rich as to pay "readily" the fine of 100 marks exacted for the slaying of the unhappy castellan of Hertford...

One of the reasons for this prosperity was due to its advantageous position on Watling Street that ran from Canterbury in Kent through the centre of the City of London, and onward to *Viriconium* or Worcester located on the River Severn in Shropshire some 50 miles directly upstream of Kempsey. Watling Street was the important Roman arterial road connecting St. Albans to the City of London only 20 miles away, and passing within a couple of miles of Winslow as its route crossed Buckinghamshire.

Mark Hagger suggests that the main reason for writing *Gesta* was to ward off competing property claims from institutions like the Benedictine monks of Ely, and from individuals like the Bishop of Lincoln.[9] Disputes with the St. Albans townsfolk remained a feature of Abbey life into the fifteenth century.[10] The prosperity of St. Albans had grown quickly with its local merchants trafficking goods as far as France; a French commercial class had existed in St. Albans since Domesday. Initially King Henry II had granted exclusive liberties to the Abbey, but by 1253 King Henry III dismantled some of those privileges.

Friction between the townsfolk and the Abbey provoked frustration resulting in protracted and occasionally violent disputes, sometimes over seemingly innocent issues like rights to grind grain. The Winslows are seen to be playing a role in defending townsfolk's rights. Underlying resentment continued to fester until serious violence eventually broke out during the Peasant's Revolt in 1381 with the town striving to replace the Abbot's overlord status by a more conventional and less prescriptive structure of governance led by the King and the Commons.[11]

Two members of the Winslow family moved to the village of Little Horwood next to Winslow in 1352, one of whom was Holton's *John Winslow*, later married to

---

[7] Originally published in 1908 in vol. 2 of The Victoria History of the County of Hertfordshire
[8] Rushbrook Williams, p. 126
[9] Mark Hagger, Gesta Abbatum Monasterii Sancti Albani: Litigation and History at St. Albans, August 2008, article pp. 373-398
[10] City of St. Albans, The Borough, History of County of Hertford vol. 2, ed. William Page, London, 1908, p. 477
[11] Page, William 1908, op. cit., quoting Walsingham, Hist. Angl. (Rolls Ser.), i., 472

Edward Winslow's English Origins

Mariota Crouchman. Unwittingly the Winslows were to become embroiled in disputes with the Abbey. To understand the context of the dispute we first need to understand the rules under which the Winslows of Little Horwood were operating, and then to discover the imprudence of the Winslows in accepting the terms of their tenancy.

Williams sets out the social structure for the three classes of tenant living under St. Albans jurisdiction: the free tenants, the villeins *or villani*; and lastly the serfs, or *nativi*.[12] He starts with the onerous rules relating to villeins:

> *No villein may sell his land even to other villeins—quia plurima destructio est: [it is too disruptive].*
>
> *No freeman may enter upon a villein tenement.*
>
> *If any villein buys land, the House [The Abbey of St. Albans] is straightway to enter into possession of it.*
>
> *No villein may sell either corn or cattle without express permission.*
>
> *No villein is to accumulate in his hands more than one single villein holding.*
>
> *On the death of any villein the heriot [death tax] is to be exacted without delay.*

Rushbrook Williams next describes the even more onerous life of serfs, the *nativi*.

> *As late as 1302 the tenure of a bondman of St. Albans exhibited all the old features of earlier and harsher days. He must work upon his lord's land so many days in the week, in addition to the "boondays" at harvest and the like: and although the quantity of the work was fixed, the lord might demand it when and where he chose. Further, the bondman had to pay the hated "merchet of flesh and blood", the price for permission to marry away his daughter: he had no legal status except in the court of his lord against whom he had no protection. In common with his like, he was subject to arbitrary taxation—in sonorous legal phrase "talliabilis de alto et basso ad voluntatem Domini Abbatis" [taxable from top to bottom according to the will of the Lord Abbot].*

The specific rules applicable to serfs or *bondmen* are prescriptive and demeaning:

> *Bondmen may not stand surety for freemen.*
>
> *Bondmen are incapable of having heirs, for all their property belongs to the House.*
>
> *Bondmen who leave the land are to be sought diligently until they are recaptured.*
>
> *Sons of bondmen may not leave the manor on which they are born, but must take up their father's holding.*

Rushbrook Williams concludes that *no more oppressive system could well be imagined than that which is here outlined;* but adds that *a survey of the later history of the Abbey suggests doubts as to whether it was ever carried out in its entirety.*

The reason for setting out the regulatory structure of the Abbey in such detail here is to provide context to explain why the Abbey reacted so aggressively to the business activities of John Winslow *Maunciple* and how, despite the setbacks, John

---

[12] *Rushbrook Williams, pp. 53-54, pp. 125-131*

managed subsequently to rise to such spectacular prominence. The cause of his discomfiture was that when he took up residence in Little Horwood he had unwittingly accepted a tenancy classifying him as a *serf*, and Abbot Thomas's team adopted the confrontational stance towards him whose repercussions were considerable and are described below.

The Winslow family does not feature at all in Volume 1 of *Gesta*, but in Volumes 2 and 3 they are mentioned eight times in the context of the Abbey's profligacy.[13] Book 2 of *Gesta* opens in 1290 with the recent death of an Abbot triggering recurrent and crippling expenses associated the election of his successor, Abbot John of Berkhamsted, to be followed by yet more expenditure for the customary visit to the Pope. The Abbey, already in financial straits, cannot afford to pay its way. To make matters worse in this case, King Edward I has sent in an escheator, and he promptly misappropriates some of the Abbey's assets.[14]

Abbot John plans his trip to the Pope in Rome, but first has to raise funds in London to finance the trip; and on arrival in Rome is obliged to borrow further funds direct from the Pope. On his return Abbot John cannot afford the repayments, and King Edward attempts to embezzle further sums out of Abbey funds earmarked for the Pope. Continuing attempts over several years to misappropriate other assets place the Abbey in a solvency crisis. In an obituary the *Gesta* chronicler denigrates Abbot John as an affable fool detested by some, and habitually incautious in his *largesse*.[15] *Gesta* is more a story of political machination than a handbook of Christian ethics and spirituality.

Abbot John's successor is John de Maryns who resumes the cycle of poor financial husbandry, and remarkably his successor Abbot Hugh of Eversden manages to impoverish the Abbey even further. By this time the *Handmill* has been invented, a device allowing grain to be milled at home, and it arouses a dispute quaintly termed *The Subtraction of Multure*. Rushbrook Williams calculates that the traditional Abbey mills generate as much as three percent of total Abbey revenue. The Abbey's tenants want to use their new handmills to save the grinding fee. But the abbot disagrees, insisting that its tenants have no such right. In his view the obligations forcing them to use Abbey mills have existed *since time immemorial*, so handmills are banned, and the dispute intensifies.[16]

Around the time of Edward III's accession in 1327, another revolt breaks out in the town and culminates in further litigation. The chronicler is reporting that Abbot Hugh has been profligate, needlessly burdening the Abbey with debt, and mortgaging so much of the Abbey's property that even the manor of Winslow has

---

[13] *Gesta, vol. 2, pp. 198, 249; vol. 3, pp. 67, 379, 417, 425, 480, 484*
[14] *Gesta, vol. 2, p. 3*
[15] *Gesta, vol. 2, p. 51*
[16] *Rushbrook Williams op. cit. p. 127*

now been effectively mortgaged to an income *Farmer*, Simon Fraunceys. In this atmosphere of confrontation and just as feelings are running so high, so the Winslows start to become involved in local affairs following the election of Abbot Richard of Wallingford in 1327.

Son of a blacksmith, Abbot Richard is best remembered to history as a gifted engineer. He designed and oversaw the construction of the famously sophisticated clock, arguably the most complex timepiece in all Europe at that time, a landmark invention of the fourteenth century. This chronological masterpiece in the Abbey church displayed not only the time, but also reported true solar time, the positions of lunar phases and even the height of tide at London Bridge. Sadly the clock was destroyed during the Reformation. Despite the Abbey's parlous financial state, Abbot Richard's first action is to travel to meet the Pope, now resident in Avignon rather than Rome, and incurring additional costs approaching £1,000.

Around this time, Brother *William de Winslow* makes his appearance as *coquinarius* or Kitchener, one of five monastic *obedientaries*. He stands accused of misconduct for not paying Abbot Richard his share of the tithes due. Abbot Richard threatens physical chastisement and excommunication, later commuted to penance under pressure from senior monks, possibly signalling Brother Winslow's youthful age.[17] The dispute with the *obedientaries* may have place within a couple of years of the Abbot's accession in 1326. It is also highly likely that this Brother *William de Winslow* is the same person later running the Winslow Manor Court in 1340-44, a son of Walter Winslow *Muster* as discussed below.

Abbot Richard decides at this point to impose his own interpretation of the Abbey's rights and privileges.[18] A leading townsman called John Taverner is summoned for adultery; and an ensuing scuffle involving the Abbot's esquire escalates into violence, resulting in the death of both men. A coroner is sent for. Initially blame for the incident is directed to Abbot's staff and latterly attaches to the Abbot himself; but subsequently the responsibility for law-breaking is attributed to the townsfolk themselves. Simon Fraunceys, Winslow Manor's *Farmer*, supports the townsfolk, assisted by Thomas Lincoln, *Serviens de Banco*, professional London Lawyer.[19] These events probably occur around 1330.

The *Gesta* chronicler reports how the prosecution team comprising seasoned Trailbaston judges Robert de Grey, John of Cambridge and Robert le Bourcer is lavishly entertained before a hearing at Hertford Priory, well away from St. Albans. The outcome is predictable and somewhat inevitable: victory for the Abbot, imprisonment for some of the townsfolk. Even the original coroner is indicted for daring to bring charges against the Abbot. Taken with what else has been

---

[17] *Gesta, vol. 2, p. 198*
[18] *For his abbacy see Gesta, vol. 2, pp. 186 et seq.*
[19] *Gesta, vol. 2, p. 222*

developing since the 1290s, these two incidents under Abbot Richard from around the 1330s illustrate the toxic climate of antagonism developing between the Abbey and the St. Albans townsfolk.

At this point a fresh dispute breaks out over *Handmills,* and three distinct iterations of legal activity ensue. It is difficult to date events and durations with precision, but the sequence leads up to 1332. Two of the sessions which occupy multiple pages of the *Gesta* text have already had inconclusive outcomes. The third session involves thirteen pairs of litigants jointly challenging the Abbey's right to invoke precedent as a rationale for blocking private use of handmills.

For this third session, *Gesta* introduces two new individuals, *Richard Winslow* and *John Baldwyn of St. Albans,* one of the thirteen pairs of litigants.[20] In contrast to previous iterations, this report barely fills a single page of *Gesta* text, and despite listing all twenty six claimants in detail.[21] This time the chronicler, normally happy to trumpet the humiliation of the Abbot's opponents, confines his observation to one laconic sentence:[22]

> as for the judge's conclusion, I didn't find it.

The outcome was probably not as the Abbot intended. For this study, who were *Richard Winslow* and *John Baldwyn?* We find out shortly.

Moving on to the contents of *Gesta* Volume 3 and the abbacy of Thomas de la Mare, 1349-96, the name of *John Winslow* appears prominently as someone accused of serious transgression or *gravamen,* resulting in a huge fine of £20, the largest single financial penalty ever recorded in the entirety of *Gesta.*[23] What had this John Winslow done that was so wrong? The incident is given coverage in three different sections of Volume 3, each one conveying a subtly different underlying message.

The first section describes Winslow's apparent offence as having disposed of a property called *Blakette,* and despite holding valid legal title. The narrative extends over several pages with the chronicler criticising Abbot Thomas's poor stewardship. We hear how entitlements such as twice-yearly gifts of deer have been squandered, rental income has gone uncollected; and widespread needless asset disposal has been permitted, including one property settled for an unduly advantageous price *because of carnal affection.* The criticism is directed at poor standards of management and not specifically at *John Winslow,* and ends with a weary resignation about deplorable administrative stewardship under Abbot Thomas.

What rankles the chronicler here is not so much John Winslow's execution of a property transaction *per se,* but rather the implicit breakdown in governance that

---

[20] *Gesta, vol. 2, p. 249*
[21] *Gesta, vol. 2, p. 249*
[22] *Gesta, vol. 2, p. 250*
[23] *Gesta, vol. 3, p. 67*

should have prevented its disposal. From the original text it is difficult to ascertain exactly how John was in any way to blame, and indeed whether he was in fact acting on behalf of the Abbey:[24]

> *Terrae insuper, et tenementa, quondam "Blakette" vocitata, quae Johannes Wynslowe, nativus ejusdem Abbatis, adquisierat, et ob hoc per seisinam debite ad ejus pacificam possessionem devenerant , alienata.*

> Lands and tenements once called "Blakette", which John Winslow, a serf of the same Abbot had acquired, and through which he had duly obtained valid possession and title, were disposed of..

The Abbey's problem was that a valued property had been lost; and to make it worse, John Winslow as a mere *serf*, someone totally devoid of property transfer rights, had no entitlement to be leading such transactions. The chronicler fails to provide the background to the particular breakdown in governance that triggered John Winslow's harsh punishment.

The next section mentioning John Winslow conveys a different message, this time focusing on Abbot Thomas's robust disregard for rank and title. The chronicler reels off a long list of all the prominent figures in England successfully confronted and challenged by the Abbot, including Kings Edward III and Richard II, together with leading members of the various classes of nobility, some senior churchmen; and somewhat incongruously the list ends with the names of two individuals *whom the abbot has vigorously reconsigned to their rightful condition* [of servitude].[25] John Winslow appears as one of the two individuals so named and shamed.

The third section about John Winslow includes his name in the list of those victims suffering punitive financial penalties imposed by the Abbot. The entry is clearly dated to 1356-7.[26]

> It was found thus in the Great Roll for the thirtieth year of the reign of King Edward ...twenty pounds fine for John Wyselowe (sic) for law breaking, extortion and offensive behaviour...

Perhaps in his glee the chronicler even manages to spell John Winslow's surname incorrectly. We will find later from WMCB what the sequence of events 1356-7 entailed.

The final two references to Winslows in *Gesta* are to *Prior William Winslow*. After the death of Abbot Thomas in 1396, Prior William is ranked second in the St. Albans monastic community during the election of Abbot Thomas's successor, John de la Moote.[27] The other reference referring to *Prior William of Hertford* follows the death of this Abbot John de la Moote.[28] That would make *Prior William* a very elderly gentleman well into his eighties if indeed he is recognised both as the

---

[24] *Gesta, vol. 3, p. 417*
[25] *Gesta, vol. 3 p. 379, "ad conditionem eorum debitum viriliter revocavit"*
[26] *Gesta, vol. 3 p. 67*
[27] *Gesta, vol. 3, p. 466*
[28] *Gesta, vol. 3, p. 480*

recorder of Winslow Manor Court mentioned in 1342 and the *Brother William* punished for breaking tithing rules between 1326 and 1335, and who emerged as this *Prior William* after 1396. If that sounds implausible, it is worth recalling that Abbot Thomas de la Mare's age at his death on September 15 1396 is documented as being eighty seven years, a considerable age in any epoch.[29] Evidence presented later will show that Thomas de la Mare had been William's immediate predecessor as Recorder of Winslow Manor Court, placing him perhaps a few years older than Brother William, and remarkably Prior William would continue to remain alive until at least 1400.

The implication of what has been found from *Gesta* is considered in greater depth in Chapters 3 and 4 as further corroborative evidence is uncovered.

2.2   *Winslow Manor Court Books*

Winslow Manor Court Books or *WMCB* provide a unique historical record of the Winslow family in its dealings with St. Alban Abbey. Translated by historian David Noy in 2011, *WMCB* provide valuable information about virtually contemporary life for the Winslows in their Buckinghamshire home town of Winslow.[30] A copy of the original WMCB escaped the general destruction of Abbey manuscripts during the 1381 Peasants' revolt[31] and was given to Cambridge University in 1715.[32]

The surviving Winslow Manor Court Books span the periods from 1327-77 and from 1423-60. Numerous references to Winslow family members wholly unavailable from other sources are found in the first WMCB volume, allowing Holton's Winslow chart to be rolled back three further generations. While Holton

Figure 2-1 Winslow and Little (Parva) Horwood, distances in miles

restricts his comments to the statement that John Winslow was *of great repute* in London about 1350, WMCB records offer a detailed account of John and brother John living under Abbey's jurisdiction in Little Horwood between 1352 and 1357.

Residents of Winslow classed as *serfs* rather than *villani* enjoyed a status little better than slavery.[33] Noy has separately suggested that the Winslow family held

---

[29] *Gesta, vol. 3, p. 422*
[30] *Winslow Manor Court Books, Vols. i and ii, David Noy ed., Bucks Record Society, nos. 35-6, 2011*
[31] *Noy, WMCB, vol. i, intro., p. xi*
[32] *The surviving Cambridge University record is Ms. Dd. 7.22*
[33] *So Rushbrook Williams, op. cit., passim*

Edward Winslow's English Origins

an elevated status in the town, setting them apart from the general residents, and probably explaining why their eminence enabled them to monopolise the usage of the Winslow byname.[34] It makes the brothers' adoption of serfdom all the more inexplicable

WMCB court sessions were conducted under the jurisdiction of the St. Albans Abbey Cellarer,[35] with social obligations similar to those described above by Rushbrook Williams for *serfs* and *villeins* of St. Albans. In the extant court records documenting the lives of the Winslows we find administration of justice occasionally transferred a *Farmer* like Simon Fraunceys, located earlier in *Gesta*. Fraunceys acted as *Farmer* for Winslow between around 1330 and 1342, and was later elected Mayor of London, and called to Parliament before his death in 1358.

The administrator of the Manor Courts under Fraunceys between 1340 and 1344 was William Winslow *Cellarer,* also found earlier in *Gesta*. Given their unique status in the town as freeholders it might be expected that the Winslow children were educated locally. The two surviving volumes of the WMCB report a total of twenty five instances of fathers applying to send their sons to *clerical school*. Twenty two such requests span the 50 years between 1327 and 1377, but only three for the 37 years between 1423 and 1460. No application from the Winslow family is recorded in either extant volume, perhaps reflecting the possibility that the Winslows did not spend their childhoods there, a subject picked up later, but also possibly because their elevated social status in Winslow precluded any need to register. The descent of this possible privilege can be followed in the family chart at the end of this chapter using the unique suffixes described on page vi of the Preface.

The first Winslow family member found in WMCB appears as early as page 2 of the surviving WMCB record: *Geoffrey de Wynselowe*, suffix *Galfrid,* son of *William Winslow* and married to Alice, daughter of Walter Roberd.[36] The only William Winslow identifiable with children on the chart so far is William Winslow *Wodyam,* but we will discover later that he is too young to be father of Geoffrey de Wynselowe.

Geoffrey de Wynselowe is not mentioned again in WMCB after this entry, but his interfamilial relationships with the Roberd family can be established from other WMCB references, revealing relatives on his wife's line a generation earlier. Walter Roberd transfers property to his son-in-law, Geoffrey Wynselowe, an action prefaced by this statement that reveals more of the Roberd ancestry:

[34] David Noy, Winslow in 1556, The Survey of the Manor, Buckinghamshire Archaeological Society, 2013, p. 15
[35] Noy, WMCB, intro., pp. xii-xiii
[36] Noy, WMCB, vol. 1 p. 2

Walter, son of William Roberd, the brother and heir of John, son of William Roberd, after the death of the said John whose heir he is, came and paid gersum [tax] for two messuages with two appurtenances...[37]

By 1342 Brother William of Wynselow *Cellarer* is acting as court recorder,[38] a role he continues to perform until 1344, the period when Simon Fraunceys is acting as *Farmer* of Winslow. At this stage there is insufficient evidence in WMCB to determine Brother William's family origins.

The next reference is to Walter de Wynselowe *Muster,* recently deceased in May 1346, and the subject of Holton's 1322 reference. At his death Walter de Wynselowe reportedly held a cottage and a storehouse in Winslow[39] which his son William Winslow *Wodyam* will inherit, and has both paid for the continuity of tenure and is due to perform the requisite dues and accustomed services. Evidently Walter also had landholdings elsewhere. His *heriot* or death tax in Winslow is half a mark, 3/4d. By October of the same year the court records mention *distraint* or threat of legal action, suggesting that William Winslow *Wodyam* has failed to perform required services, an omission covered in Chapter 3.

The onset of Black Death in England occurs in 1348-49. Abbot Michael falls victim and is succeeded in 1349 by Abbot Thomas de la Mare, incumbent for almost half a century until 1396. Brother Thomas de la Mare was Brother William's immediate predecessor in the role of Winslow Court recorder, and presumably already familiar to many Winslow residents.

Next comes Thomas Wynselowe *Homicide* in May 1350, son and heir of William Winslow *Wodyam* who has just died. The reason for the *Homicide* identifier becomes apparent later. Thomas Winslow *Homicide* is set to inherit in villeinage the cottage and storehouse left to his father by grandfather Walter *Muster* in 1346.

An adjacent entry concerns *Wodyam's* spouse Alice, also recently deceased. She has a separate cottage and three acres that she leaves to Thomas in villeinage as sole beneficiary.[40] We still have no indication about the eventual fate of Geoffrey Wynselowe *Galfrid.*

By January 1352 John Wynselowe is taking over from John le Irmonger a messuage in Little Horwood, and within Winslow manorial jurisdiction. The holding comprises a virgate of land with appurtenances and a meadow *to hold for himself and his heirs in bondage, at the lord's will, through due and accustomed services.*[41] The fine is 2 marks, and John has unwittingly adopted the status of a *serf.* By 1353 the *Cellarer* is referring to John Winslow as a *Maunciple,* a purveyor of foodstuffs, and hence

[37] Noy, WMCB, vol. 1 p. 318
[38] Noy, WMCB, vol. 1 p. 132
[39] Noy, WMCB, vol. 1, p. 178
[40] Noy, WMCB, vol. 1, p. 253
[41] Noy, WMCB, vol. 1, p. 269

Edward Winslow's English Origins

his suffix in this work.[42] To qualify for his landholding in Horwood, John de Wynselowe must have been of age, which Noy interprets as above 20 years old.[43] John Winslow *Maunciple* was therefore born before January 1331, marking him as around 70 years old when he died 1399-1400.

Whatever the outside interests of John Winslow *Maunciple* around this time, compliance with manor rules was not his priority. By May 1353 John has been placed into the tithing of Thomas atte Wode,[44] and a sequence of amercements commences, the first when John Winslow *Maunciple* in violation of the rules of *serfdom* attempts to transfer the recently acquired Horwood property to his younger brother John Winslow, identified here as *Hunsdon*. The Court Books note that in December 1353:[45]

> John de Wynselowe maunciple, demised his land to his brother John without licence of the lord; therefore amerced 6d. And it was ordered to take the land into the lord's hand etc.

The reason why John Winslow *Maunciple* was so keen to transfer his Horwood property interest to his younger brother John Winslow *Hunsdon* is not explained. John is fined a further 6d for a service default in May 1354,[46] repeated in January 1355 when he is amerced only 3d, but the penalties continue:[47] 3d in June 1355 along with a default relating to frankpledge, without specification of cost.[48] In October 1355 he is amerced 3d in court and 6d for frankpledge.[49] May 1356 brings a 3d penalty for default,[50] while a fellow defaulter at the same court is reported to be *John Beaufiz* from Little Horwood, and a name previously encountered in connection with the descent of Trumpington Manor. A further 3d amercement is levied in November 1356.[51]

At this point things go badly wrong. John Winslow *Maunciple* abruptly surrenders the Horwood messuage in May 1357 along with its virgate of land, its appurtenances and its meadow, notionally home to himself and his brother since 1352,[52] but WMCB does explain why. The timing of the event in *Gesta* is clearly stated as in the thirtieth year of Edward III's reign, pointing to 1356-7. In WMBC the session where John Winslow is fined for non-attendance occurs on 14th November 1356, the thirtieth year of Edward III's reign, and by next court hearing on May 1357 John Winslow *Maunciple* has paid his heriot of ten shillings for release

---

[42] Noy, WMCB, vol. 1, p. 286
[43] Noy, WMCB, vol. 1, intro., p. xxii
[44] Noy, WMCB, vol. 1, p. 285
[45] Noy, WMCB, vol. 1, p. 286
[46] Noy, WMCB, vol. 1 p. 289
[47] Noy, WMCB, vol. 1 p. 294-5
[48] Noy, WMCB, vol. 1 pp. 299-301
[49] Noy, WMCB, vol. 1 p. 305-6
[50] Noy, WMCB, vol. 1 p. 309
[51] Noy, WMCB, vol. 1 p. 312
[52] Noy, WMCB, vol. 1 p. 318

from his tenure. Without doubt the two references are addressing the same individual.

No further references are found for the Winslow family in Volume 1 of WMCB which runs to 1377. Volume 2 of WMCB running from 1423 to 1460 has only a single reference: in May 1435 a William Wynslowe, here given the suffix *Attorney,* is acting as legal representative to a Winslow resident, Henry Thomas or Thomlyn.[53]

An observation worth making at this stage is that no connections have yet been established with any Winslow family with Worcestershire.

In a separate work, Noy's research has uncovered a 1556 survey of Winslow conducted by the Crown seeking to augment its tax revenue by re-establishing entitlements and reassessing personal wealth by studying landholdings, registers of births and deaths and associated records.[54] Noy has identified the only free tenant in Winslow in 1556 as *Richard Dele.*

Evidence of this is apparent in the WMCB from 1346 when William of Winslow assumes a cottage and 2 acres of *copyhold* on the death of his father Walter of Winslow. By 1517 this holding, later to be Richard Dele's, is described in the court rolls as formerly of *Walter of Winslow.* The freehold land is not mentioned specifically in the 14th century Court books, but the court orders *the heir of Walter of Winslow to do the outstanding relief and fealty,* which Noy interprets as evidence of freehold tenure. Noy concludes that only Edmund Paxon remained a freeholder by 1660.

Noy's further research suggests that Walter Winslow was indeed outright owner of freehold land, an arrangement seemingly at variance with the terms of Offa's original gift of Winslow town to St Albans Abbey in 793 AD. These five references located in the medieval sources suggest that Walter was a man of affluence with property holdings in Swanbourne and Winslow. Walter's landed wealth probably explains his call to fight the *Scotts* in 1322 as

Figure 2-2 showing Winslow and Swanbourne adjacent to Drayton Parslow

reported by Holton. The evidence and implication of this will be further considered in Chapter 3. Noy's theory about the Winslows' unique freehold tenure in Winslow manor is corroborated by finding William Winslow *Patriarch* with the Swanbourne

---

53 Noy, WMCB, vol. 1 p. 562
54 David Noy, Winslow in 1556, The Survey of the Manor, Buckinghamshire Archaeological Society, 2013, p. 15

Edward Winslow's English Origins

landholding obtained through his wife in 1278, daughter of Walter Godard, also covered in Chapter 3. Were William a *serf* or *villein*, this tenure would not be permitted, suggesting that the Winslows as Anglo Saxons had enjoyed this unique status perhaps as far back as the Norman Conquest.

Updated Winslow Family Chart

Winslow Family Connections from WMCB and Medieval Sources c. 1225 to 1435. Paternity of John Winslow *Maunciple* not yet established

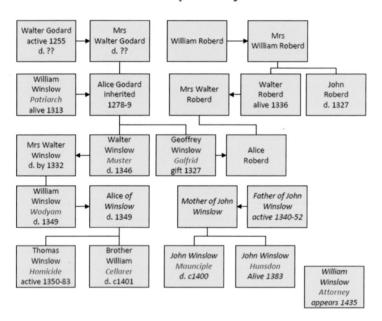

Chart 2-3 Winslow Family Connections as found through the WMCB, adding the Godards

3   Distinguishing the Individuals

Introduction

Incorrect or incomplete data found in the historical tradition of the Winslows has led to inconsistencies and misleading conclusions about the descent of the Winslow family line, as already discussed in Chapter 1. As far as possible these obvious anomalies have now been identified and eliminated. Chapter 1 has also demonstrated the risk of misidentification between the distinct clusters of English families who share variants of the *Winslow* family name. They originate from different and geographically separate parts of England, and are unlikely to be related by blood.

Chapter 2 has introduced some additional primary source material about the Winslows found in *Gesta* and the WMCB, and this new data has been incorporated in rework and extension of Holton's chart at the end of the previous chapter.

This chapter reviews the 800 or so primary references uncovered for the Winslows and some of their family associations covering the period up to the early 1430s when Fradd locates Henry Winslow in the manor court in Kempsey. These primary records from contemporary medieval sources stretch back to the mid-thirteenth century. Some twenty-five people bearing the Winslow family name have been traced, now uniquely distinguishable by their suffixes as listed in the table immediately before Chapter 1.

We will consider each Winslow family member in turn, checking events and associations for each individual, and mapping wider family connections based on content. Chapter 4 combines this primary data with additional circumstantial evidence to derive the family's wider patterns of social interaction and geographical dispersion.

Robert Winslow *Bercarius*

A single undated record for this Robert Winslow has been located for the village of *Sideham*, modern-day Sydenham in Oxford.[1]

> *Oxford. C. 5663. Grant by Isabel relict of Adam Franchum of Sideham, widow, to Peter Delapole of Sideham and Emma his wife their heirs and assigns of her right in ½d. rent in which Robert de Winslowe, shepherd (bercarius), and his heirs were bound yearly to her and her heirs for a part of her messuage which she sold to Robert; also ½d. rent in which Nicholas de Bertone of Thame was bound to her for 1a. of her land which he bought of her*

---

[1] *Descriptive Catalogue of Ancient Deeds: Volume 6, ed. H C Maxwell Lyte (London, 1915), Entry 5663*

Edward Winslow's English Origins

in the town of Sideham. Witnesses:— Ralph Grimbaud, Nicholas Bussard, and others (named). The said 1d. of rent is payable at Michaelmas yearly.

Sydenham village jointly formed one knight's fee with neighbouring Chinnor in the 1250s. Both villages skirt the ancient Icknield Way on the edge of the border between Oxfordshire and Buckinghamshire, with Winslow town in Buckinghamshire located about 20 miles north. Isabel, widow of Adam Franchum, has sold *a part of her messuage* to *Robert de Winslowe*, whose surname and proximity suggest origins in adjacent Winslow.

The oppressive rules applied to the villeins and serfs in Winslow Manor outlined earlier would have restricted Robert's options even to hold property, so we can assume that Robert was operating not as some indentured farm labourer, but more likely as an independent specialist in the profitable medieval sheep farming sector, and that Isabel Franchum valued his expertise highly enough to sell him part of the family's dwelling. We will return to Robert Winslow in the light of other information uncovered.

William Winslow, *Patriarch,* Entries 1284-1313

The Parish of Swanbourne in Buckinghamshire is important for understanding the descent of the Winslows. WMCB earlier introduced Geoffrey Winslow *Galfrid* whose father was stated to be *William,* but without identifying William's lineage. Datable references for William Winslow *Patriarch* are as follows:

DATE	ACTIVITY
1284-86	Godard Fee in Swanbourne held by Willelmus de Wineslowe, Thomas de Walda
1302-3	Willelmus de Winslawe, jury duty for 6, Honour of Berkhamsted
1302-3	Fee in Swanbourne
1313	Property transaction for Doygnel, West Tockenham, Wiltshire, 1313

Table 3-1 Timeline for William Winslow, Patriarch

Swanbourne, a village adjacent to Winslow, contained a manor known as *Weldes* where *Thomas de Walda* or *de la Welde* held a knight's fee in 1284,[2] and with an adjacent estate known as the fief of *Mortain*. The Passelewe and the Chenduit families held interests here, and a dispute with the Abbot of Woburn had resulted in half the *Mortain* fee in Swanbourne being held of the lord of Langley, formerly William Chenduit. The Chenduits remained as tenants, and the Godard family holders in fee. These Godards intermarried with the Winslows. The name of *Richard Godard* appears in spring 1251 in connection with a landholding:[3]

---

[2] *Feudal Aids, vol. 1, p. 84*
[3] *Feet of Fines Buckinghamshire, 7 Richard I to 44 Henry iii, Bucks Archaeological Society, ed. M. W Hughes, vol. 4, 1942, p. 95*

Walt. s. Ric. de Swaneburn' quer. and Ric. Godard deforc.; 2 caruc, land in Swaneburn'; R. ackn. right of W. as of his gift, to hold for ever; W. and his heirs henceforth will pay each year for the whole life of R. 4 mks. of silver.

Walter Godard was holding 2 hides in 1255,[4] and by 1278 had transferred the estate to his daughter and heir who married William de Winslow *Patriarch* as confirmed by this entry from 1302:[5]

> *Thomas de Walda and William de Winslow who has the heir of Walter Godard for his wife, are holding three hides of land as a third part of one fee in Swanbourne from John Passelewe, and the same John holds from the Queen of England, in connection with her Manor of Langley.*

William *Patriarch* continued to hold in the right of his wife in 1284 and in 1302, and the property was still being held by William's son Walter de Winslow *Muster* on his death in 1346.

The Feudal Aids entry from 1302 reports an inquisition where six jurors, including *Willelmus de Winslawe* and Edmund Godard, have delivered sworn oaths about their testimony.[6] *Willelmus de Winslawe* is advantageously married, has clearly earned respect and trust from his peers, and perhaps is familiar with the legal process. A 1313 entry suggests that William Winslow *Patriarch* is now acting for the *Doygnel* family in connection with property transactions in Wiltshire and Buckinghamshire:[7]

> *34. Oct. of S.J.B. Peter Doygnel and Amice his wife, pl. William de Wynselawe, def. I messuage and 4 virgates of land in Westokham. To hold to pl.*

The background to the 1313 entry is found in an inquisition held in 1293 when Peter Doygnel was aged only 14, seeking to establish whether Peter's late father Sylvester held due entitlement to three estates. Huish and West Tockenham are both located in Wiltshire, while

Figure 3-2 showing Drayton Parslow next to Winslow

Drayton Parslow [Passelewe] was a Buckinghamshire landholding close by Winslow as shown below, suggesting social or commercial connections between the Doygnels and Winslows.[8]

---

[4] *Hundred Rolls, (Rec. Com.), i, 27*
[5] *Feud. Aids, vol. 1, p. 77*
[6] *Feud. Aids, vol. 1, p. 107*
[7] *Abstract of Feet of Fines Relating to Wiltshire, Edward I and ii, ed. R. B. Pugh, p. 84*
[8] *Abstract of Feet of Fines Relating to Wiltshire, Edward I and ii, ed. R. B. Pugh, p. 84*

Edward Winslow's English Origins

97.   SILVESTER DOYGNEL alias DUYNEL, DOYNEL. Writ, 24 May, 21 Edw. I.

WILTS. Hywysch. [Huish] 80a. land, 40a. poor land, 6a. meadow, pasture, 75s. 8d. rents, &c., and the advowson of the church...

Hywysch and West Tokham [West Tockenham]. The said Silvester and Margaret his wife were jointly enfeoffed by John Doignel and Simon de Ordeston of a virgate and 1a. land in Hywysch...

BUCKINGHAM. Drayton Passelewe. A messuage, 93a. arable, 6a. meadow, and 5s. rents of free tenants, held of the abbot of Woubourn...

William de Wynselawe *Patriarch*, mentioned in the 1313 property transfer and acting as deforciant in the West Tockenham property transaction, is neither enfeeoffed in his own right, nor apparently acting as agent on behalf of a third party; the property remains in Doygnel family ownership. More likely, William de Wynselawe *Patriarch* is operating here on behalf of Silvester's son Peter as trustee or legal intermediary to complete the inter-generational transfer between father Sylvester Doygnel and his son who is now of age, further suggesting that William *Patriarch* probably possesses expertise in aspects of property law and administration.

We do not know when William *Patriarch* died. If his death occurred shortly after the 1313 reference to the Doygnels with William roughly seventy years old, William's date of birth would be around 1245; but William may have lived beyond 1313. The extant WMCB resuming in 1327 makes no reference to William's death or succession, so we can be confident that William *Patriarch* had already died before that date.

At best, any such estimates of age as these are informed guesswork. If we project William's year of birth as around 1250 with his death around 1320, and if we know that Walter died in 1346 perhaps aged 70, then we can estimate his son Walter's year of birth may have occurred around 1275, a not unreasonable assumption. Walter was called to muster in 1322, making him 47 if his birthdate were 1275; we may judge that age far too advanced for someone to be entering a military campaign until we find that John Winslow *Maunciple* is acting similarly in the 1390s by which time he would be in his mid-sixties.

For the next generation, we can project that Walter's son William Winslow *Wodyam* was possibly born around 1300. Unquestionably Geoffrey's father must have been the William Winslow *Patriarch* from the preceding generation on the basis that we know that Geoffrey *son of William* and his wife were gifted property from her father in 1327. By that date a twenty seven year old William Winslow *Wodyam* would presumably have been far too young to have fathered the already married Geoffrey Winslow *Galfrid*. So Galfrid's father named *William* was someone older, and William Winslow *Patriarch* is the obvious candidate.

Edward Winslow's English Origins

We can therefore see that the line of Winslow inheritance descended from William *Patriarch* through Walter *Muster,* onward to William *Wodyam* and eventually to Thomas *Homicide.* Noy's theory that the Winslows enjoyed a landholding status unique in Winslow is supported by finding William Winslow *Patriarch* with property in Swanbourne outside the jurisdiction of the Winslow Manor courts as early as 1302.

The confirmation of the subsequent property descent is found in the record from 1346 for the Hundred of Berkhamsted, referring to the holding between *Thomas de Walda* and Walter Winslow *Muster* previously held by William Winslow *Patriarch* and Thomas de la Welde senior.[9] The separate record from 1346 about the transition of the fractional fief of *Mortain* to Walter Winslow *Muster* from his father William Winslow *Patriarch* for *40d.* indicates the continuity of its retention:[10]

> *De Willelmo de Wynselowe et Thoma de Walda pro octava parte un. f. m. in Swanebourne, xld.*

The village of *Drayton Parslow* in Buckinghamshire takes its name from the family of *Passelewes,* the established Buckinghamshire family introduced earlier. The fee held in Swanbourne by Walter Winslow was previously held of *John Passelewe,* and evidently the *Passelewes* worked for the King. Ten commissions from July 1247 are addressed to members of the Passelewe family instructing them to distribute gifts from the Royal Forests, such as the deer out of Rockingham Forest destined for Eleanor Countess of Leicester, King Henry III's sister.[11]

Given an intermarriage with a prominent local family like the Godards and connections with the Doygnels, the Winslows by 1275 are shown to have been well established in the structure of Buckinghamshire society. Potentially they may have been so for generations, but sadly the extant public records do not stretch back that far.

Richard Winslow, *Barrowden*, Entry 1296

Richard Winslow is the next Winslow located from primary source materials. The entry in the 1296 Rutland Subsidy Roll for the town of Barrowden records his property assessment at 2s 4½d out of the total Barrowden tax roll of £7 19s 4d.[12] It is not possible to deduce the identity of this Rutland resident from the limited primary information located so far, nor to explain his reason for being in Rutland.

Date	Activity
1296	Barrowden, Rutland, Richard Winslow taxed on Lay Subsidy property

Table 3-3 Reference for Richard Winslow, Barrowden

---

[9] *Feud. Aids, vol. 1, p. 132*
[10] *Feud. Aids, vol. 1, p. 128*
[11] *Cal. Close, Henry iii, vol. 5, 1242-1247, p. 518*
[12] *Rutland Lay Subsidy, 1296/7, David Postles, Leicester University, undated, available online*

Edward Winslow's English Origins

His status is clarified in Chapter 4 from unlikely circumstantial evidence.

Walter Winslow *Muster*, Entries 1322-46

Holton introduced us Walter *de Wynslaive*, the Buckinghamshire resident summoned to fight against the Scots as noted in Chapter 1. Based on what we have found about his father William *Patriarch*, we can speculate that the summons to war was issued to fulfil feudal obligations arising from his landholding in Swanbourne. These are references found to Walter Winslow *Muster*:

DATE	ACTIVITY
1322	Walter de Wynslaive ex Buckinghamshire, muster at Newcastle
1329	Walter de Wynselawe of Swanbourne, witness March 20
1334	Walter de Wynselowe, priest, Sussex 1334
1345	Sir Walter de Wynselowe. Resignation, *ix Kal. Jun.*, 24 May 1345
1346	Walter de Wynselowe, property Swanbourne, previously of William de Winslow
1346	Walter Wynselowe dies 29 May 1346, son William is heir

Table 3-4 Timeline for Walter Winslow, Muster

WMCB tells us that Walter died in 1346, having survived his Scottish campaign of 1322, and the Close Rolls place him in his home town of Swanbourne in 1329 among a large group of witnesses to a quitclaim in favour of the Thomas de la Welde, co-holder of the Swanbourne fee. The names of *Ed. Godard* of Swanbourne and *John de la Welde* of Mursley demonstrate the continued bond between this social group of local landholders. Walter *Muster*, son of William *Patriarch*, was an active participant in his local social circle:[13]

> Christiana, late the wife of Richard de Messingge, to Thomas de la Welde of her right and claim in all the lands, rents, services, bondmen and their goods, and the lands held by them in villeinage in Swanebourne, co. Buckingham... Witnesses: Hugh de Waltham, clerk; Stephen de Waltham, clerk; Nicholas Ponge; John Brid; Henry de Norhampton; James le Sherman; John Pedewardyn; John Frere, 'skynner'; John Pisselege of London; John son of Walter Yerdele of Syncleburgh; John de la Welde of Mursle, Thomas le Bran of Northmershton, Walter de Wynselawe of Swanebourne, Ed. Godard of the same, of co. Buckingham. Dated at London, on Thursday after St. Martin the Bishop, 2 Edward III.

WMCB does not confirm whether Walter *Muster* has siblings, and Walter's wife's death is nowhere mentioned, nor is there any record of her forename. Maybe she had also died before 1327 when the extant WMCB narrative resumes.

The *Register of Bishop Robert* de *Stratford* dated 12 November 1334 styles Walter Winslow *Muster* as *Sir Walter*, describing him as a *priest*. Barely 12 years after the summons to Newcastle in 1322, Walter has been *collated*, presented to an

---

[13] *Cal. Close, Edward iii, vol. 1: 1327-1330, p. 532*

ecclesiastical benefice at Aldingbourne in Sussex, close to the English South Coast and well away from Winslow town some ninety miles North.[14]

> *12 Nov 1334. On resignation of Sir Geoffrey de Sydlesham, Sir Walter de Wynselowe, priest collated (at Aldyngbourne). From Bishop Robert de Stratford's Register: — ix Kal. Jun. (24 May). 1345. On resignation of Sir Walter de Wynselowe, John Sakeuille, clerk, collated (at Iden). iii Kal Mar (28 Feb) 1352 Sir Michael de Nourne collated (at Aldyngbourne). Later, in Bishop Robert Rede's time, Sir John Lemyngton, chaplain, was collated on 4 Feb. 1399...*

Holton had described Walter as *gentleman at arms* in the 1322 summons for the Scottish campaign, probably a translation of *Armiger* from the Parliamentary Rolls text now lost. The title *Sir* applied here is perhaps an honorific ecclesiastical designation analogous to *Monseigneur,* and not suggesting that Walter had been elevated to a knighthood. The final reference to Walter Winslow *Muster* located is the report of his death on May 29 1346 in WMCB, confirming succession to his son William Winslow *Wodyam.*[15] Holding *by rod* implies copyhold tenure analogous to *freehold.*

> *Horwood. Walter of Wynselowe has died, who held from the lord a cottage and a storehouse and two acres of land by rod, as was found out by the jurors. And William his son is his nearest heir, of full age. He came and made a fine for the said cottage, storehouse and land, to hold for himself and his heirs by rod, performing due and accustomed services for them. And he paid a fine for entry 3s 4d. And Walter paid as heriot 6s 8d.*

William Winslow, *Wodyam*, Entries 1332-1350, and 1433

Wodyam is perhaps a family nickname affectionately applied to William Winslow. A piece of land described as a *toft with enclosure and curtilage* held by the recently deceased Juliana Adam is recorded in WMCB in 1433 and belonged to *William, son of Walter of Wynselow's, otherwise called Wodya(m).*[16]

DATE	ACTIVITY
1332	Warks Lay Subsidy, Bernaston or Barston in Barlichway Hundred, Warks, 2/7d, 1332
1346	Heir of Walter of Wynselowe, fealty 1346
1350	William & Alice Wynselowe both dead, Thomas inherits May 24
1433	55 / 45 acres of land formerly of Wodyam son of Walter Winslow, Jun 8

Table 3-5 Timeline for William Winslow, Wodyam

We established earlier that William Winslow *Patriarch* died between 1313 and 1327. The entry in the Warwickshire Lay Subsidy Rolls for 1332 under the Hundred of Hemlingford for the village of Barston in Warwickshire[17] is therefore unlikely to be referring to William Winslow *Patriarch*. In the absence of other candidates from

---

[14] *Sussex Notes and Queries: A Quarterly Journal of the Sussex Archaeological Society, vol. 5, 1935, p. 184*
[15] *WMCB, vol. 1, p. 178*
[16] *WMCB, vol. 2, p. 550*
[17] *Lay Subsidy Warwickshire, Dugdale Society vol. 6, 1926, W.F. Carter ed., p. 72*

Edward Winslow's English Origins

this time named *William Winslow*, we therefore assume that the addressee is William Winslow *Wodyam*, son and heir of Walter Winslow *Muster*.

The Hundred of Hemlingford is recorded in the Pipe Rolls around 1160 as *Humilieford*.[18] The entry for *Bernaston* or Barston states that *William de Wynselowe* has a taxable worth of 2s. 7d out of a total taxable of £1 1s. 10¾d. Barston is 55 miles distant from both Winslow in Buckinghamshire and from Rutland, the base for Richard Winslow *Barrowden* in 1296.

The 1346 entry reports the death of Walter Winslow *Muster,* with *Wodyam* stated to be his heir. *Wodyam's* relative Geoffrey *Galfrid* is nowhere mentioned in the WMCB record.[19] Finally the death of William Winslow *Wodyam* is reported shortly afterwards on 24 May 1350, along with that of his wife Alice. Next heir is Thomas of Wynselowe who will *hold for himself and his heirs in villeinage, by rod, at the lord's will, through due and accustomed services,*[20] maintaining the Winslow family's unique status.

If William Winslow *Wodyam* was born around 1300 as suggested, then the deaths of William Winslow *Wodyam* and his wife Alice both in 1350 may have occurred before their time was due. This is further explored in Chapter 4.

Brother William Winslow, *Cellarer*, Entries 1326-1401

There are six events located for Brother William *Cellarer*:

DATE	ACTIVITY
1326-35	Brother William de Wynslowe Coquinarius, fined
1340-44	Brother William of Wynselow is St Albans Cellarer, Winslow Manor
1342	Brother William of Wynselow acts as court recorder
1374	William of Winslow elected Prior of Beaulieu, 1374, month unstated
1396	William Wynslowe, Prior of Hertford, Oct 9
1401	William Wynslowe, Prior of Hertford, 1401

Figure 3-6 Timeline for William Winslow Cellarer

We only know the *Cellarer* by the forename *William*. Postulants entering the noviciate of St. Albans may have been issued a new forename on arrival, and he may not have been christened *William*. Whatever the truth, we know him only as *Brother William Winslow*. William's early misadventures with unpaid tithes and his involvement with Winslow Manor Court were covered in Chapter 2.

Noy's introduction to WMCB provides a chronological list of Cellarers in whose names the Winslow Manor Courts operated, and Brother William's name appears between 1340 and 1344.[21] The name preceding his in 1339 is given as *Thomas*

---

[18] *Pipe Rolls, Henry II 1161-2, vol. 5, 1885, p. 2*
[19] *WMCB, vol. 1, p. 178*
[20] *WMCB, vol. 1 p. 253*
[21] *WMCB, v. 1 intro., p. xiii*

Mare, and this is presumably the same *Thomas de la Mare,* under whose abbacy between 1349 and 1396 John Winslow *Maunciple* suffered penalties over the *Blakette* property affair, as reported previously in the section about *Gesta*.

There is a thirty two year gap between Brother William's activities as the Winslow Manor court recorder and his 1374 appearance in Beaulieu located in the New Forest a few miles away from Southampton.[22] Beaulieu was a cell of St. Albans Abbey which fell under the responsibility of the diocese of Lincoln, and despite its closer proximity to both Canterbury and Ely. Later, according to *Gesta,* William Winslow *Cellarer* was Prior of Hertford in 1396 and 1401.[23] If so, by 1396 William Winslow would have been a venerably old man indeed. If William for his first reported appearance as court recorder around 1342 was in his early twenties, then by 1400 he would have been in his eighties; unusual perhaps, but not exceptional. We noted earlier that Abbot Thomas, senior to Brother William and his predecessor in the Winslow Manor Court, marking Abbot Thomas as aged eighty-seven. Maybe William was born around 1320.

Two other entries relating to a *William Winslow* associated with ecclesiastical matters have been located in medieval records, but both are omitted from consideration here because the links to Brother William of St. Albans cannot be substantiated. The two places are *Willesford*[24] in Lincolnshire, and *Lidford,*[25] a Devon town connected to commercial administration of tin mining.

Geoffrey Winslow, *Galfrid,* Entry 1327

There is only a single reference to Geoffrey in WMCB dating from June 1327. Reported as son of William de Winslow and Alice, daughter of Walter Roberd, Geoffrey is granted possession of Winslow properties previously held by Walter Roberd.[26]

It is uncertain whether Geoffrey Winslow occupied these properties or not, and WMCB does not mention him again in the rest of the continuous sequence from 1327 to 1377, strongly suggesting that Geoffrey had moved away from Winslow, or had simply died. Under the terms of the original bequest, his tenure would probably have reverted to the family line of Walter Roberd on the deaths of Geoffrey and Alice.

---

[22] *Linc. Epis. Reg., Inst. Gynwell, 388d*
[23] *Gesta, vol. 3, pp. 425 & 480*
[24] *Cal. Pat., Richard ii, vol. 3, 1385-89, p. 268*
[25] *Cal. Pat., Richard ii, vol. 4, 1388-92, p. 151*
[26] *WMCB, vol. 1, p. 2*

Edward Winslow's English Origins

John Wynslou, Single Entry 1337

A writ dating from 1337 addressed to Thomas Wogan, the king's escheator of Ireland from James Butler, Earl of Ormond, names a *John Wynslou* as tenant in Tipperary in an inquisition taken at Cassel, 23 March, 12 Edward III. The free tenants for a place called *Obin* include *Adam fitz Stevyn and John Wynslou:*[27]

> *Obin. Half a carucate of land held by Adam fitz Stevyn and John Wynslou for 1d. rent.*

There is insufficient evidence to link this entry with any Winslow family member, and indeed there may be no Buckinghamshire family connection at all.

Richard Winslow, *Handmills*, Single Entry c. 1332

This Richard Winslow *Handmills* appears with John Baldwyne of St. Albans as a litigant in the Handmills legal dispute reported in *Gesta* possibly around 1332 covered in Chapter 2. What is not apparent is why this Richard Winslow *Handmills* has no previous record in the locality. There is no further information about him in either WMCB or in *Gesta*.

John Winslow, *Bailiff*, Entries 1340-c. 1375

Based on the evidence presented below, this John Winslow seems to have operated for a time as *Bailiff* of St. Albans for the Abbot, later transferring to a different role in legal and property administration before leaving St. Albans and moving to the Hertfordshire town of Hunsdon.

DATE	ACTIVITY
1340	Legal enforcer houses of Benedictine monks
1340	John Wynselowe & Andrew Mentemore re apostate monk, 1340
1347	John de Wyneslowe, bailiff of St. Albans, May 1347 1348
1352	John Wynselowe Bailiff of St. Albans, witness re Sopwell Lane St. Albans, Feb
1352	John Wynselowe, "then" Bailiff of St. Albans, witness re Sopwell Lane St. Albans, Sept
1352	Winslow, John Wynselowe, alienate land to the abbot, 1352
1352	John Wyncelowe of St. Albans & Andrew Mentemore sell St Albans property, Dec 9
1353	John de Wyncelowe of Honesdon, De Bohun funding, 20 marks, Jan 21
1353	John Wynselowe and Thomas Morteyn, their bailiffs re saddlers, July
1375	John Winslow Bailiff is deceased by this date

Table 3-7 Timeline for John Winslow, Bailiff

The responsibilities of a bailiff are described in a broader description of the governance of St. Albans found in an extract taken from *Gesta* from the time of Abbot Richard, 1326-35.[28] A constable was appointed for each of the four parishes, and a single *bailiff* oversaw the documentation relating to the coroner, the process of goal delivery, the accounting for the chattels of criminals and general

---

[27] *Cal. Inq. p.m., Edward iii, vol. 8, File 55*
[28] *Gesta, vol. 2 p. 205*

administration of documents notifying fines and amercements marked with a green wax seal to assure their authenticity. That means that the bailiff officeholder needed to be both literate and numerate, and well versed in the law.

The downside was that because the bailiff was representative and enforcer for an Abbot who was frequently unpopular with the townsfolk, bailiffs were often hated by both tenants and villeins alike. John Winslow is seen acting as a representative of the abbot in this entry from February 1340:[29]

> *Appointment of Andrew Mentemore and John Wynselowe to take William de Somerton, an apostate monk of the Benedictine monastery of St. Albans, and to hand him over to his abbot to be chastised according to the rule of his order.*

Binham Priory, close to Blakeney on the North Norfolk coastline, served in medieval times as a *cell* or outpost to St Alban's Abbey, and nominally under the Abbot's control. English Heritage Website notes *Binham Priory's* scandalous reputation. Apparently Somerton, Prior of Binham intermittently from 1317 until 1335, maintained established malpractice by embezzling Priory assets to fund his experiments in alchemy, crippling the priory with debt.

The controversy is covered extensively in Volume 2 of the *Gesta* where the chronicler mentions Somerton in no fewer than ten separate entries, and with multiple paragraphs of coverage. No mention is made in *Gesta* about involvement by John Winslow *Bailiff* in Somerton's 1340 arrest. In an earlier incident, Somerton had absconded from the Priory during the abbacy of Hugh 27th Abbot, 1308-26, but did not simply withdraw from public view; instead Somerton made an extraordinary expedition, journeying all the way to Rome where he gained audiences with the Pope seeking support for policies opposed by the Abbey.

Accordingly, on his return to England, Somerton was arrested and brought before King Edward II, but released on instructions of Queen Isabella. By Abbot Michael's election in 1335, Somerton's profligacy had resumed and he absconded a second time, reportedly leaving considerable debts.[30] *Gesta* do not specify the date of this new disappearance, presumably shortly before this summons to arrest him in 1340.

John Winslow is specifically addressed as *Bailiff* in the next reference involving a property transfer relating to modern-day *Holywell Street* in St. Albans, May 1347:

> *Grant by Rosia Gryndecobbe, late the wife of William Gryndecobbe, of St. Albans, to John Elyse, son of Geoffrey Elyse, of a messuage in Halywellstrete, St. Albans. Witnesses: John de Wyneslowe, bailiff of St. Albans, & others. Thursday after St. Martin the Bishop, 21 Edward III.*[31]

John is similarly addressed as *Bailiff* in February 1352, this time for Sopwell Lane:

---

[29] *Cal. Pat., Edward iii, vol. 4, 1338-40, p. 485*
[30] *Gesta, vol. 2, p. 302*
[31] *Descriptive Catalogue of Ancient Deeds: vol. 1, p. 532*

B. 3370. Grant by Richard Gardyner of Bishops Hatfield, to William Fraynshe of St. Albans, and Agnes his wife, of a messuage with a curtilage in Sopwellane, St. Albans, abutting on the stream of water running from Halywelle to Sopwelle mill. Witnesses:—John de Wynslowe, bailiff of St. Albans, and others [named]. Thursday the Purification, 26 Edward III.[32]

Another St. Albans property transfer from September 1352 suggests that John's term of office as *Bailiff* has ended:

A. 1012. Grant by Roger ate Dore to Nicholas le Sawyere, both of St. Albans, of a tenement in Soppewelle-Lane, St. Albans, next the mill of Soppewelle. Witnesses:—John Wynslowe, then bailiff of St. Albans, and others... Sunday next after the Invention of Holy Cross, 26 Edward III.[33]

A subsequent document from 1352 involving a property transaction omits John's title, again suggesting that John's term of office has concluded: [34]

Licence for the alienation in mortmain to the abbot and convent of St. Albans, in satisfaction of 60s. of £100 yearly of land and rent which they have the king's licence to acquire, of the following:—

...by John Wyncelowe of St. Albans, a messuage, a shop, 8 acres of land, 2 acres of wood and 12d. of rent in the same town,

...by William son of Walter de Langeleye, four messuages and five shops there, and by Andrew de Mentemore and the said William de Langeleye, a messuage there.

A couple of months later in January 1353, John Winslow *Bailiff* is being addressed as *John de Wyncelowe of Hunsdon*. Hunsdon, a small village in Hertfordshire, is situated some 20 miles east and slightly to the north of St. Albans. Sir Oliver de Bohun has lent 100 marks to three debtors including John Winslow *Bailiff*, with additional funds personally to John Winslow *Bailiff* which he has already repaid:[35]

John atte Watre of Ware, Robert de la Lee of Reyndon and John de Wyncelowe of Honesdon acknowledge that they owe to Oliver de Bohun, knight, 100 marks; to be levied, in default of payment, of their lands and chattels in the county of Hertford. Cancelled on payment.

John de Wyncelowe of Honesdon acknowledges that he owes to Oliver de Bohun, knight, 20 marks; to be levied etc. in the county of Hertford. Cancelled on payment.

Maybe Sir Oliver de Bohun is subsidising John Winslow *Bailiff* during the transition from his former post as *Bailiff*. From a different source we find Sir William de Bohun, Earl of Northampton, reportedly acting on behalf of his relative Sir Oliver de Bohun and John Engayne, lord of Hunsdon Manor, in a deed from 1346, and maybe that association is John's reason for relocation.[36]

---

[32] *Descriptive Catalogue of Ancient Deeds: vol. 1, p. 396*
[33] *Descriptive Catalogue of Ancient Deeds: vol. 1, p. 117*
[34] *Cal. Pat., Edward iii, vol. ix, 1350-54, p. 365*
[35] *Cal. Close, Edward iii, vol. ix, 1350-54, p. 523*
[36] *National Archives, DL 27/184*

Edward Winslow's English Origins

Of the other two creditors mentioned, *John atte Watre* of Ware was connected with the City of London through the Cutlers gild[37] and is found borrowing funds in 1332.[38] Two separate members of the *de la Lee* family served as high sheriffs for Hertfordshire Essex, in 1304 and 1310, connecting the family to the local judiciary.

John Winslow is described as *Bailiff* in a 1353 document whose phrasing hints at irritation with an unnecessary protraction of legal process, perhaps attributable to John's exit from his role of bailiff:[39]

> 112. The same to the Prior and Convent of the Town of Seynt Auban (St. Albans). A similar letter to the above, desiring them to command John de Wynselowe and Thomas Morteyn, their bailiffs, to allow the said Roger Hackesalt and Robert de Shilyngtone to follow their trade, and not to hinder them as they from malice had done, that there might be no necessity to bring the matter before the King and his Council, nor to annoy their folk repairing to London, which thing they (the writers) would be loth to do. The Lord, Etc. London 21 July.

The Morteyn name is familiar from Walter Winslow's interest in the half fief in Buckinghamshire mentioned earlier. With John Winslow now living in Hunsdon, nothing further is heard about other family members in the location until a John Winslow name appears in 1366.[40] Yeoman of the Chamber *Reynold de Neuport* has been permitted to trade a quantity of grain with Flanders, and John Winslow *of Hunsdon* has been granted a similar privilege, but with twice the volume of *Neuport's* entitlement. We recall from WMCB that one of the Winslow family, John Winslow *Maunciple* deals in provisions:

> Licence for Reynold de Neuport to buy 200 quarters of wheat in the counties of Kent and Essex, and take them to the parts of Flanders to make his profit thereof. By C…. The like for the following:—John Wyncelowe of Hunsdon, to ship 400 quarters of wheat in the port of Kyngeston-upon-Hull, for Flanders…

And so it proves, but the references to Hunsdon create a new linkage: the two John Winslows found living in Little Horwood between 1352 and 1357 are related to the *Bailiff*. From the evidence they have joined John Winslow *Bailiff* in Hunsdon sometime after leaving Little Horwood. The proof of this is disclosed in an agreement dated October 1375 following the reported death of John Winslow *Bailiff*. John Winslow *Maunciple* is now the *elder*, and brother John Winslow *Hunsdon* the *younger*, and on the basis that: [41]

> Writing of John Wyneslowe of Honysdon the elder, being a quitclaim with warranty to John Wynselowe the younger his brother, William Eynsham, Philip Yonge, John Cosyn citizens and pepperers of London and John Wiltshire of Heydon co. Essex, their heirs and assigns, of all right present or future in all the lands, rents and services now held by his said brother

---

[37] *Calendar of Letter Books of City of London vol. F, 1337-52, HMSO 1904, pp. 57, 92, 110*
[38] *National Archives, C 241/104/192*
[39] *Calendar of Letters from the Mayor and Corporation of the City Of London c. 1350-70, pp. 52-53*
[40] *Cal. Pat., Edward iii, vol. xiii 1364-7, p. 248*
[41] *Cal. Close, Edward iii, vol. 14, 1374-7, p. 257*

and the others in the town of Honysdon sometime of John Wynselowe his father... Dated
Honysdon, 19 October 49 Edward III.

John Winslow *Maunciple* has evidently involved some colleagues described as
pepperers in the execution of the quitclaim. The *Pepperers* formed one of the most
prestigious of all the London mercantile gilds. The William Eynsham mentioned is
Chamberlain of the City of London Guildhall,[42] one of the three most important
senior City roles alongside the Common Clerk and the Common Serjeant at law.[43]
Colleague Philip Yonge, based in Cheapside, will be appointed a tax collector in
1369. By July 1993 John Cosyn will become an Alderman of the City.[44]

The involvement of such senior City figures finally vindicates Holton's observation
in his chart that John Winslow was *of great repute* in London, albeit twenty years
later than Holton had envisaged. Eighteen years had now elapsed since John and
his brother John had quit Little Horwood in 1357 to join their father John in
Hunsdon. The transition from acrimony to commercial success is remarkable.

This new evidence may partly explain the principal cause of John's frequent
amercements for non-appearance in the Winslow Manor Court. He had clearly
served an apprenticeship as a Pepperer in the City of London at some stage of his
career. If his period of indenture in the City had commenced before 1357, John's
apprenticeship would have dictated that he remain resident with his master in
London. Such a commitment would have caused extended periods of absence from
Little Horwood, and might explain his early eagerness to transfer the Little
Horwood holding to his younger brother John.

Thomas Winslow, *Homicide,* Entries 1346-83

We already found Thomas Winslow *Homicide* to be the heir of William Winslow
Wodyam and grandson of Walter Winslow *Muster.* Like his grandfather, Thomas
Winslow *Homicide* has served in the military under the Earl of Northampton as
evidenced by the terms of his pardon for good service issued in 1360. Thomas
Winslow has caused someone's death, and hence his suffix for this book as Thomas
Homicide. But significantly just as John Winslow *Bailiff* has also taken up residence
in Hunsdon, so apparently has Thomas, and perhaps around the same time:[45]

> Westminster. *Pardon, for good service done in the war of France to ...Thomas de
> Hundesden alias Thomas Wynselowe apprentice of John Turk, 'fisshmongere' of London, in
> the company of the Earl of Northampton for the death of Robert Cook, late servant of the
> said John Turk. By ...*

---

[42] *City Letter Books vol. G., pp. 153, 229, 263, 315, 326 etc.*
[43] *See in particular Gwyn A. Williams, pp. 94-96*
[44] *City Letter Books vol. H, 1375-1399, folio cclxxxiii b*
[45] *Cal. Pat., Edward iii, 1360, vol. xi, 1358-61, p. 391*

Edward Winslow's English Origins

The Earl of Northampton here is William de Bohun, a distant relative of the Oliver de Bohun who had lent £20 to John Winslow *Bailiff* in the first mention of any connection with Hunsdon in 1352-3.

The other factor to consider here is the date when Thomas Winslow *Homicide* signalled his intention to relocate from the family ancestral home in Buckinghamshire. He had disposed of the Swanbourne holding in 1352, and there could have been compelling reasons for doing so, whether to take up his apprenticeship with the Turk family or to serve in France with William de Bohun. Whatever the date or reason for choosing to change his place of residence, his long-term decision was to move away, and most surprisingly as senior family member he decided to recombine the disparate branches of the wider Winslow family.

Proof of such strong linkages between the two branches of the Winslow family was not previously apparent. William Winslow *Patriarch* had married advantageously into a family local to Winslow while Richard Winslow *Barrowden* had moved away to Rutland; John Winslow *Bailiff* had moved away to St. Albans, with his sons stationed in Little Horwood. Now the entire family was reconvening.

Entries for Thomas Winslow *Homicide* and for some related events are as follows:

YEAR	WINSLOW	SUFFIX	ACTIVITY
1346	Walter	*Muster*	Walter Wynselowe dies 1346 29 May, son William is heir, WMCB
1346	William	*Wodyam*	William Wynselowe, heir of Walter, fealty 1346, WMCB
1346	Thomas	*Homicide*	Thomas loses his grandfather, WMCB
1350	William	*Wodyam*	William & Alice Wynselowe both dead, WMCB
1350	Thomas	*Homicide*	Thomas inherits May 24 1350, WMCB
1351	Thomas	*Homicide*	Thomas de Wynselowe, Swanbourn, Black Prince's Register
1352	John	*Maunciple*	John le Irmonger's property to John de Wynselowe, 1352 Jan
1352	Thomas	*Homicide*	Likely date for surrender of Swanbourne property
1353	John	*Bailiff*	John de Wyncelowe now of Honesdon
1357	John	*Maunciple*	John Wynselowe surrenders Horwood, May 22, heriot 10s.
1360			Peace through Treaty of Brétigny, 8 May 1360
1360	Thomas	*Homicide*	Pardon: Thomas de Hunsdon alias Wynselowe, apprentice, Jul 1
1375	John	*Bailiff*	John de Wyncelowe now deceased of Honesdon
1375	Thomas	*Homicide*	Thomas Winslow of Hunsdon £20 debt December 12
1383	Thomas	*Homicide*	John Wynselowe Younger, Sir Robert Turk & Thomas, Hunsdon

Table 3-8 Timeline for Thomas Winslow Homicide

WMCB confirms Walter's date of death as May 29 1346. Walter's son and heir William Winslow *Wodyam* performs fealty for his inheritance in 1346, but the deaths of both William *Wodyam* and his wife are reported on 24 May 1350, leaving Thomas as heir. References to Thomas *Homicide* in WMCB cease after this date.

Edward Winslow's English Origins

We know that Thomas was still in the Buckinghamshire area in 1351 from a reference in the Black Prince's Register, with Thomas addressed as *Thomas de Wynselowe of Swanbourne*:[46]

> May 3, London. Order to Sir Ralph Spigurnel, steward and constable of Walyngford, or his lieutenant, to supersede until the octave of Midsummer next the distraint he is making against the Abbot and convent of La Bruere, and in the meantime to certify the prince as to the reason for such distraint. A like letter of the same date to Roger le Graunt, constable of Berkhamstede, in favour of Thomas de Wynselowe of Swanbourn.

Spigurnel and Thomas de Wynselowe *of Swanbourne* appear to be recovering monies from a monastic establishment, and for reasons unstated. Roger le Graunt, constable responsible for Berkhamsted, adjacent to Thomas's Swanbourne home village, is being directed to challenge a distraint action, suggesting that Spigurnel and Winslow remain in England in May 1351. Furthermore, Thomas Winslow is now in the service of the heir apparent, Edward the Black Prince. From the absence of any further mention of the Swanbourne property, the likelihood is that around 1352 Thomas Winslow *Homicide* has surrendered the Swanbourne family estate to a new tenant, Thomas Williams:[47]

> ...it is found that the tenements in Swanebourn are two messuages and two carucates of land whereof Thomas Williames holds a messuage and a carucate, and William atte Welde holds the other messuage and carucate, which tenements were held of Nicholas by the service of a knight's fee and 6d. yearly, and Nicholas held those lands of John de Clynton of Makestoke..

The Feudal Aids reference from 1346 previously noted implied fractional entitlement to the Swanbourne property between *Thomas de Walda* and Walter Winslow; this reference from an inquest suggests that Thomas Winslow *Homicide* has totally given up his interest.

It is hard trace to Thomas's exact whereabouts between his grandfather's death reported in 1346 and his subsequent pardon in 1360. Thomas had lost his grandfather, father and mother in quick succession. It is unclear whether by this time Thomas was already committed to an apprenticeship in the City with John Turk, Fishmonger, and also to the military campaign in France. The question of whether the apprenticeship predated his military duties cannot be determined with certainty from the text of the 1360 pardon quoted above.

Acceptance as an apprentice fishmonger with the Turk family would have carried significant social status. Like the Pepperers, the Fishmongers were a prestigious City gild, and commercially one of the most successful. Gwyn Williams explains[48] how during the half century of the reigns of the first two Kings Edwards between 1272 and 1327, the identities of a thousand or so of the City counsellors are known,

---

[46] *Register of Edward the Black Prince Pt. 4 (England) 1351-55*, London 1933 p. 12
[47] *Cal. Close, Edward iii, vol. ix, 1349-54*, pp. 563-4
[48] Gwyn Williams, *Medieval London, From Commune to Capital*. London, Athlone Press, 1963, p. 165

and remarkably no fewer than two hundred of their number were fishmongers. Williams regards them as strongest single mercantile interest in the City of London measured by the political power they exercised, and describes their wards as *strongholds of the middle-class,* an echo of Rebecca Fraser's description of Kenelm Winslow, yeoman of Droitwich.

But the fishmongers did not confine themselves to dealing in fish nor in adhering to the class of tradesmen; and thanks to the nature of their business, they possessed maritime transport resources. Unsurprisingly, before long the leading men in the mistery had diversified into the wine and wool sectors, and as Williams describes it had established themselves *among the patriciate,* so developing a power base that they would retain throughout the later middle ages.

We cannot be certain when Thomas *Homicide* moved to Hunsdon, but he evidently retained connections with the City of London because in 1375, and still described as *Thomas Winslow of Hunsdon,* Thomas Winslow *Homicide* is borrowing £20 with Helmyng Leget in attendance, son of one of the Yeomen of the Chamber; later High Sheriff of Essex, and an MP in his own right. Thomas Makewilliam was a grocer:[49]

> Debtor: *Thomas Winslow of Hunsdon. Creditor: Thomas Makewilliam, and Godfrey Marshall. Amount: £20. Before whom: William Walworth, Mayor of London; Helmyng Leget, Clerk. When taken: 31/05/1375 First term: 01/08/1375 Last term: 01/08/1375 Writ to: Sheriff of Herts Sent by: John Ward, Mayor of London; Helmyng Leget, Clerk.*

Eight years later on December 14, 1383, Thomas Winslow *Homicide* and John Winslow *Hunsdon* appear as witnesses in Hunsdon to a property disposal by the Goldyngton family in the company of Sir Robert Turk, distinguished elder son of the same John Turk fishmonger with whom Thomas *Homicide* had previously served his apprenticeship.[50]

> Witnesses: *Robert Turk knight, John Wynselowe, William Rokesburgh, John Quenyld, Thomas Wynselow. Dated Honesdone, 14 December 7 Richard II*

Thomas de Hundesden alias Thomas Wynselowe after leaving Swanbourne had maintained his residence in Hunsdon until at least 1383. Meanwhile as we have seen, John Winslow *Bailiff* has been living with the two Johns now identified as his sons, and all three branches of the Winslow family, formerly dispersed and separated in Little Horwood, St. Albans and Swanbourne, have now converged to dwell in the same village some thirty miles away from Buckinghamshire, demonstrating the enduring bonds between Winslow family members.

Evidence suggesting that they shared the same dwelling in the town of Hunsdon is discussed further in Chapter 4. We do not know when Thomas Winslow *Homicide* died, and as yet we do not know how Thomas and John Winslow *Bailiff* are related. But it is time to move on to the Winslow of greatest interest to Holton's research,

---

[49] *N. R. A., Ref C 241/157/11*
[50] *Cal. Close, Richard ii., vol. 2, 1381-85, p. 405*

Edward Winslow's English Origins

John Winslow *Maunciple*, because at this point he is leaving Hunsdon in 1375 to set up home with new bride Mariota Crouchman in Hempstead, Essex.

John Winslow, *Maunciple*, Entries 1352-1405

Thanks to the Winslow Manor Court books and the *Gesta* we have two additional sources of information about John Winslow presumably unfamiliar to Holton.

Principal findings so far indicate that John is described in WMCB as a *Maunciple*, someone involved in the food supply chain.[51] We found no information about him prior to 1352 when he acquires a tenure in Little Horwood along with his brother, also John. As a result of his sojourn in Little Horwood with the nominal status of *serf*, John is later drawn into a property dispute with his overlord the Abbot of St. Albans leading to a significant financial penalty, although we have no definitive evidence that the £20 debt was ever enforced or paid.

No one else called John Winslow connected to Buckinghamshire has been located around the 1350s apart from John's brother John *Hunsdon,* subject of the next section. The sequence for John Winslow *Maunciple* opens in Little Horwood in 1352 placing him in his early twenties if he were born around 1330, and above the 20 years age threshold which Noy considers the minimum to qualify for a tenure in the village. The spectacular trajectory of the *Maunciple's* career path is unusual, and comprises five phases.

The first, his upbringing, may not even have taken place in Buckinghamshire. The second was his time in Little Horwood with the other John Winslow *Hunsdon.* The third is when he moves to Cordwainer Ward in London and joins the gild of *Pepperers*, later the *Grocers*. The fourth, concurrent with the third, is his time on his ever-growing estates following his marriage.

The final phase, overlapping with the fourth and probably the least expected, is his adoption of military service and his subsequent expedition to Ireland. This fifth phase takes on an ironic twist – just as John is elevated to King Richard II's personal entourage for the campaign to avenge the death of the Earl March, so King Richard is deposed by Henry Bolingbroke, later King Henry IV. There is no evidence of how long John Winslow *Maunciple* remained alive after the overthrow, or indeed whether his death resulted from it.

The entries below provide sufficient continuity of sequence to suggest that they all relate to the same individual.

YEAR	ACTIVITY
1352	Transfer of John le Irmonger's Horwood property to John de Wynselowe 1352 Jan
1353	John de Wynselowe placed in Thomas Atte Dode's tithing, Horwood 1353, May 20
1353	John Wynselowe *Maunciple*, demised land to brother John; therefore amerced 6d, Dec 16

---

[51] *WMCB, vol. 1, p. 286*

Edward Winslow's English Origins

Year	Activity
1354	John Wynselowe (6d), committed default, amerced May 20, Horwood
1355	John Wynselowe (3d), amerced, Jan 12, Horwood
1355	John Wynselowe (3d), amerced, Jun 15, Horwood
1355	John Wynselowe (3d), amerced, Oct 26, Horwood
1356	John Wynselowe (6d), amerced, May 16, Horwood
1356	John Wynselowe default twice along with John Beaufiz once, Horwood
1356	John Wynselowe (3d), amerced, Nov 14, Horwood
1356	John Wynslowe £20 fine per 1340 County of Hertford re *Blakette*. Date imprecise
1357	John Wynselowe surrenders the Horwood property, May 22, heriot 10s.
1366	John Wyncelowe of Hunsdon, ship 400 Q of wheat, "make his profit"
1373	John Winslow {Wyncelowe}, citizen and Pepperer of London, Creditor, Oct 18
1374	Not recorded in Cordwainer St. donors list, Nov
1375	John Wyneslowe of Hunsdon elder quitclaim to John Wynselowe younger, Oct 19
1375	Quitclaim John W of property sometime of John Wynselowe, his father, Oct 19, Hunsdon
1375	Marriage of Mariota and John Wynselowe, Hempstead
1383	Legal challenge re fitness of justices on bench in Cambridge, undated
1383	Legal challenge re fitness of justices on bench in Cambridge cont. Dec
1384	John Wyncelowe Cordwainer ward re mayoral election, Nicholas Brembre, undated
1384	John Wynslowe of London, mainprise for Edmund Fraunceys of London, Jun 22
1384	John Wyncelowe, Cordwainer Street, re Mayor Brembre, July 1384
1384	John Wyncelowe Cordwainer Street: Common Council, Oct 13
1384	John Wyncelowe, Debtor re Harlow £100, Oct 13 1384, 3 sources
1385	John Wynslowe of London & Culham, recognisance re £400 loan, Jan 17
1385	Crouchmans estate Hempstead etc. to Wynselowes
1385	Citizen and grocer of London, debtor June, Chancery: Extents for Debts, Series I June 25
1385	Start of 5-year records spanning multiple property transactions in Cambridgeshire
1386	John Wynselowe of London, mainpernor with Fraunceys, £170, Feb 8
1386	John Wyncelowe citizen and Pepperer of London, debtor £100 May 3, not actioned
1386	Ref to John Wynselowe "of Norffolk" re £500 mainprise re Carthusians, Jul 1
1387	John Wynselowe, Newnham property, Cambridge 1387 Apr 3
1387	John Wynslowe is to be again sought and imprisoned for £400 debt, July 10
1387	John Wynslowe is to be again sought and imprisoned for £400 debt, Aug 25
1387	John Wynslowe £400 debt, John Walcote to hold property until recovery, Nov 12
1392	John Wynselowe, pardon for non-appearance re £140 debt, London, Jun 29
1392	John Wynselowe, witness in Hempstead Sept 3
1393	John Wyncelowe and wife Mary, heiress of William Crocheman, inherits; Jan 29
1393	John Wyncelowe, trespass in Hempstead family property, spring 1393

Edward Winslow's English Origins

YEAR	ACTIVITY
1394	John Wynslowe, landlord Trumpington re inquest, March 17
1394	History of Parliament misidentification, 1387-94 re *Maunciple*
1394	John Wynselowe citizen and grocer, prison and debt pardon, May 10
1394	John Wynselowe of Hempstede, co. Essex, Irish Campaign with William W, Sept 24
1396	John Wyncelowe, esq., Irish Campaign with Roger, Earl of March, Jan 24
1397	John Wyncelowe esquire £100 debt, Essex, Feb 13
1397	John Wynselowe, Esq, protection with Roger Earl of March, Lieutenant of Ireland, Oct 11
1398	John Wynselowe property, Newnham, Cambridge, Cokking Yard, Sept 11
1399	John Wynslowe, of Cambridge, alias of Essex, protection to Ireland, April 18
1399	Winslow, John Wyncelowe, esquire, tarrying in England, July 4
1399	John and Mary Wyneslowe, had bought Wood Hall, Finchingfield, Michaelmas
1401	Moiety of one knight's fee in Hempstede held by John Wynselowe at 50s, Feb 26
1405	John and Mary Wyncelowe, deforciant, Essex property, Ashdon etc., Michaelmas
1406	Death of Mary Crocheman former wife of John Winslow, Dec 8
1410	Mary Crocheman former wife of John Wyncelawe of Oxford, Dec 8
1418	Homages and Services of the heirs of John Wynselowe, re Essex property, 1418 Sept 29
1430	John Winslow deceased, reference to former Hempstead land 1430, Feb 22

Table 3-9 Timeline for John Winslow Maunciple

Many of the early references from *Gesta* and WMCB have already been covered in detail in Chapters 1 and 2 above, as has the licence to ship grain in 1366 addressed to *John Wyncelowe of Hunsdon*.[52] John's focus has shifted from acting as *Maunciple* into sales of property, and then back to wholesaling of provisions. We do not know how it was arranged, but at some stage John Winslow *Maunciple* must have been offered an apprenticeship with the gild of *Pepperers* in the City: an entry found in the 1373 court records describes him as a *Pepperer* while he is pursuing John Boys for a debt. By this time John evidently has access to funds: this notice dates from October 1373:[53]

> Debtor: John Boys, of Dunmow in Essex. Creditor: John Wyncelowe, citizen and pepperer of London. Amount: £10. Before whom: William de Walworth, Mayor of the Staple of Westminster. Date: 1373 Oct 18

Gwyn William associates *Pepperers* with the elevated status of the *patrician fraternities: drapers, pepperers, goldsmiths, mercers and vintners*.[54] In his table of *Trade Designations of the Aldermanic Class* between 1230 and 1340, Williams

---

[52] *Cal. Pat., Edward iii, vol. 13, 1364-7, p. 248*
[53] *N. R. A., Kew , ref. C 241/155/129*
[54] *Gwyn Williams, p. 45*

places *Pepperers* in fifth place out of the seventeen trade designations in this group.[55]

Historically, membership of the Pepperers' gild or *mistery* would have descended from father to son. The *Pepperers* go back a long way: established by King Henry II in the late twelfth century, their expertise was associated with exotic locations further afield than typical domestic traders. As long-distance shippers they combined or *engrossed* various cargoes, the etymological root for the term *Grocers.* A separate formal *mistery* of Grocers was created in 1345, later to merge with the Pepperers, and John Winslow styled himself as both *Pepperer* and *Grocer.*

John's marriage to Mariota in 1375 has already been noted, and a reference from around 1383 places John in nearby Cambridge following his move to Hempstead in Essex. Although Cambridge is an inland town focused on agriculture, the rivers Cam and Ouse connect it directly with the sea at *Lenne,* modern-day King's Lynn, making it a valid commercial hub from which a maunciple could ship grain and other provisions. Mariota, aged only around 17 years at this time, is specifically mentioned in a petition regarding legal conflicts of interest:[56]

> *John and Mary Wynselowe request that whereas they have arraigned an assize against Holt and others of certain tenements in Cambridge, which Holt therefore cannot judge, that the assize be directed to Thyrnyng and Tresilian, Pinchbeck and Brokhole.*

The request to redirect the case hints at a knowledge of legal process and personal acquaintance with senior members of the judiciary: Sir Robert Tresilian would later become Chief Justice of the King's Bench between 1381 and 1387; and William Thirning rose to become Chief Justice of the Court of Common Pleas.

John and Mariota are busy between 1385 and 1390 with property transactions in and around Cambridge.[57] Three of these appear around 1386-7 without specific calendar dates, and the final entry is from around 1393:

> *70 Thomas Ward and others v. John Wynselow and Maria his wife of the manor called Crochmans in Trumpynton.*

> *71 John Pejoun of London and Matilda his wife v. John Wynselowe of London grocer, and Maria his wife in Cantebrigg.*

> *73 Robert Foxton of Cantebrigg and Margery his wife v. John Wynselowe of London Grocer and Maria his wife in Cantebrigg.*

> *116 Henry English v. John Wynselowe of London and Maria his wife in Cantebrigg.*

John's social status in the City of London is evidently on the ascendant. A summons in 1384 from his home ward of Cordwainer to the inauguration of Sir Nicholas Brembre is addressed to him not as a functionary of the council, but as someone

[55] *Gwyn Williams, p. 319*
[56] *N. R. A., SC 8 - Special Collections: Ancient Petitions, SC 8/215/10744*
[57] *Fines relating to the County of Cambridge, ed. Walter Rye, CAS 1891, pp. 134-5*

Edward Winslow's English Origins

described in a footnote to the Plea Rolls as among *the more sufficient men of the city*:[58]

> *.. the mayor with the assent of sixteen aldermen at least should cause the Common Council to be summoned against that day, with others of the more sufficient men of the city, to make the same election etc.*

Such is the level of esteem in which John Winslow *Maunciple*, by now probably aged in his early fifties, was held by 1384. *John Wynslowe of London* is one of four guarantors standing for the good behaviour of *Edmund Fraunceys*, a fellow London grocer, and possibly related to the former *Farmer* of Winslow in the 1330s, Simon Fraunceys:[59]

> *Memorandum of a mainprise under a pain of £200. made in chancery 23 this year by Hugh Fastolf of London, John Farewelle, Reynold Aleyn and John Wynslowe of London for Edmund Fraunceys of London, that he shall do or procure no hurt or harm to Thomas Chardesley notary..*

The Calendar of City letter books record John Winslow's attendance at Mayor Brembre's subsequent inauguration:[60]

> *Be it remembered that at a congregation of the Mayor, Aldermen, and good and sufficient men summoned from the Wards as a Common Council the last day of July, 8 Richard II. [A.D. 1384], there being present Nicholas Brembre, the Mayor, William Walworth, William Cheyne, the Recorder...and the following from the several Wards, viz.*
>
> *Cordewaner stret (17): Robert Lyndeseye, William Pountfret, Geoffrey Walderne, Robert Harengeie, Richard Hatfeld, John Hoo, Henry Stacy, William Culham, Andrew Coggeshale, Thomas Sibsay, Thomas Heyward, John Bradfeld, Robert Dane, John Chyngford, John Suttone, John Wyncelowe and Simon Aylesham.*

Shortly afterwards in October 1384, John Winslow *Maunciple* is borrowing money. The loan is secured on assets in London:[61]

> *Recognisance of John Wyncelowe, citizen and pepperer of London, to William de Humbreston, parson of Harlow for, £100 to be levied in default of payment of his lands and chattels in London.*

We know that the loan was not repaid because the outstanding sum is subsequently pursued through the courts:[62]

> *Debtor: John Wyncelowe, citizen and pepperer of London. Creditor: William de Humbreston, parson of the church of Harlow. Amount: £100, before whom: Chancery.*

A writ for the recovery was sent to the Sheriff of Herts, Essex and Cambridgeshire, and in an endorsement Sheriff Geoffrey Brokhole replies that the writ was delivered too late to be executed within the time allocated. This was the same

---

[58] *Calendar of the Plea and Memoranda Rolls of the City of London, vol. 3, pp. 84-125*
[59] *Cal. Close, Richard ii, vol. 2, 1381-5, p. 568*
[60] *Calendar of Letter-Books of the City of London: H: 1375-1399 pp. 224-249*
[61] *Cal. Close, Richard ii, vol. 2, 1381-5, p. 577*
[62] *N. R. A., ref. C 131/202/47*

Brokhole sought by John and Mary Winslow as an alternative justice in place of Holt during the case over his Cambridge property transactions in 1383. The next event is possibly a move to establish unequivocally the Winslows' legal tenure of the Crouchman Essex estate:[63]

> *Michaelmas. Thomas Warde, pl. John Wynselowe and Mary his wife, def.*
>
> *The manor called 'Crochemans' in Hempstede and 4 tofts, 3 carucates of land, 10 acres of meadow, 60 acres of wood and 30 acres of pasture in Great Samforde, Little Samforde, Fynchyngfeld, Radewynter and Bumstede. Def. and the heirs of Mary to hold of the chief lords.*

A parallel reference suggests that the tenure of the Crouchman Trumpington estate in Cambridge is being similarly established the same year:[64]

> *Thomas Warde gave the King 20s for license to grant John Wynselowe and wife Mary the manor called Crocheman's in Trumpyngton, co. Cambridge, Mich.,9 Richard II.*

A loan offered to John Winslow dating from January 17 1385 is an undertaking of a completely different order of magnitude:[65]

> *Westminster. William Culham and John Wynslowe of London to John Chitterne clerk. Recognisance for £400, to be levied etc. in the city of London.*

Fellow Grocer Culham from Cordwainer Ward had attended Mayor Brembre's inauguration with John. The purpose of the original loan is unstated, and the first indication that anything is wrong is found in an entry from July 1387 where John is evidently being pursued for debt. Culham is no longer mentioned. It is bad news:[66]

> *Debtor: John Winslow, citizen and grocer of London. Creditor: John Walcote, citizen and merchant of London. Amount: £400. Before whom: William Walworth, Mayor of the Staple of Westminster. Writ to: Sheriff of Cambridge Sent by: Chancery.*

John's property has been sequestered in his absence. In an endorsement, Sheriff Robert Paris confirms that John Winslow *was not found in the bailiwick*, and his lands and goods are being taken into the King's hands. The extent of the Winslow estate is considerable, and its complex liquidation covers several manuscripts identified in the Chancery records as *M.2* to *M.5*.[67] The reason for the detail becomes apparent later.

> *Date given for return to Chancery: 25/08/1387.*
>
> *M.2: Inquisition made before Robert Paris, Sheriff of Cambs., Sat. 24/08/1387, at Cambridge. John Winslow held on the day of the recognisance five messuages in Cambridge worth £4. He held the manor of Trumpington called Crochmans Beaufuse except for the third part, which Matilda, once the wife of John Elmond holds. The two parts of the manor are worth after expenses 10m. He held six cottages in Caldecote worth 20s. a year,*

---

[63] *Essex Feet of Fines, 9 Richard ii, 1385, entry 200, p. 203*
[64] *Plea Rolls, De Banco, Mich., 9 Richard ii, m. 437*
[65] *Cal. Close, Richard ii, vol. 2, 1381-5, p. 603*
[66] *N. R. A., 1385, Ref.: C 241/175/151*
[67] *N.R.A., ref.: C 131/35/7*

and an annual rent of 20s. a year. Dorse: Memorandum that 28/09/1387 John Walcote received the lands, tenements and rents.

M.3: Writ from Chancery to the Sheriff of Essex and Herts., dated 04/07/1387 about the same debt. Dorse: John Ruggewene, Sheriff, replies that John Winslow was not found in the bailiwick. All his lands and chattels have been seized into the King's hands.

M.4: Inquisition made at Hempstead before John Ruggewene, Sheriff of Essex, Fri. 19/07/1387. John Winslow held on the day of the recognisance in Essex the whole manor called Crochemannes with its parts in the vills of Hempstead, Finchingfield, Great and Little Sampford, Radwinter, Ashingdon, Helions Bumpstead and Steeple Bumpstead, worth in all £44 10s after services to the chief lord. He pays £10 annually from the manor to Matilda who was the wife of William Crocheman. After Matilda's death the manor is worth £44 10s. John Winslow has in the vills of Great Sampford and Hempstead the crop of 125 acres sown with wheat worth 5s. an acre; the crop of 5 acres sown with barley worth 5s.; the crop of 40 acres sown with peas worth 3s. an acre; the crop of 72 acres sown with oats worth 2s. 8d. an acre; the crop of 4 acres sown with dredge worth 40d. an acre; hay from 49 acres of meadow worth 100s.

M.5: Writ from Chancery to the Sheriff of Essex and Herts., dated 28/09/1387, reiterating MM. 3-4, and instructing him to hand over lands, tenements, goods and chattels of the value of the debt of £252 11s. 4d. The same writ was sent to the Sheriff of Cambs. Dorse: John Ruggewene replies that he has handed over all the lands, tenements, goods and chattels of John Winslow, except the rents, in part satisfaction of his debt. John Winslow was not found in the bailiwick.

The investigation is extended: a report dated November brings further bad news:[68]

Endorsement: Robert Parys, Sheriff, replies that he has delivered to John Walcote two parts of the manor, and the messuages, cottages, and rents within. John Winslow was not found in the bailiwick.

Inquisition and return: Date given for return to Chancery: 12.11.1387. The sheriff replied to an earlier writ that John Winslow was not found in the bailiwick, but on the day of the recognisance he had the manor of Trumpington called Crochemans and Beaufuse, apart from the third part of the manor which Matilda, formerly the wife of John Esmond, holds as dowry; 5 messuages in Cambridge, and 6 cottages in Caldecote, worth in all £11 13s. 4d a year, and also an annual rent of 20s. from Caldecote. He has no goods or chattels. John Walcote is to hold the property until he recovers £93 13s. 4d, with costs and expenses. The Sheriff of Essex and Herts is to hand over to John Walcote goods and chattels worth £53 15s. 4d, and lands and tenements in Essex worth £34 10s. a year to meet the residue of the debt of £400, with costs and expenses.

To clarify what is going on, these assets are not being *confiscated*. The loan repayment will be achieved from net annual income taking labour cost and rental fees into account, and afterwards the property will be handed back. Title to the underlying property tenure is unaffected. Evidently no interest is chargeable. The writs (M2, M4) give the assets shown in the left-hand column, and the next columns

---

[68] *N.R.A., ref. C 131/204/16*

Edward Winslow's English Origins

show deemed annualised revenue value followed by the sub-total of revenue per asset group per county. The totals in red can be reconciled with the writs:

5 messuages in Cambridge, and 6 cottages in Caldecote, worth in all £11 13s. 4d a year, and also an annual rent of 20s. from Caldecote.

The Sheriff of Essex and Herts is to hand over to John Walcote goods and chattels worth £53 15s. 4d, and lands and tenements in Essex worth £34 10s. a year to meet the residue of the debt of £400, with costs and expenses

ASSET	NOTIONAL VALUE	NET £
M2 5 messuages CAMBRIDGE	£4	£4
M2 Crochmans Beaufuse CAMBRIDGE	10 Marks	£6 13s 4d
M2 6 cottages Caldecote CAMBRIDGE	20s annual	£1.00
	Total RENTAL CAMBRIDGE	£11 13s 4d
M4 Crochemannes ESSEX	£44 10s less £10, ESSEX RENTAL	£34 10s
M4 125 acres Wheat	5s per acre	£31 5s
M4 5 acres Barley	5s per acre	£1 5s
M4 40 acres peas	5s per acre	£10
M4 72 acres oats	2s 8d per acre	£9 12s
M4 4 acres dredge	40d	13s 4d
M4 49 acres hay	100s	£5
	Annual Crop Value ESSEX	£57 15s 4d

Figure 3-10 Annualised Revenue from John Winslow Maunciple's Assets

The difference of £4 between £57 15s. 4d and £53 15s. 4d is possibly attributable to the cost of labour for the harvesting. The duration of the legal charge over the properties is not indicated. Calculation of the net residual value of outstanding debt as £252 11s. 4d is not explained either, perhaps representing the balance of the £400 after other assets have been handed over.

The good news is that John Winslow *Maunciple* and his wife Mary can now recover possession once the revenue collection period is served. This medieval debt management system carries significance for when we encounter Walcote again.

From the above we learn that Mariota Crouchman's father William Crouchman *C4* left a widow named Matilda, previously unknown, and her annual entitlement from the annual income from the Manor in Hempstead is £10, respecting her legal status as a preferential creditor. John Winslow still holds the Crouchman manor in Trumpington, described in the writ as *Crochemans* and *Beaufuse*, signalling a previously undisclosed but significant family connection to be covered in Chapter 4.

Edward Winslow's English Origins

Where does this leave the public standing of John Winslow *Maunciple*? From the evidence found, largely unaffected. Despite some possible public embarrassment, his credibility and links with the City of London remain intact, and no disgrace attaches to the misfortune. One beneficiary is London Merchant John Chingford whom John Winslow, despite his own problems, has generously assisted at personal financial risk in February 1386:[69]

> *To the sheriffs of London. Order to deliver to John Chyngeforde of London merchant £85 by them arrested at the king's command; as at the said merchant's suit, averring that goods and merchandise of his to the value of £155 were taken at sea by the king's enemies of France and Flanders... and John Hattefelde, John Wynselowe and Edmund Fraunceys of London have mainperned in chancery under a pain of £170 to answer to the king for the said money, if hereafter it shall be proved that it was of his friends and not of his enemies*

In July 1386, John Winslow, described as being *of Norffolk*, has volunteered to help another fellow Grocer, Reynold Aleyn. [70] The reference to Norfolk suggests that John and Mary have now quit their Hempstead manor indefinitely while the estate income is being farmed on behalf of their creditors:

> *Memorandum of a mainprise under a pain of £500, made in chancery 29 June this year by John Bretoun of Norhamptonshire, John Herlyngton of Cambridgeshire, John Wynselowe of Norffolk and William Wyndham for Reynold Aleyn of London 'grossere,' that he shall do or procure no hurt or harm to the prior of the house of the Salutation of St. Mary by London of the Carthusian order, his men or servants.*

John is making no attempts to evade his creditors. His associates are fully aware of the situation, and they know where he is. *John Bretoun* is described elsewhere as *the king's serjeant, yeoman usher of his chamber*[71] and as *yeoman of the king's chamber*[72] on his death in 1399, and as already explained John Winslow *Maunciple* has developed strong royal connections, however unlikely that propect may have appeared when he was being fined by the Abbot's team in Little Horwood.

As for John Herlyngton, he is a former sheriff of Cambridgeshire.[73] Reynold Aleyn was one of the mainpernors with *John Wynslowe of London* when they supported *Edmund Fraunceys of London* earlier. Despite his own financial turmoil and the scale of financial liability, John Winslow also chooses to extend financial support to his fellow Grocers' gild member backed by other sponsors from the wider social circle. Winslow is evidently generous.

In April 1387 a property transaction takes place involving *John Boldham* and *Matilda his wife* and a tenement in Newnham, adjacent to the centre of Cambridge, and described as located next to a *tenement of John Winslow* and abutting onto *the*

---

[69] *Cal. Close, Richard ii, vol. 3, 1385-9, 1386, p. 56*
[70] *Cal. Close, Richard ii, vol. 3, 1385-9, 1386, p. 247*
[71] *Cal. Close, Richard ii, vol. 3, 1385-9, 1387, p. 345*
[72] *Cal. Close, Richard ii, vol. 6, 1396-9, p. 401*
[73] *Cal. Close, Richard ii, vol. 6, 1396-99, May 1398, p. 309*

garden of the said John Winslow, proving that John has retained entitlement to this property.[74]

We also know from various inquests that John's son William Winslow *Armiger* was born on November 1st, All Saints Day, in either 1387 or 1388 in Cranworth, a small Norfolk town some sixty miles north east of Hempstead. [75] The next reference found after William's birth appears in June 1392:[76]

> *Pardon to Hugh Mice of Ware of his outlawry in the Husting, London, for not appearing before the justices of the Bench to render £4 to Simon Wynchecombe... The like to the following:*

> *John Wynselowe, for not appearing to answer William Venour, citizen of London, touching a debt of £140, London*

William Venour was ex-Lord Mayor of London. The reason and circumstances for the pardon are unstated, but by now John is now free to re-enter his properties. The recovery of the £400 debt has been satisfied. John has evidently returned to Hempstead by 3rd September 1392 because his name appears among a list of witnesses to a local property transaction involving *Ralph de Boyton.. ..and all his lands and tenements in the vills of Great Sampford and Hempstead.*

Other witnesses present include *Robert de Langham* of Hempstead Hall, successor to the *Sir William de Langham of Hempstead Hall* visited in 1347 by Sir William Crouchman, a further sign that John's social rehabilitation is complete. The original medieval charter of these events has not been sighted; but a copy of the manuscript was recorded on the internet as having come up for auction around 2016, even though its current whereabouts are unknown. Further activity to restore family entitlements in Hempstead is reported in 1393:[77]

> *To William Gildryche escheator in Essex. Order to remove the king's hand and meddle no further with 153 acres of land, 4 acres of meadow, 1 acre of pasture, 4½ acres of wood and 18d. of rent of assize in Great Sampforde, delivering to John Wyncelowe and Mary his wife any issues thereof taken; as the king has learned by inquisition, taken by Thomas Coggeshale late escheator, that William brother and heir of John son and heir of William Crocheman at his death held the premises in his demesne as of fee of Joan daughter and heir of William de Welle, who was within age and in the late king's ward, by the service of paying yearly 36s. 10d., and that the said Mary, being daughter of the said William brother of John, is his next heir and of full age.*

John Winslow complains about a trespass on his Hempstead property in 1393, suggesting that not only is he back in Essex, but indeed reasserting his rights to the property vacated during his financial *imbroglio*.[78] An entry from March 1394 about

---

[74] *Corpus Christi College Cambridge, CCCC, ref. 09/13/55*
[75] *Cal. Inq. p.m., Henry iv, vol. 19, entry 898*
[76] *Cal. Pat., Richard II 1392, vol. 5 1391-96, p. 252*
[77] *Cal. Close, Richard ii, vol. 5, 1392-96, 1393, p. 45*
[78] *Select Cases of Trespass from the King's Courts 1307-99, Hilary 1393, Morris S. Arnold 1985, ref. KB 27/527, pp. 27-28*

Edward Winslow's English Origins

the Trumpington Manor after the death of its tenant *Joan late the wife of John Hosterle or Osterlee* lists the several parcels of property she held, reconfirming that John still holds Trumpington Manor despite previous indebtedness:[79]

> *Trumpyton. 50a. land, held of Edmund atte Pole by knight's service; a parcel of a tenement, 50a. land and 4a. meadow, held of John Wynselowe, by knight's service .... 2 cottages held of the heirs of Roger de Trumpiton by knight's service.*

Although no connection has been established, the *Edmund Atte Pole* with the 50 acres of Trumpington was Knight of the Shire for Buckinghamshire in 1377 and 1383 and the family with Robert Winslow of Sydenham around 1286. The final entry relating to John's debts is found a month or so later in May 1394:[80]

> *Pardon to John Wynselowe citizen and grocer of London, of his outlawry for not appearing before the justices of the Common Bench to pay to Christiana, late the wife of John Rede, citizen and brewer of London, £9. 14s. and 40s. damages, in an action of detinue, he having now surrendered to the Flete prison and paid both debt and damages, as is certified by Robert de Cherlton, chief justice. London.*

This is when John, now aged probably in his early sixties, takes an unlikely course of action. Perhaps to prove his social rehabilitation or perhaps as a result of feudal obligation after re-confirmation of the family estate, John joins his King in the upcoming Irish military campaign. By September 1394 his attorneys are nominated:[81]

> *John Wynselowe of Hempstede, co. Essex, nominating Robert Hethe and Henry Halle.*

And then an even bigger surprise; the attorneys are switched:

> *The said John, nominating John Walcote and Edmund Heryng.*

John's second nominees are *Edmund Heryng* and *John Walcote*, the same Walcote who had pursued John Winslow *Maunciple* for debts of £400 previously. In view of all that had preceded it, the episode tells much about the respect and warmth that John Winslow must have generated and enjoyed in the City of London, and despite previous uncomfortable moments.

Indeed, this improbable switch of support to Walcote leads Carole Rawcliffe, Walcote's biographer, to conclude that the two John Winslows mentioned were actually separate individuals.[82] While she accepts that Walcote is acting as John's attorney, she identifies the previous debtor as an unrelated party, a *Grocer*, and despite the overlapping circumstantial evidence of locations, contexts and professions all pointing to the same individual.

John's first expedition to Ireland in September 1394 is clearly satisfactory, because it is followed in January 1396 by a second when he returns to campaign in the

---

[79] *Cal. Inq. p.m.*, vol. 17, Richard ii, pp. 147-164
[80] *Cal. Pat., Richard ii, vol. 5, 1391-6, p. 406*
[81] *Cal. Pat., Richard ii, vol. 5, 1391-6, p. 506*
[82] See *Hist. Parl, 1386-1421, 1993, vol. 4, p. 734*

company of the heir presumptive to King Richard II, fourth Earl of March Roger Mortimer, the King's Lieutenant in Ireland. As the eldest son of Edmund 3rd Earl of March, Roger's claim to the English throne derived though his mother Philippa of Clarence, granddaughter of King Edward III.[83]

> Protection with clause volumus for one year for John Wyncelowe, esquire, staying in Ireland on the king's service in the company of Roger, Earl of March, the king's lieutenant there.

John Winslow is now being styled with the title *Esquire,* underlining how far he has advanced socially since leaving Little Horwood with his brother in 1357. By July 1396 John has returned home, but still incurs some royal displeasure:[84]

> Revocation of protection with clause volumus for one year, granted 24 January last to John Wyncelowe, esquire, as staying on the king's service in Ireland in the company of Roger de Mortuo Mari earl of March, because he tarries on his own affairs in England..

His absence in England is reconfirmed by February 13 1397 when we find John Winslow back in Essex raising funds again. The Close Rolls report:[85]

> John Wyncelowe esquire to Thomas Scotton and Nicholas Freton. Recognisance for £100, to be levied etc. in Essex.

The next reported event from February 1397 reconfirms the ongoing Winslow interest in the Trumpington estate. The tenure is clarified.

> ...Writ of devenerunt, 18 February, 20 Richard II CAMBRIDGE. Inq. (indented) taken at Cambridge, Tuesday after St George, 20 Richard II.

> Trompyton. A messuage, a garden, 100a. land and meadow, a dovecot and 3 tofts, part held of Edmund de la Pole, knight, by knight's service and service of 7s. 6d. yearly, part held of John Wynselowe by knight's service and service of 9s. 8d. yearly, and part held of the heirs of Henry Bresele by knight's service and service of 1d. yearly.

The entry provides clues about why John is in Ireland – knight's service. October 1397 sees reinstatement and extension of John Winslow's military service and protection:[86]

> Protection with clause volumus for one year for John Wynselowe, esquire, staying on the king's service in the company of Roger de Mortuo Mari, Earl of March, Lieutenant of Ireland.

John Winslow's *Cokking Yerde* property in Newnham, Cambridge is mentioned again in September 1398 after the first reference to the property in April 1387, indicating that John still has title to the property:[87]

---

[83] *Cal. Pat., Richard ii, vol. 5, 1391-6, p. 667*
[84] *Cal. Pat., Richard ii, vol. 6, 1396-9, p. 7*
[85] *Cal. Close, Richard ii, vol. 6, 1396-9, p. 87*
[86] *Cal. Pat., Richard ii, vol. 6, 1396-99, p. 212++*
[87] *Corpus Christi College Cambridge, CCCC 09/13/57, 1398*

Edward Winslow's English Origins

One garden lies next to a garden of John Ratilesden, barker, called 'Pondyerd' and the other next to a garden of John Wynselowe commonly called 'Cokking yerde'. Witnesses: Robert de Brigham, mayor; John Herrys; John Blaunkpayn.

Reports of John's whereabouts become less frequent after his ongoing military service is reconfirmed in October 1397. We assume that John was in attendance in 1398 when the Earl of March, aged only 24, was killed in a skirmish. His death angered King Richard sufficiently that the King personally undertook an expedition to Ireland the following year. This time John Winslow *Maunciple* travels not with the heir presumptive but in the King's own company. This announcement from April 1399 recorded in *Rymer's Fœdera* confirms that royal protection is being extended again to John Winslow for the new Irish campaign.[88]

> *Protection with clause volumus for one year for Richard Vernon of Harleston co. Stafford, knight, going to Ireland in the company of the king. The like for the following:*
>
> *...John Wynslowe, of the county of Cambridge, alias of Essex...*

Was John Winslow *Maunciple* really travelling in the King's company? A quick inspection indicates that he was. Among his fellow-campaigners we find many of the people found in the royal entourage: the King's secretary, John Lincoln; several valets of the Crown; the Earl of Gloucester, Thomas Despenser; John Beauchamp of Holt, godson of King Richard II, knighted around this time to become *Sir John Beauchamp*. Evidently the Winslows are now personally connected to additional members of the Beauchamp family. No fewer than ten of the royal entourage carry the honorific title *Armiger*, Esquire, including John Winslow *Maunciple* himself.

Unhappily for the King, Henry Bolingbroke chose to return from exile in France during the King's absence in Ireland, landed in Yorkshire, gathered his supporters and claimed the throne, all with little resistance. By 19 August, former King Richard is promising to abdicate if his life is spared. He leaves Bolingbroke to be crowned Henry IV on the feast of Edward the Confessor, October 13 1399. The course of King Richard II's subsequent fate is less clear because he was dead by the following February 1400 in unexplained circumstances, perhaps from starvation. Thomas Despenser the Earl of Gloucester was executed 13 January 1400. And as for John Winslow *Maunciple,* he died in unexplained circumstances, but to establish his date of death we need to consider some events leading up to 1400.

John had borrowed £100 as recorded in February 1397:[89]

> *Debtor: John Winslow {Wyncelowe}, esquire. Creditor: Thomas Scotton and Nicholas Fredon Amount: £100 Before whom: Chancery When taken: 13/02/1397, First term: 22/04/1397, Last term: 22/04/1397, Writ to: Sheriff of Essex [and Cambs]. Sent by: Chancery.*

---

[88] *Rymer's Foedera, vol. 8, entry ref. O. viii. 78. H. iii. P. iv. 159*
[89] *National Archives, C 131 / 215 /1*

Edward Winslow's English Origins

Endorsement: Edward Benstede, Sheriff, replies that the writ arrived too late to be executed in the time set. 1400 May 13.

This is now the fifth phase of John's life, and here he is being addressed as *Esquire* and not as *Grocer* or *Pepperer*. We do not know why John Winslow is borrowing this new sum of £100, but around this time he was acquiring a new home, *Wood Hall* adjacent to Winslow Hall in Hempstead but closer to Finchingfield, a property these days known as *Shore Hall*. The Court of Common Pleas from late 1399 provides some background to a related dispute.[90]

> *Term: Michaelmas 1399. County: Essex. Writ type: Detinue. Damages claimed: £100. Case type: Detention of goods; Safe keeping*
>
> *Pleading: John Kent states that he delivered a chest containing muniments to John Vautot for safe keeping, the documents including a charter by which John and Mary Wyneslowe granted to John Kent and William atte Fen lands in Finchingfield, called the Wood Hall, which had been purchased from John Kempe, and also a bond by which JW was bound to Kent in £100. However, neither John V nor his widow have returned it.*
>
> *Pleading: Joan Vautot states that she is prepared to hand over the chest, but that JK and JW had given it to her husband to be restored under certain conditions, but she does not know if these have been fulfilled. Sheriff to summon JW at octave of Hilary to answer whether the chest should be restored to JK.*
>
> *Postea text: Writ arrived too late, sicut prius to quindene of Easter.*
>
> *Postea text: JW did not come, sheriff said he had been summoned by Chunne and Langham, therefore the court orders that JK have delivery of the chest. Joan V sent without day.*

John Winslow was clearly instructed by the court to confirm by Easter 1400 whether the chest should be returned, but he failed to attend the hearing. By 1400 John would have been aged about 70 years, and maybe the real reason behind the reported failure to execute the writ in time was because John had unexpectedly died. *Chunne* was a Hempstead neighbour and *Langham* still occupied Hempstead Hall. Their ignorance of his whereabouts by May 13 1400 in the second *Postea* text may point to a death connected to the 1399 deposition of Richard, and a breakdown in communication after the regime change. Did John even die defending his King? There is no record.

While several references to John Winslow are found after 1400, we cannot be sure that he remained alive. No will for John Winslow *Maunciple* has been located, and no evidence of a tomb exists in Hempstead church, a place for which John's son William *Armiger* clearly had affection, as evidenced in his will.

In a long list of names in 1401 in connection with the death of Alice, wife of the Earl of Oxford, John Winslow's holding in Hempstead and Finchingfield is simply

---

[90] *Court of Common Pleas, CP 40/555, Michaelmas 1399*

Edward Winslow's English Origins

acknowledged. His son William Winslow *Armiger* is not yet of age, and another long sequence of inquests is yet to begin:[91]

> To the escheator in Essex. Order to give Alice who was wife of Aubrey de Veer late earl of Oxford livery of the knights' fees and parts of fees of her husband in his bailiwick which the king has assigned to her in dower; as of those fees etc., which are in his hand by reason of the nonage of Richard son and heir of the earl, with assent of John Pygot the younger clerk her attorney, the king has assigned to her: [long list, including]
>
> ..the moiety of one knight's fee in Hempstede held by John Wynselowe at 50s...

The statement reflects the *status quo* of John Winslow's knight's fee while Alice's husband Aubrey de Vere, Earl of Oxford was still alive. Aubrey died on St George's day, April 23 1400, and news of John's death may not even have reached home yet. Similar grounds for uncertainty relate to the last reference to John Winslow found the Feet of Fines for Essex in the Michaelmas term of 1405, 6 Henry IV, mentioning the additional family landholdings in *Asshedon, Steventon and Berkelowe*[92] comprising the Manor of Ashdon that William Winslow Armiger proudly refers to in his will of 1415.

To summarise, it is likely that John Winslow *Maunciple* was born around 1330 and died around 1399-1400. While he attracted some commercial controversy both in his early and his middle years, he rose to an early prominence sustained to his death.

Of all the Winslows in medieval times, John Winslow *Maunciple* emerges from the public record as the most flamboyant, a prosperous personality held in considerable respect by his peers and with connections both to the Crown and to John Beauchamp of Holt. The contrast between the five phases of his life was remarkable, and the related impacts of his death on the rest of the Winslow family is covered in the next two chapters.

John Winslow, *Hunsdon*, Entries 1353-1383

This is the sequence of events for John Winslow, *Hunsdon:*

YEAR	ACTIVITY
1353	John Wynselowe *Maunciple*, demised land to brother John; therefore amerced 6d, Dec 16
1375	John Wynselowe *Maunciple* passes his Hundson inheritance to his brother John *Hunsdon*
1383	John Wynselowe with Sir Robert Turk & Thomas W, witness Hunsdon 1383

Figure 3-11 Timeline for John Winslow, Hunsdon

Over his lifetime, John Winslow *Hunsdon* spent considerable time between 1352 and 1375 in proximity to his brother John Winslow *Maunciple*.

---

[91] *Cal. Close, Henry iv, vol. 1, 1399-1402, p. 251*
[92] *Feet of Fines for Essex, vol. 3, entry 97, p. 242*

Edward Winslow's English Origins

We have not yet established where the boys spent their earliest years before 1352, nor the age difference between them. We know that the two boys shared a residence in Little Horwood from 1352 to 1357, before moving to Hunsdon where John *Maunciple* is subsequently reported to have given him tenure of their father's Hunsdon home having inherited it before moving out to marry Mariota Crouchman.

All we can determine so far is that this John Winslow *Hunsdon* was reportedly the younger brother of John Winslow *Maunciple,* and that John Winslow *Bailiff* was their father. The unusual coincidence of a father and two sons all bearing the same forename *John* raises questions addressed later.

Walter Winslow, *Kimpton,* Entry 1368

There is only one entry for this Walter Winslow, *Kimpton*. He and his wife Emma are giving up property in Luton and Kimpton on the Hertfordshire / Bedfordshire border.

Year	Activity
1368	Walter Wynselowe and Emma, his wife, deforciants, Luton & Kimpton

Figure 3-12 Reference to Walter Winslow, Kimpton

We may speculate from his forename that Walter descended from the lineage of Walter Winslow *Muster,* and may have been the son of William Winslow *Wodyam*, but no other specific evidence has been located.

William Winslow, *Candlewick,* Entries 1370-1400

Someone assumed to be a member of the Buckingham Winslow family who received no mention in either WMCB or *Gesta* is William Winslow *Candlewick*. The only references to him place him exclusively in London where he is described as a *Tailor*. No connections with the Winslows of Buckinghamshire or of Yorkshire have yet been established.

William Winslow's profession may have been as a tailor, but like other Winslows he and his wife Joan have an appetite for property transactions.

Year	Activity
1370	William de Wyncelowe, citizen & tailor of London, wife Joan his wife, property deal 1370
1371	William de Wyncelowe, citizen & tailor of London, wife Joan his wife, property deal 1371
1371	William Winslow, citizen and tailor of London, Creditor Jul 25
1372	William de Wyncelowe, citizen & tailor of London, wife Joan his wife, property deal 1372
1374	William Wynselowe, citizen & merchant tailor and wife Joan, St Katherine's Jun 14
1376	William Wynselowe, City of London, Mainprise Garton's Somerset property, Sep 14
1376	William Wyndeslowe, City of London, Mainprise Garton's Soton and Kent property, Sep 27
1376	William Wynselowe, City of London, St Katherine's, Sherborne Lane property, Sep 29
1377	Winslow, William Wenselowe, of City of London re Whitley Surrey Dec 8

Edward Winslow's English Origins

Year	Activity
1378	William de Wynslowe, house in Candelwyk strete London, Feb 25
1386	Creditor: William Winslow, citizen and tailor of London. Amount: £278.
1399	William Wynslowe, Candlewyck St. London citizen & tailor dies. Will proved May 9
1400	Bequest in William Wynselowe's will

Figure 3-13 Timeline for William Winslow, Candlewick

References to William Winslow *Candlewick* are plentiful and stretch almost thirty years from 1370 to 1399. In the first two, William and his wife Joan are involved in property transactions in Barking in the years 1370 and 1371, a town some seven miles downstream from London Bridge.

> *1625. Trin. John Monek of Berkyng and Sarah his wife, pl. William Wynselawe of London and Joan his wife, def. 7 acres of land in Berkyng. Def. quitclaimed to pl. and the heirs of John. Cons. 100s.[93]*

> *1648 Trin. Master John de Torkeseye, clerk, William de Mirfeld, clerk, and John Beauteyn, clerk, pl. William de Wyncelowe, citizen and tailor of London, and Joan his wife, def. i messuage in Berkyng. Def. quitclaimed to pl. and the heirs of William. Cons. 10 marks.[94]*

The third entry places William Winslow, *citizen and tailor of London* as a joint creditor pursuing John Hamond of Southwark for £8 due before William de Walworth, the Mayor of the Staple of Westminster.[95]

> *Endorsement: William Neudegate, Sheriff, replies that he has sent the writ to the bailiff of the liberty of the Archbishop of Canterbury of Croydon who extended and valued all the lands, tenements, goods and chattels of John Hamond.*

The bad news arrives in a subsequent attachment to the original entry dated September 1371. John Hamond's property is found to be worth only £1. 10s.

> *Inquisition made at Southwark, Wed. 30 July 1371, before the seneschal of the liberty of the Archbishop of Canterbury. John Hamond had a messuage in Southwark worth 2½m after expenses. No goods and chattels. Date: 1371 Jul 25*

The next entry also relates to Barking. From other public documents we can deduce that William Colkirk was a mariner,[96] and the property deal dates from 1372:[97]

> *1708. Trin. Sarah late the wife of William Colkirke, pl. William Wynselowe and Joan his wife, def. 1 messuage in Berkynge. Def. quitclaimed to pl. and her heirs. Cons. 10 marks.*

An entry from 14 June 1374 indicates that William and wife Joan have acquired a sizeable plot of land in the precincts of St Katherine's Hospital to the East of the Tower of London.[98] The space is described in detail:

---

[93] *Essex Feet of Fines, vol. 3, entry 1625 p. 160*
[94] *Essex Feet of Fines, vol. 3, entry 1648, p. 162*
[95] *Nat Archives, Chancery: Extents for Debts, Series I, ref. C 131/19/25*
[96] *So: ...master of a ship called 'le Holygost' of Jernemuth, Cal. Close, Henry iv, vol. 2, 1402-5, p. 199*
[97] *Essex Feet of Fines, vol. 3, entry 1708, p. 166*
[98] *Cal. Pat., Edward iii., vol. xv, 1370-1374, p. 450*

extending in length 150 feet, and in breadth 33 feet on the north side and 27 feet on the south side, which lies between the tenement of Stephanetta Olneye on the west and the brethren's cloister on the east and extends from the great ditch in the garden on the north as far as the churchyard of the hospital on the south as the tenement of Stephanetta does, so that they may build on the plot at their pleasure and hold it so built upon for life without rendering anything therefor.

The next two entries date from September 1376. William Wynselowe, here described as a draper rather than as a tailor, is acting as mainpernor with John Blanket, a skinner, in a commitment to *John Basse, citizen and clothier of London* to provide support to the son of John de Garton in respect of property in Southampton and Kent.[99] In the Close Rolls, Basse is described as a draper.[100] The second entry repeats the principle, but extends the undertaking to a manor in North Newton near Bridgwater in Somerset.[101] The issue, also reported in Calendar of City letter-books,[102] is of sufficient interest that it taken up by Barbara Hanawalt in her book about the role of *Women, Law and the Economy.*[103]

An entry from a couple of days later on September 27 indicates that the plot of land adjacent to the *mansion of William Wenselowe* in the hospital of St. Katharine by the Tower of London has been granted to *Robert Chaumberleyn.. granting him a void plot of land in the hospital between the mansion of William Wenselowe on the west and the north corner of the church of the hospital.* Evidently *William Wenselowe* has taken up residence in a new mansion constructed in the two years since 1374, outside the walls of the City of London and in a prime position next to the Tower of London. It is unclear whether William's wife Joan is still alive at this stage. The site of this property was eventually excavated in the 1820s to create St. Katherine's dock, still visible as a working yacht haven to the east of the Tower of London.

A further reference to William in 1376 involves John Hermesthorp or *Hernesthorp* who has been master of St. Katherine's Hospital by the Tower and continues in the post until at least 1406,[104] and he is mentioned in both the property transactions above. He reappears in the next reference from the Fine Rolls from December 8 1377 relating to the upkeep of one of the royal mansions in Whitley in the county of Surrey:[105]

..to John de Hermesthorp, clerk, by mainprise of Robert Medle and William Wenselowe, both of the City of London..

---

[99] *CFR Edward iii., vol. viii, 1369-77, p. 364*
[100] *Cal. Close, Richard ii, vol. 1, 1377-1381. p. 58*
[101] *CFR Edward iii., vol. viii, 1369-77, p. 363*
[102] *Calendar of letter-books of the city of London, 1375-1399, p. 52*
[103] *The Wealth of Wives: Women, Law, and Economy in Late Medieval London, Barbara Hanawalt, OUP, 2007*
[104] *Court of Common Pleas, CP 40/583, rot. 514*
[105] *CFR, Richard II 1377, vol. ix, 1377-83, p. 37*

Edward Winslow's English Origins

This record may imply that William Winslow *Candlewick* may have had commercial interests in the upkeep of the fabric of royal property. The next reference written in French relates to a City of London property belonging to *William de Wynslowe* located in Candlewick Street, modern-day Cannon Street, dated March 1377:[106]

> *Indenture made between Roger de Brimmisley of Brandeston chaplain and Robert Pegge of Prestwold, being a lease with warranty during the lessor's life of all the said Roger's lands etc. ...rendering to the lessor or to William de Wynslowe in the said William's house in Candelwykstrete London 4 marks a year. Dated Braundeston by Croxton, Saturday after St. Gregory 1 Richard II.*

Whether by this time the mansion next to the Tower of London has been sold or surrendered is unclear. We can be pretty sure that a house in Candlewick Street, possibly the same house, may have been occupied by a later Winslow family member, suggesting that for some decades Candlewick Street was one of the bases for Winslow activities in the city of London. *Candlewyck*, one of the Wards of medieval London, was only about a hundred yards away from *Cordwainer* where John Winslow *Maunciple* evidently had a residence, possibly since the 1360s.

By 1386 William is conducting high value transactions. John Clerk, son of William Clerk of Kingston-on-Hull owes him the substantial sum of £278.[107] One of the last references to William Winslow *Candlewick* some thirteen years later is his will dated 9 May 1399 describing him as *citizen and tailor of London*. He expresses his wish:[108]

> *..to be buried in churchyard before the church of St Mary Abbechurch next Candlewykstrete.*

The will mentions his daughter Emma who is under age, and she is the beneficiary of various bequests, suggesting her year of birth as postdating 1378. In his lifetime William Winslow *Candlewick* has been active, engaging early in property transactions, prepared to act as a guarantor, and his generosity is also apparent. The account books of the Merchant Taylors contain an Anglo-French inscription dated August 1400, the first year of Henry IV:[109]

> *"Fait a remembrer que ceux sont lez acomptz de Clement Kyrton, Mestre de la Fraternite Seint Johan le Baptistre des Taillours en Londres de les biens du dit Fraternite, renduz le xxme jour de August l'an du regne Roy Henry quarte puis le conquest primer.*

Be aware that these are the accounts of Clement Kyrton, master of the fraternity of St. John the Baptist of the London Tailors and of the goods of the said fraternity, rendered on the 20th of August in the first year of King Henry IV since the conquest.

---

[106] *Cal. Close, Richard ii, 1374, vol. I, 1377-81, p. 124*
[107] *N. R. A., C 241/174/103*
[108] *Commissary Court of London Wills, no. 425, Courtney*
[109] *Memorial X: Accounts, Memorials of the Guild of Merchant Taylors of the Fraternity of St. John the Baptist in the City of London, 1399-1400, p. 65*

Edward Winslow's English Origins

Under a heading in the accounts marked *from gifts and testaments* in the shillings column, we find that forty shillings have been left by William Winslow *Candlewick* to the London Taylors' Fraternity.

> *del testament William Wynslowe, par Johan Creek: XL*

John Winslow, *Chesham*, Entries 1392-1423

Another John Winslow who first appears in 1392 lives on to 1423. According to his will reproduced in 6.1 below, John Winslow *Chesham* is a member of the Drapers' Gild. The first two entries below connect him to Chesham Bois in Buckinghamshire, situated some twenty-five miles south east of Winslow, and only fourteen miles west of St. Albans Abbey, increasing the likelihood that John Winslow *Chesham* is somehow related to the Buckinghamshire Winslows.

YEAR	ACTIVITY
1392	John W presented to church at Chesham Bois
1393	John Wynselowe, London citizen & draper, mainpernor, March 19
1398	John Winslow, citizen and draper of London, Creditor, Jan 18
1399	Not *patriarch* John Wynslowe, Attorney to Richard Brevvos, Ireland, April 14:
1406	John Wynselowe of London, mainprise, Jan 16
1413	John Wynselowe, creditor of the Bruces, Jan 30 1413
1413	John Winslow, citizen & draper, debtor of John Cornwall & John Brewes, 6 Oct 1414.
1423	John Winslow, willed Chesham Bois to wife Philippa, reversion to son John, died 1423
1423	John Wynslowe or Wynselowe, Draper of London, will 1423 Nov 3

Figure 3-14 Timeline for John Winslow Chesham

Who had owned the Chesham Bois manor previously? The Feet of Fines for Buckinghamshire records two transactions for the *de Breous* family in 1368 and 1377. [110] A reference from 1277 mentions *John de Breous* and Little Brickhill, about ten miles away from Winslow, and the *Brewos / Braose* / Bruce family were evidently acquainted with the Winslows as they were later with the Crouchmans; we can recall that Sir William had dealings with the Bruces in 1341. In November 1351 Peter de la Brewese was complaining about damage to his property at Chesham Bois where he was still residing in 1365.[111]

At some point the property transferred into *the possession of the family of Winslow, Citizens of London.*[112] No entry in the Feet of Fines for Buckinghamshire has been traced, but someone from the Winslow family, presented to the church there in 1392. Based on an entry from March 1393, the *De Brewes* and John Winslow *Chesham* were connected:[113]

[110] Travers, *Buckinghamshire Feet of Fines 1259-1307*, BRS, entries 105 and 229, pp. 17 and 37
[111] *Cal. Pat., Edward iii*, vol. 9, 1350-54, p. 200
[112] Lipscomb, *The History and Antiquities of the County of Buckingham*, George, vol. iii, QQQ p. 270
[113] *Cal. Close, Richard ii*, vol. 5, 1392-96, p. 132

Edward Winslow's English Origins

Westminster. To the sheriffs of London. Writ of supersedeas, by mainprise of Simon Ingram, John Wynselowe, John Creyke and William Crowemere citizens and drapers of London, in favour of Thomas de Brewes knight at suit of William Scut clerk for debt.

Taken with the evidence from his will in 1423, this entry is unmistakeably referring to John Winslow *Chesham*. Although he joined a different gild, John *Chesham* separately followed family members Thomas *Homicide*, William *Candlewick* and John *Maunciple* into apprenticeship in London, pursuing an opportunity with evident advantages.

In an entry from January 1398 John Winslow, *citizen and draper of London*, is seeking redress as a creditor following a default over a £60 loan by *John Prendergast, knight, of Northumberland*. This partially damaged text dated January 18 1398 perhaps tells something of the contemporary drapery trade, providing an inventory of some of Sir John's possessions, including:[114]

...a gold brooch, a cawl of pearls worth 66s. 8d, filets of pearls worth 30s. 8d, and 40d., ... a girdle of silk encrusted with silver and gold.... furs, and other [illegible] valuables.

The Irish campaign is mentioned in a reference from April 13 1399 but this time is probably addressing John Winslow *Chesham* and not John Winslow *Maunciple* who is already abroad. A John Winslow is acting as attorney to one of the *Brewos/Braose* family members, here Richard *Brewos*, and previously tenant in Chesham Bois:[115]

Richard Brewos has the like letters nominating Thomas Anleby and John Wynslowe. William Roudon, clerk, received the attorneys as above.

The *Thomas Anleby* mentioned here is probably the individual remembered later in John Winslow's will in 1423: *ten marks goes to Thomas Legeard of Anleby*, and associating this reference with John *Chesham* rather than John *Maunciple*. As for *Richard Brewos,* the Bruces would remain a significant Anglo-Norman family whose surname probably derives from *Briouze* in the South of Normandy. After the Conquest the family benefited from gifts of landholdings in both England and Scotland and have played a significant role in both English and Scottish history. One wonders how many Scots would be surprised to discover that national hero *Robert the Bruce* was really an Englishman of Norman ancestry.

John Wynselowe *Chesham* in 1413 is a frustrated creditor of Sir John Brewese and the outcome of debt recovery action is not found:[116]

To the sheriffs of London. Writ of supersedeas, by mainprise of Edmund Breudenell of Bukinghamshire, Richard Wakehurst, John Waleys of Sussex and John Impay of Bukinghamshire, in favour of John Brewese knight at suit of John Wynselowe for a debt of £213 6s. 8d. Like writ in favour of John Brewes knight in regard to a debt of 37l. 3s. 1½d.

---

[114] N. R. A., Kew, 1398, ref. C 131/46/18
[115] Cal. Pat., Richard ii, vol. 6, 1396-99, p. 520
[116] Cal. Close, Henry iv, vol. 4, 1409-1413, p. 416

But an entry barely a year later suggests that John Winslow *Chesham* now owes £100 to John Brewes and John Cornwall[117] confirmed at a hearing before Richard Whittington, these days better known to young theatregoers as pantomime hero *Dick Whittington*.

The last reference to John Winslow *Chesham* is found in his will dated 12 July 1423, proved in November 1423,[118] and reproduced in the Appendix 6.1. A long codicil directs that timber in *my manor of Cheshamboys in the county of Buckingham* is to be felled, and that funds *to the value of 100 marks of sterling* be swiftly realised to pay specific bequests directed *first of all to Agnes, bastard daughter of John Wynselow, my son, towards her marriage, ten marks of sterling*.

He goes on to leave *ten marks* to *Emme, wife of the said Walter Frebarn, my kinswoman*. Another ten marks goes to *Thomas Legeard of Anleby in the county of York*, presumably the *Thomas de Anleby* mentioned above. Thomas's son is also left a small legacy. The residue is left to his wife Philippa for her lifetime, and thereafter to *the said John Wynselow, my son, and the heirs of his body lawfully begotten*. So John Winslow *Chesham*'s son John, now identified as John Winslow *Junior*, stands to inherit Chesham Bois Manor; but the property will eventually pass to the Cheynes in a deed dated January 1433:[119]

> B. 910. Indenture between John Popham, knight, and Thomas Wedon, John Underwoode, of Chesham in the co. Buckingham, and others relative to a yearly rent payable to him out of the manor of Chesham Boys; and also to a demise to him of the manor of Rolleston in the co. Buckinghamshire. Leicester. 4 January, 11 Henry VI. Seals.

The date of death of John Winslow *Chesham* places him in the generation succeeding John Winslow *Maunciple,* although the identity of his father has not been established, a topic to be considered later.

John Winslow, *Hostytter*, Entry 1365

All the John Winslows associated with Buckinghamshire and London found in the extant historical record up to the 1390s have now been accounted for: John *Maunciple,* John *Hunsdon,* John *Bailiff* and John *Chesham*; apart from one:

YEAR	ACTIVITY
1365-	John de Wynselowe and Alice his wife, executrix of Henry Sket

Figure 3-15 Entry for John Winslow Hostytter

During the nearly ten years between leaving Little Horwood in 1357 and emerging in 1366 to ship supplies to Flanders from Hull, John Winslow *Maunciple* is not mentioned. In reviewing the life of John Winslow *Maunciple* so far we have found that he has many attributes: entrepreneurialism, a willingness to take risks;

---

[117] PRO, C 131/225/19
[118] N. R. A., PCC Will Registers, Luffenam, ref PROB 11/3/31
[119] N. R. A., Records of the Court of Augmentations and the Augmentation Office, Ref E 329/230

Edward Winslow's English Origins

generosity; a wily team player, loyal, supportive, socially adept, connected, inspiring loyalty, someone who recovers from adversity. We know him later as a *pepperer* or *grocer*.

The entry unidentified is for John Winslow who is described as a *hostytter*, a keeper of an inn or lodging-house, and seemingly in trouble. He and his wife Alice, are first mentioned on 16 June 1365 when:[120]

> *John Wynselowe, hostytter, and Alice his wife, executrix of the will of Henry Sket, were committed to prison till they paid the sum of £24 due to Joan and Anne, the testator's daughters*

Immediately mainprised by William Whetele, Cordwainer, events move on; and by September, the same source document exonerates Winslow as blameless:

> *Pleas held before the Mayor, Aldermen and Sheriffs on 25 Sept. Ao 39 Edw. III [1365]*
>
> *William de Whetele, cordwainer, was summoned to answer John de Wynselowe and Alice his wife, executrix of Henry Sket, cordwainer, in a plea that he render them an account of 70 dozens of white prepared leather, value £40, and thirteen quaternions of black prepared leather, value 30s, and other hides of black oxhide and cowhide fully prepared for making boots and shoes, value £30, all of which he had received from her, when she was sole, to trade therewith on her behalf, and to render account to her, which he now refused to do.*
>
> *The defendant pleaded that he never received any hides on such terms, but that immediately after the death of the above-mentioned Henry Sket, he purchased from the widow, the plaintiff Alice, oxhide and cowhide to the value of £29, which sum he paid in cash except £9 8s 11d, for which he gave a tally. Subsequently he paid that sum, by the plaintiffs' instructions, to a certain John Canoun, who was a creditor of the late Henry Sket, and the tally was thereupon cancelled. Both parties put themselves on the country, but the plaintiffs afterwards withdrew from their action. Judgment that they and their pledges be in mercy and that the defendant go thence without a day.*

We recall that Cordwainer Ward was the location from which John Winslow would be summoned to the inauguration of Sir Nicholas Brembre in 1384. Gwyn Williams[121] mentions another Cordwainer resident *William Servat* whose activities are further considered in Chapter 4.

William Winslow, *Pavilioner*, Entries 1381-1414

The lifetime of William Winslow *Pavilioner* is well documented, but his origins are obscure. William occupies leading roles in royal circles, initially as Yeoman of the Chamber and later as King's Pavilioner. In the court of King Richard II, the significance of Yeomen of the Chamber shifted as they assumed positions with wide-ranging political and sometimes diplomatic responsibilities, and were generously rewarded for their loyalty. William Winslow, *Pavilioner* was no exception.

---

[120] *Calendar of Plea & Memoranda Rolls, City of London, v. 2, 1364-1381 Roll A 10: (ii), 1365, p. 30 et seq.*
[121] *Gwyn Williams, pp. 141-3*

Edward Winslow's English Origins

An informative article by James Gillespie analyses the careers of some prominent yeomen in Richard's court, and assesses their significance. Gillespie notes the increase in the number of Yeomen under King Richard, and argues that Richard's aim was to foster his own internal group supportive of royal policies without initiating major structural change, mainly as a defensive measure to sustain royal authority over an increasingly assertive aristocracy.[122]

Gillespie considers the *Yeomen of the Chamber* as being treated far more liberally that the *Yeomen of the Crown,* and this is apparent from the generosity extended to William Winslow *Pavilioner.* Gillespie notes how at least three Yeomen of the Chamber undertook quasi-diplomatic expeditions,[123] and he cites[124] one such expedition undertaken by Ralph Tudor who was generously rewarded in December 1398 for *a journey to France on the King's secret business.*[125]

Yeomen of the chamber fulfilled civic administrative functions and well as household and military duties.[126] An area that Gillespie does not cover in detail is the line of command between monarch and the yeomen. Gillespie mentions Sir Simon Burley and his appointment for life as under-chamberlain of the King's household, positioning him in the mid-tier of administration. Previously Burley had worked for Richard's father, Edward of Woodstock the Black Prince, and he served as tutor to the young Richard II after his accession in 1377. Thomas Winslow *Homicide* appears in the Black Prince's Register in 1351, as previously noted.

Parliament attempted to elect its own candidate for the Stewardship of the Household, an imposition unacceptable to the Crown, and instead Richard named his own man, the Sir John Beauchamp whom we encountered earlier. The King was godfather to Beauchamp's son John. In the ensuing power struggle, the Merciless Parliament headed by the King's opponents was in session from February to June 1388 and issued an order to confine a group of the King's supporters *incommunicado* on February 24.[127]

> *To John Devereux constable of Dovorre [Dover} castle and warden of the Cinque Ports, and to his lieutenant. Order by advice of the council to cause John Beauchamp of Holt, Thomas Tryvet, John Salesbury knights and John Lincoln clerk of the receipt of the exchequer with all speed to come before the king and council in this parliament at Westminster; as for urgent causes it was by the king granted and by the council declared and ordered that they should for a time be kept severally in custody in divers places within Dovorre castle, so that none should have speech with another for counselling or entreating him, and none of them*

---

[122] Gillespie, James L. "Richard II's Yeomen of the Chamber." *Albion: Quarterly Journal Concerned with British Studies,* vol. 10, no. 4, 1978, pp. 319–329
[123] Gillespie, p. 324-5
[124] Gillespie, p. 325
[125] N.R.A., E. 403/561
[126] Gillespie. p. 323
[127] Cal. Close, Richard ii, vol. 3, 1385-89, p. 382

Edward Winslow's English Origins

should send aught save to the great council, with proviso that one might greet another in public. By K. and C.

The like to ...William de Neville constable of Notyngham castle and his lieutenant, concerning Simon de Beurly [Sir Simon Burley] and William de Elineham knights.

Gillespie does not mention Sir Simon Burley among those impeached for treason, but his execution took place on 5 May 1388 by order of the Commons. Another among many victims was John Beauchamp, now Baron Beauchamp of Kidderminster, executed on Tower Hill on May 12,[128] and by May 14 portions of his transferrable estate were already being dispersed.[129] John Beauchamp was succeeded by his son, John Beauchamp of Holt, whom we will revisit later.

Against this instability of courtly confrontation and hostility we are introduced to the William Winslow known here as *Pavilioner,* with documentation relating to him running from 1381 to 1414.

YEAR	ACTIVITY
1381	Grant of Mildenhall land to William Wynselowe Mar 19
1382	Grant to William Wynselowe, Standon, adjacent to Hunsdon, Feb 10
1382	Grant of Kayo to William Wynselowe May 21
1382	Grant of Standon Park, update to William Wynselowe Sept 10
1382	Grant of Mewes *Meaux* to William Wynselowe Sep 10
1384	William Wynslowe, re Mildenhall including Tresilian Feb 7
1385	William Wyncelowe re Mildenhall, Feb 4
1385	William Wyncelowe cedes Mildenhall, Feb 24
1385	William Wyncelowe, St John Colchester gift March 22
1386	William Wyncelowe, yeomen chamber, Chiltern Langley parker, Apr 26
1386	William Wyncelowe accepts post of Parker of Chiltern Langley with a swap, Aug 4
1386	William Wyncelowe, yeoman chamber, king's Stannary, Cornwall Dec 13
1387	William Wyncelowe accepts post of parker of Chiltern Langley swap, Apr 9
1387	William Wyncelowe payment for post of parker of Chiltern Langley park Oct 1
1387	William Wynslawe to receive 10 marks a year from Preston estate, Sussex, Oct 11
138x	William Wynselowe marries Mary Beaufeu, daughter of William Beaufeu's son John
1388	William Wynslawe, Preston Sussex benefit, case heard in Cambridge, Sep 28
1389	William Wyncelowe king's yeoman Pershore Abbey, Worcester, August 16
1389	William Wyncelowe and post of parker of Chiltern Langley park again Oct
1390	Winslow, William Wyncelowe, Chiltern Langley, Jan 29
1390	Winslow, William Wyncelowe, Chiltern Langley back pay, Oct 3
1390	William Wenselawe, woodwardships, Dyntheleyne & Iscorvay, co. Carnarvon, Nov 20

[128] Hist. Parl., vol. 2, 1386-1422, p. 153
[129] Cal. Close, Richard ii, vol. 3, 1385-89, p. 494

Year	Activity
1391	William W takes Sandford Ferry, surrenders Chiltern Langley, Jan 12
1391	William Wyncelowe, Yeoman of the Chamber, former under-parker, May 16
1391	William Wynselowe, takes Sandford fair, Jul 12
1391	William Wynselowe, cedes Chiltern Langley, Jul 12
1393	William Wyncelowe, Kings serjeant, surrenders Pershore, Worcestershire, Jun 28
1394	William Wyncelowe, gift Evyonyth N Wales, (Eifionydd) commote, Caernarvonshire, Feb 11
1394	William Wyncelowe military service Ireland, Sept 20
1395	William W takes office of the king's Pavilioner, May 22
1396	William Wyncelowe, King's Esquire & Pavilioner, pardon for loss of pavilions, Calais, Dec 20
1397	William Wynselowe pavilioner, and John Beaufitz, pavilions repair Oct 30
1399	William Wyncelowe, nominating Gaunstede and Pygot attorneys, April 18
1399	William Wynselowe loses office of the Pavilioner, October 8
1399	William Wynselowe, Wenslawe, Wyncelowe, royal grants, Nov 3
1403	William Wyntelowe deceased? Pershore March 6
1403	William Wyncelowe, Sandford Ferry tenancy extended, Nov 19
1406	History of Cambridge inaccuracies Volume 8 (pp. 248-267)
1409	William Wyncelowe, Sandford ferry rights, Nov 9
1412	Bradmore, death of former surgeon of Pavilioner, 1412
1414	William Wyncelowe deceased, re Meaux, Feb 22
1414	William Wyncelowe, deceased, re-grant of ferry called Samfordhithe, March 4
1414	William Wyncelowe deceased re abbot and convent of Colchestre, March 22

Figure 3-16 Timeline for William Winslow Pavilioner

The first entry for William Winslow *Pavilioner* for March 1381 is recording a royal gift to the *Pavilioner* comprising land in Mildenhall in Suffolk previously forfeited to the Crown after an inquisition established legal irregularities in an earlier transfer. William is one of the yeomen of the Chamber who benefits:[130]

Grant, for life, to William Wynslowe, one of the yeomen of the chamber of two messuages, two cottages, seventy acres of land, nine of meadow and sixteen of pasture in Mildenhale, co. Suffolk, of the yearly value of 100s., late of Richard de Chadenhalk, who acquired them partly from John Stafford and partly from Alan Exnyng, which were forfeited to the Crown because [without licence] he enfeoffed John Traas, John Palfreyman, chaplain, William Fermer, chaplain, and John Claver and their successors, chaplains of a chantry in Mildenhale, of the premises, and because, also without licence, Laurence Crowemere, Robert Shastbury, Thomas Fennowe, Alexander Kechynghog and John de Rougham, chaplains of the same chantry, acquired the premises in mortmain, as appears by inquisition of William Berard, Escheator.

---

[130] *Cal. Pat., Richard ii, vol. 1, 1377-81, p. 612*

Edward Winslow's English Origins

By the time of the next entry dated February 1382, the Peasants' revolt has been suppressed. Gillespie notes how Yeomen of the Chamber had some scope among themselves to influence, exchange and trade their royal gifts. With the death of Edmund Mortimer, third Earl of March killed in Cork on one of the Irish campaigns in December 1381 and during the minority of his heir, King Richard allocated a number of Mortimer's assets to the Yeomen of the Chamber, including this gift to the *Pavilioner. Stondon* is the modern-day village of Standon in Hertfordshire:[131]

> Grant for life, during the minority of the heir, to William Wynselowe, yeomen of the chamber, and the office of the custody of the park of Stondon county Hertford, part of the possessions of Edmund, late Earl of March.

Next in May 1382 we find William being offered a gift in Wales:[132]

> Grant, for life, to William Wynselowe, one of the yeomen of the chamber, of the office of the constableship of the commote of Kayo without rendering aught therefor, in the same manner as John Henxteworth, deceased.

Kago or *Kayo* is located in *Cantrefmaur*, these days part of Carmarthenshire, Wales. Cantref Mawr comprised seven *cwmwdau* bounded by the rivers Tywi, Teifi and Gwili, the Towy and Telvy. The Constableship presumably offered William Pavilioner a source of income in an area of outstanding natural beauty.

A further reference to Standon is found in the Close Rolls from September 1382, confirming that the gift as custodian of *Standon Park* is generating income:[133]

> To the keeper, bailiff, farmer or receiver of the manors of Stondon for the time being. Order to pay to William Wynselowe yeoman of the king's chamber every year the wages and fees belonging to the office of keeper of Stondon park co. Hertford, and the arrears since 10 February last, on which date the king granted to the said William for life, so long as the same shall remain in the king's hand, the office of keeper of the said park, which is in his hand among other lands of Edmund de Mortuo Mari earl of March. Et erat patens.

An entry[134] shortly afterwards confirms the promise of a weekly gift of a bushel of grain for life to another member of the Household, John de Massyngham yeoman, from the same Standon estate.

The next reference for William *Pavilioner* also dates from 1382, and this time it is for his lifetime from a property in Meaux Abbey, located in Beverley, East Riding of Yorkshire. The reference is dated September 10:[135]

> William Wyncelowe yeoman of the king's chamber is sent to the abbot and convent of Mewes to take for life such maintenance of that abbey as Lucy who was wife of John atte Wode knight otherwise called Lucetta de Gaynesburgh deceased had at the late king's command.

---

[131] *Cal. Pat., Richard ii, vol. 2, 1381-5, p. 93*
[132] *Cal. Pat., Richard ii, vol. 2, 1381-5, p. 118*
[133] *Cal. Close, Richard ii, vol. 2, 1381-5, p. 151*
[134] *Cal. Close, Richard ii, vol. 2, 1381-5, p. 195*
[135] *Cal. Close, Richard ii, vol. 2, 1381-5, p. 213*

Edward Winslow's English Origins

Meaux Abbey previously owned the land of Wyke which King Edward I purchased in 1293 to create the major seaport town of Kingston upon Hull, and from whose new docks John Winslow *Maunciple* was to ship his 400 quarters of grain in 1368. It was also the Delapoles' home town. Two years later in February 1384 a dispute occurs over the land in Mildenhall:[136]

> To Robert Tresilyan and his fellows, justices appointed to hold pleas before the king. Order by writ of nisi prius to command an inquisition which remains to be taken between the king and William Wynslowe suing for him and John Trace and John Claver, whether William Childeston the younger, John son of Bartholomew de Childeston and Robert le Soutere were before Monday after St. Gregory the Pope 6 Richard II enfeoffed of two messuages, two cottages, 69 acres of land, 9 acres of meadow and 16 acres of pasture in Mildenhale or no, to be taken before one of the king's justices..

There is a follow-up to this request for an enquiry in February 4 1385:[137]

> Grant in aid of the king's esquire, William Takel and in consideration of his service in war heretofore, and of his offer to serve at his own charges for half a year whenever required, to Robert Hethe of the reversion, in lee, of lands and tenements late of Richard Chadenhalke in Mildenhale, now held for life by William Wyncelowe. By signet letter.

An entry from a fortnight later on February 24 confirms that the issue is resolved:[138]

> Vacated by surrender and cancelled

In this matter William Winslow *Pavilioner* can be judged to have behaved with ready compliance, a disposition that works to his advantage, as the evidence shows: he is immediately offered an alternative on March 22 1385:[139]

> William Wyncelowe, yeoman of the king's chamber is sent to the abbot and convent of St. John Colchestre, to take of that house such maintenance as John Mareys deceased had.

The gift in Colchester at only forty miles away is marginally more convenient than more distant Suffolk. In April 1387 another opportunity arises in Chiltern Langley, a location better known now as *Kings Langley,* close by St. Albans and located within the royal Hundred of Dacorum.[140] We encountered Langley earlier with William Winslow *Patriarch*'s connections:

> Thomas de Walda and William de Winslow who has the heir of Walter Godard for his wife, are holding three hides of land as a third part of one fee in Swanbourne from John Passelewe, and the same John hold from the Queen of England, in connection with her Manor of Langley.

Now the Langley estate becomes relevant again in April 1387:[141]

---

[136] Cal. Close, Richard ii, vol. 2, 1381-5, p. 360
[137] Cal. Pat., Richard ii, vol. 2, 1381-5, p. 533
[138] Cal. Pat., Richard ii, vol. 2, 1381-5, p. 543
[139] Cal. Close, Richard ii, vol. 2, 1381-5, p. 625
[140] Cal. Pat., Richard ii, vol. 3, 1385-9, p. 288
[141] Cal. Pat., Richard ii, vol. 3, 1385-9, p. 202

Edward Winslow's English Origins

Grant, for life, to the king's servant William Wyncelowe, one of the yeomen of the chamber, of the office of parker of the king's park of Chilternelangle, at the supplication of John Chaundos, yeoman of the chamber, to whom it was lately granted and who has surrendered his letters patent thereof. Vacated by surrender and cancelled, because the king granted to the said William the office of under-parker thereof, 13 October, 13 Richard.

A follow-up in August 1387 states:[142]

Grant, for life, to John Chaundos, yeoman of the chamber, of the office of parker of Chilterne Langele park as held by Roger Cokerel, deceased. By signet letter.

December 1386 had produced a new appointment for William Winslow *Pavilioner*.[143]

Grant, during pleasure, with the assent of the Council, to William Wyncelowe one of the yeomen of the chamber, of the office of controller of the king's stannary in Cornwall, in the room of Walter Raynold. By p.s.

Stannaries are tin mines, and Cornwall has been associated with tin since at least Roman times. Historically the mines have produced significant profits. The office of *Lord Warden of the Stannaries* connected with coinage and Assay has existed since 1197. A new office was instituted during the early years of King Richard's reign, later evolving to be known as *Deputy Lord Warden of the Stannaries*. Evidently Walter Reynold was the first appointee, and in March 1386 a successor is reported:[144]

Grant, during good behaviour, to the king's servant Nicholas FitzHerberd, of the office of controller of the stannary in Cornwall as held by Walter Reynold.

Richard Breton is appointed new Bailiff of the Stannary on April 1 1386,[145] and William Winslow succeeds FitzHerberd on December 13 the same year:[146]

Grant, during pleasure, with the assent of the Council, to William Wyncelowe one of the yeomen of the chamber, of the office of controller of the king's stannary in Cornwall, in the room of Walter Raynold. By p.s.

Creation of this new office under Richard II might reflect a need for better accountability. After Edward the Black Prince had died without succeeding to the throne, Edward III directed that one third of the profits of the stannaries be directed to Joan *The Fair Maid of Kent*, widow of Edward the Black Prince:[147]

To Richard Sergeaux steward of all the lands and lordships in Cornwall and Devon which were of Edward prince of Wales etc. ....Order to deliver in dower to Joan who was wife of the said prince, or to the receiver by her now appointed, a third part of all moneys and

---

[142] *Cal. Pat., Richard ii, vol. 3, 1385-9, p. 202*
[143] *Cal. Pat., Richard ii, vol. 3, 1385-9, p. 248*
[144] *Cal. Pat., Richard ii, vol. 3, 1385-89, p. 107*
[145] *Cal. Pat., Richard ii, vol. 3, 1385-89, p. 129*
[146] *Cal. Pat., Richard ii, vol. 3, 1385-89, p. 248*
[147] *Cal. Close, Edward iii, vol. 14, 1373-77, pp. 407-8*

Edward Winslow's English Origins

profits arising from the stannary and stampage of tin in Cornwall and Devon since the prince's death..

After its creation, the post of *Deputy Lord Warden of the Stannaries* was maintained for almost the next five hundred years, with William Winslow *Pavilioner* as the third incumbent. His predecessor Nicholas FitzHerberd went on to become an auditor, and later an MP.[148] William's successor was Thomas Trewyn, who took over nearly a year later on 21 Nov 1387.[149] Meanwhile on October 1 1387, the pay rate for William Winslow's post as under-parker of Chiltern Langley is upgraded to that of a full parker.[150] An additional source of royal income is provided on October 11, a week or so later:[151]

> Grant, for life, during the minority of Thomas, son and heir of Robert Tregos, knight, to the king's esquire, Thomas Brounflete, of, 10 marks a year from the issues of the manor of Preston, co. Sussex, in the king's hands by reason of the said minority. The like to William Wynslawe yeoman of the chamber.

The impact on the yeomen of the chamber arising from the upheaval at the royal court caused by the Merciless Parliament is not evident from the written record, and as a group they emerge broadly unaffected. The stream of gifts is interrupted until August 1389 when William is granted further benefits. In this case we have Pershore, a market town located in Worcestershire, England, on the banks of the River Avon, and barely seven miles from Kempsey:[152]

> Westminster. William Wyncelowe the king's yeoman is sent to the abbot and convent of Percheor, to take of that house for life such maintenance as Walter Hayne deceased had therein at the late king's request.

The previous holder of this gift had been one of the King's favourites, Sir John de Beauchamp. After the merciless Parliament had opposed the King over new rules that the Steward of the Household must be appointed in parliament, Richard II reacted by granting Sir John a knighthood, and this new Lord Beauchamp of Kidderminster was beheaded on Tower Hill on 12 May 1388 as already noted. Now William Winslow becomes the recipient of further royal generosity, marking another connection between the Winslows of Buckinghamshire, the county of Worcestershire and the Beauchamp family.

The benefits to William Winslow *Pavilioner* so far have generally been described as *grants*. The three exceptions occur when *William Wyncelowe the king's yeoman* is specifically *sent* to the three religious establishments, of Meaux in Yorkshire in 1382, Colchester in Essex in 1385, and now Pershore in Worcestershire on August 16 1389.

---

148 *Hist. Parl., vol. 3, 1386-1421, p. 79*
149 *Cal. Pat., Richard ii, vol. 3, 1385-89, p. 382*
150 *Cal. Close, Richard ii, vol. 3, 1385-89, p. 347*
151 *Cal. Pat., Richard ii, vol. 3, 1385-89, p. 358*
152 *Cal. Close, Richard ii, vol. 4, 1389-1392, p. 69*

Edward Winslow's English Origins

Throughout this period of instability, the King's uncle John of Gaunt had been outside England on military campains in France and Spain. Peace was concluded on 18 July 1389 by the Truce of Leulinghem, drawing the second phase of the Hundred Years' War to a close. Neither side retained much appetite for further conflict. Political stability in England had been compromised by the fallout from the Merciless Parliament, while King Charles VI of France continued to suffer from bouts of debilitating mental illness.

The root cause of the conflict, the disputed status of the Duchy of Aquitaine, remained unresolved. William Winslow's release to travel to Pershore followed only a month later, and it is unclear whether William accompanied his monarch to Leulinghem for the treaty ratification. Meanwhile another royal servant, Thomas Armner, opted to divert one of his royal grants received in May to William Winslow on July 12 1389:[153]

> *Grant, for life or until further order, to the Kings servant, Thomas Armner, of the fair of Sandford, County Oxford.*

> *Vacated by surrender and cancelled, because the king, at the supplication of the said Thomas, granted it to William Winslow, for life, 12th July*

Sandford is a village three miles south of Oxford located on the River Thames, with the town of Winslow about twenty five miles to the south west. By October 1389, William's status as underparker of Chiltern Langley is again being reconfirmed, and this time the gift is specified unconditionally as being for life:[154]

> *Westminster. Grant, for life, to William Wyncelowe, one of the yeomen of the chamber, of the office of under-parker of the king's park of Chilternelangeley, notwithstanding that he has without warrant held it since 9 April, 10 Richard II, when the king by letters patent, now surrendered, granted to him the office of parker of the said park.*

The financial details of the agreement are more fully explained in January 1390, before there is yet a further change of plan:[155]

> *Grant, for life, the William Wyncelowe, yeoman of the chamber, of the office of under-parker at Chilternelangeley Park with the wages of 8d. a day from the issues of the manor of Chilternelangeley, 8d. a day for the time when he held the said office without warrant, and 8d. a day from 18th of October last to the present time: on his surrender of letters patent dated 9 April, 10 Richard II and 13 October 13 Richard II*

> *Vacated and surrendered and cancelled, because at his supplication the king granted the office to Thomas Armner, for life, 12 July, 15 Richard II.*

What has actually happened is that Thomas Armner has exchanged his Sandford concession for the Chiltern Langley concession held by William Winslow *Pavilioner*,

---

[153] Cal. Pat., Richard ii, vol. 4, 1388-92, p. 472
[154] Cal. Pat., Richard ii, vol. 4, 1388-92, p. 118
[155] Cal. Pat., Richard ii, vol. 4, 1388-92, p. 184

presumably for their mutual benefit, and illustrating the flexibility enjoyed by the Yeomen in dividing up royal benevolence.

William's next dealings are with Wales in November 1390. King Richard has granted management rights over areas of royal forest on the North Wales coastline near Anglesey, this time with some commotes near Caernarfon:[156]

> *Letters patent dated 20 November 14, Richard II, granting for life to William Wenselawe the office of the woodwardships of Dyntheleyne and Iscorvay, co. Carnarvon.*

Confirmations of the Chiltern Langley and Sandford reallocations between Winslow and Armner are published 12 July 1391.[157] The next references to William Winslow appear nearly two years later in 1393. Now described as the *King's Serjeant*, implying a promotion in rank, William is voluntarily conceding his lifetime residency in the Abbey of Pershore to *John Knyght of Hulle and Alice his wife*:[158]

> *To the abbot and convent of Persheor. Request to take again letters patent under the common seal of their house concerning a maintenance for life which William Wyncelowe the king's serjeant has in that abbey by grant of the king, namely such as Walter Heyne deceased had...*

On Feb 11 1394 William is offered the office of *woodward* in Evionedd.[159]

> *Grant, for life, to the Kings Esquire William Wyncelow of the office of the woodward of Evyonyth North Wales.*

By September of the same year, William Winslow *Pavilioner* is being invited to join the King's campaign in Ireland. The summons naming individuals and their attorneys had commenced a couple of months previously, and the group mustered now includes William Winslow with a diverse cross-section of knights, esquires and members of the royal household including the king's butler, John Slegh. Here is the entry from September 20:[160]

> *Protection with clause volumus for half a year for John Fekenham, going to Ireland in the king's company on his service there. The like for the following, also going in the king's company:--William Wyncelowe...*

Four days later John Winslow *Maunciple* is offered protection for Ireland on a similar basis, and with John Walcote as one of his attorneys, the first evidence of activities impacting both the *Maunciple* and the *Pavilioner*. William is in the King's company. William's performance on the Irish military expedition is evidently satisfactory, because the following May he receives an additional advancement; now he becomes King's Pavilioner, and with a supply of the formal trappings:[161]

---

[156] *Cal. Pat., Richard ii, vol. 4, 1388-92, p. 326*
[157] *Cal. Pat., Richard ii, vol. 4, 1388-92, p. 472*
[158] *Cal. Close, Richard ii, vol. 5, 1392-6, p. 221*
[159] *Cal. Pat., Richard ii, vol. 5, 1391-6, p. 366*
[160] *Cal. Pat., Richard ii, vol. 5, 1391-6, p. 482*
[161] *Cal. Pat., Richard ii, vol. 5, 1391-6, p. 568*

Edward Winslow's English Origins

22 May 1395. Grant for life to the King's Esquire William Wincelowe of the office of the king's Pavilioner and keeper of his pavilions with the fees and robes of office.

The *Pavilioner* principally managed activities connected with military logistics, and William was replacing John Savage who had died 28 August, 1394 according to church records, and was buried in a church in Blackfriars, London.[162] Savage was described as *providing, at the king's charges, the workmen and labourers for making the pavilions and tents and carriage and freight to places where necessary for the king's present expedition.*[163]

The happiness of William Winslow *Pavilioner* at his promotion was swiftly tempered by adversity. In December 1396, the royal pavilions under his stewardship were lost at sea off Calais. Despite the loss, William emerges with a pardon, and his new title of *Esquire* suggests yet another promotion:[164]

Pardon and remission to the King's Esquire and Pavilioner, William Wynselowe, of all actions and demands which the king has or can have against him on account of the loss of tents and pavilions with their furniture in his keeping, sunk by accident at sea, when the king was last at Calais.

In addition William now has a new colleague whose family name is familiar: John Beaufeu. An entry from the Patent Rolls in February 1397 had indicated that John Beaufeu had become a Yeoman of the Chamber, and already receiving royal largesse:[165]

Grant, for life, to John Beaufitz of the keepership of the castle of Kylgaren, with the wages of 3d. a day and all other fees belonging thereto, as from 1 June in the thirteenth year, when it was granted to him by letters patent under the seal of south Wales, which have been lost in a storm at sea in a ship in which the king's pavilions were lost.

Evidently all the tents and pavilions were being transported on board a single boat. Now an entry from October 1397 indicates that the misadventure had led to no recrimination; William and John are collaborating on the remediation of damage:[166]

Appointment of William Wynselowe the king's pavilioner, and John Beaufitz, yeoman of the king's pavilions, to arrest and take the necessary workmen and other labourers for making and repairing the king's pavilions and tents, and the necessary carriage and shipment thereof for the present expedition.

John Beaufitz's gift, the beautiful Cilgerran Castle in Pembrokeshire, was already a ruin by 1397, but its keepership evidently provided a source of income. Another income source was confirmed for John Beaufitz in July with a shared cash grant of 100s.[167]

---

[162] Palmer, C. F. R., *Burials at the Priories of the Blackfriars*, The Antiquary xxiii, p. 122
[163] *Cal. Pat., Richard ii*, vol. 5, 1391-6, p. 472
[164] *Cal. Pat., Richard ii*, vol. 6, 1396-9, p. 57
[165] *Cal. Pat., Richard ii*, vol. 6, 1396-9, p. 72
[166] *Cal. Pat., Richard ii*, vol. 6, 1396-9, p. 246
[167] *Cal. Pat., Richard ii*, vol. 6, 1396-9, p. 163

On April 19 1399 William is re-engaged for the Irish Campaign. Under the categorisation of those having *the like letters of general attorney* is the name of *William Wyncelowe*, nominating *Simon Gaunstede, clerk, and John Pygot the younger*, while *Thomas Stanley, clerk, received the attorneys as above*.[168] William Winslow's name appears in a subsequent document from April 26 confirming that he is operating in a group of six that includes Bishop Thomas of Carlisle and two knights, Sir Andrew Hake and Reginald Braybrook.[169]

What comes next is potentially calamitous. Henry Bolingbroke has seized power, and the first entry after Richard's deposition dated 30 September announces a change in the judiciary:[170]

> Appointment, during pleasure, of William Thirnyng as chief justice of Westminster, the Common Bench, receiving the accustomed fee.

The entries in this section of the Rolls Patent are not strictly chronological, and the entries for the first week of the new order are generally referring to senior government appointments involving the Chancery and the Rolls, interspersed with some ecclesiastical appointments. An announcement on October 8 confirms that a new Pavilioner, John Drayton, has been appointed. In the Rolls Patent records, William Winslow's is the first name singled out for replacement under the new regime.[171] Initially it is not clear why.

William's only consolation comes three weeks later on November 8 when his other offices in Wales and the right to the Sandford Ferry in Oxfordshire are reconfirmed through the Patent Rolls.[172] In practice several of the other gifts from the time of Richard II are not rescinded, and their eventual reallocation is only confirmed after William's death in 1414. Having lost his post office as Pavilioner, the references to William become far less frequent. The first whispering about William's apparent demise comes when his death is prematurely reported on March 6 1403:[173]

> William Parke is sent to the abbot and convent of Pershore, to take of that house such maintenance as William Wyntelowe deceased had therein at the late king's command.

Although his surname is misspelt, the content points unmistakably to William Winslow *Pavilioner* even if the content is erroneous; we know that William had conceded his residency to *John Knyght of Hulle and Alice his wife*. The continuity of his tenure of the Sandford Ferry is discussed within the broader context, including its associated landholding in 1403. William's tenancy is reconfirmed in November:[174]

---

[168] *Cal. Pat., Richard ii, vol. 6, 1396-9, p. 541*
[169] *Cal. Pat., Richard ii, vol. 6, 1396-9, p. 538*
[170] *Cal. Pat., Henry iv, vol. 1, 1399-1401, p. 1*
[171] *Cal. Pat., Henry iv, vol. 1, 1399-1401, p. 9*
[172] *Cal. Pat., Henry iv, vol. 1, 1399-1401, p. 111*
[173] *Cal. Close, Henry iv, vol. 2, 1402-5, p. 148*
[174] *Cal. Pat., Henry iv, vol. 2, 1401-5, p. 314*

Edward Winslow's English Origins

Whereas Richard II lately granted to William Wyncelowe for life the ferry of Sandford, Co. Oxford, in his hands by reason of the forfeiture of Robert Tresilian, knight, and the grant was confirmed by the king, and afterwards by the name of a ferry called Sandfordhith, of the value of 53s. 4d. yearly, it was taken into the king's hands by reason of the idiotcy of Roger Stanlak, son and heir of Richard Stanlak; the king grants the ferry to the said William from the time of such seisin so long as it remains in his hands, with all issues.

A lengthier clarification follows some six years later in 1409.[175] Circumstances have changed; Roger Stanlake *The Idiot* has now died; and Roger's cousins, Joan Sutton and Agnes Curteys, have taken possession. The king agrees the transfer, and suggests William's entitlement was never intended to exceed Roger Stanlake's lifetime. Later evidence suggests that William's privilege held since 1391 was not withdrawn in 1409, and actually continued past the death of Henry IV on 20 March 1413. News of the death of William Winslow Pavilioner is published in February 1414:[176]

John Clerk of Peston clerk of the crown in chancery, is sent to the abbot and convent of Meaux, to take of that house for life such maintenance as William Wyncelowe deceased had at the request of King Richard II.

John Clerk's tenure did not last as long as William's; his place at Meaux Abbey was taken by John Holton, serjeant of the King's Larder, in January 1416.[177] The Sandford Ferry gift passes to John Hill:[178]

Grant for life to the king's servant John Hill, yeoman of the larder, of a ferry called Samfordhithe, co. Oxford, which one William Wyncelowe, deceased, lately had of the grant of Richard II, of the value of 4 marks yearly, with all accustomed profits and commodities.

March 22 1414 confirms the transfer of the Colchester gift to Henry Wilymot, Esq of *such maintenance as one William Wyncelowe deceased had therein,*[179] bringing to a close the reports in the public records for the late *Pavilioner*.

But that is possibly not the end of the narrative. A medical handbook was written by the King's doctor, John Bradmore, and probably contains an unexpected reference to William Winslow. Bradmore, a recognised metallurgist as well as a leading medical surgeon, had reportedly been imprisoned, suspected of counterfeiting, and his name is mentioned in 1400 in connection with coinage irregularities.[180]

Bradmore is better known for saving the life of the future King Henry V, at that time *Henry of Monmouth,* following war wounds sustained early in his father's reign at the battle of Shrewsbury in July 1403. Although Henry IV carried the day, Henry of Monmouth took an active part in the battle and his face was impaled by an arrow

---

[175] *Cal. Pat., Henry iv, vol. 4, 1408-13, p. 145*
[176] *Cal. Close, Henry v, vol. 1, 1413-9, pp. 121, 186-7*
[177] *Cal. Close, Henry v, vol. 1, 1413-9, p. 298*
[178] *Cal. Pat., Henry v, vol. 1, 1413-6,-p. 169*
[179] *Cal. Close, Henry v, vol. 1, 1413-9, p. 122*
[180] *Cal. Close, Henry iv, vol. 1, 1399-1402, pp. 199, 206*

whose shaft snapped off after impact, leaving the metal arrowhead embedded inches deep into his face, narrowly missing both his eye socket and his brain.

Bradmore, a skilled practitioner, managed to sterilise the wound with alcohol before sealing it with honey to prevent infection. To stabilise the Prince's condition Bradmore needed to extract the arrowhead. Using his metalworking skills, Bradmore fabricated specialist tongs within a rotating cylinder. After inserting the cylinder of the apparatus, Bradmore was able to attach the tongs to the metal skirt of the embedded arrowhead, and he pulled it free. He then dressed the wound with alcohol again, and remarkably the young prince survived, albeit disfigured for life. Henry of Monmouth eventually became Henry V in 1413.

Bradmore wrote a medical and surgical handbook under the title *Philomena* documenting the process and mechanics of his advanced surgical practice and reckoned to date from between 1403 and death in 1412.[181]

A book on Life in Late Medieval England edited by Chris Given-Wilson contains a section by Simone MacDougall devoted to the subject of *Health, Diet, Medicine and the Plague*.[182] MacDougall points to a PhD thesis on Bradmore written by Sheila Lang,[183] and the underlying *Philomena* text describes the patient as:[184]

> ...a Man at Arms of the Lord King, ..at that time Master of the Lord King's tents [185]

However, Bradmore identifies his patient not by name but by his prestigious title as *King's Pavilioner*. The event is described as taking place in the first year of the reign of Henry IV, late September 1399 onwards. The diagnosis of the medical condition is cited as *wounded intestines,*[186] and the reason for the injury was a botched attempt at suicide, described as being *a result of devilish temptation.*[187]

A *baselard* is a lethal weapon larger than a dagger but smaller than a sword, as safety instructions dating from 1377 indicate:[188]

> ... no one carry any arms except a baselard by day, but a Knight to have his sword borne after him, his page having a baselard, but not a dagger...

While alone in his room, the King's Pavilioner had deliberately impaled himself on his *baselard* by holding the point of the weapon to his stomach and running into a wall, twice.[189] The incident occurred close to the Tower of London.

---

[181] *Bradmore, Philomena, British Library MS. Sloane 2272*
[182] *Given-Wilson, Illustrated History of Late Medieval England, Manchester University Press, 1996, pp. 82-99*
[183] *The Philomena of John Bradmore and its Middle English derivative: a perspective on surgery in late Medieval England, S. J Lang, PhD thesis, St. Andrews 1998*
[184] *Lang, p. 78*
[185] *Lang, quendam Armigerium domini Regis ..... eodem tempore magister tentarum domini Regis..*
[186] *Lang, ...intestina erant vulnerata..*
[187] *Lang, ...per temptationem diabolicam..*
[188] *Calendar of Letters for the City of London, vol. H, p. 269*
[189] *Lang, unum magnum et latum baselardum*

Edward Winslow's English Origins

In her thesis on *The Philomena*, Sheila Lang speculates about the name of the patient and the date of the incident, a matter of obvious interest here for understanding aspects of the Winslows' lives. On the balance of probability, Lang inclines to the view that *William Wyncelowe seems the more likely candidate.*[190] In mentioning a last will and testament from 1416, Lang mistakes the *Pavilioner* for William Winslow *Armiger*. But Lang is correct in deducing that William Winslow *Pavilioner* was someone of especial prominence:[191]

> In his descriptions of the treatment of the Prince of Wales and of the king's Pavilioner, Bradmore fulfilled several of the purposes suggested at the start of this chapter for the inclusion of such stories. He displayed the high status of his patients; he demonstrated his own skill in treating cases which seemed impossible to cure ...

Irrespective of the outcome of the failed suicide attempt, we now have a more certain timeframe for the eventual death of William Winslow *Pavilioner* based on reports circulating from early 1414 onwards, confirming the dispersal of gifts accumulated from his extended period of royal service. No will has been located for William, nor can we ascertain his date of birth nor his parentage with certainty, matters considered in more detail in Chapter 4.

William Winslow, *Armiger*, Entries 1387-1444, died 1415

The life of William Winslow *Armiger*, son of John Winslow *Maunciple* and wife Mariota, has already received coverage in previous sections. The continuity of the Crouchman line evidently continued to be troublesome. No fewer than twelve of twenty references to William relate to issues arising after his death in 1415.

We have seen that the spouse and widow of William Winslow *Armiger* was not *Agnes Poure* as Holton asserts, but *Agnes Winslow née Tibbay*, daughter of Sir John Tibbay, distinguished member of the royal household. Presented below is the timeline for William Winslow *Armiger* and for those directly connected to him, much of whose content has already been covered in Chapter 1.

YEAR	ACTIVITY
1387	(or 1388) Birth in Cranworth Norfolk, son of John & Mary, Nov 1
1406	Thomas Holgyll has taken profits since her death by king's grant
1406	William Wyncelawe, her son by her former husband John Wyncelawe, is next heir.
1409	William Wynselow son of John & Mary of Hempstead, 21st birthday Nov. 1, 1408-9
1410	William Winslow, confirmed as Crouchman heir, April 18
1411	William Wyncelawe proof of age, Thomas Holgyll to be informed. Jan 5
1413	Winslow, William, birth date of Armiger's daughter Joan, 1413-June-11
1415	William Wynslowe son of John and Mary, will, Jul 6
1415	William Wynslowe son of John and Mary of Hempstead, died 31 Aug 3 Henry V

---

[190] Lang, p. 73
[191] Lang, p. 78

Edward Winslow's English Origins

YEAR	ACTIVITY
1416	William Wynslowe, Esq, will mentioning London, Cambridge, Essex property 1416
1419	Inquest. William Wynslowe died 31 Aug 1415. Daughter Joan heir, 6 years
1420	Inquest. William Wyncelawe, armiger, tenant by knight service, 1420, Jan 20
1420	Inquest. William Wyncelawe, armiger, tenant by knight service, 1420, Jun 1
1421	Inquest. William Wyncelawe, armiger, re Joan succession Dec 8
1426	William Wynslowe's mother-in-law Joan died July 12 1426, Greyfriars wills
1426	Daughter Joan died July 20 1426, St Margaret's day, report Aug
1432	Agnes Winslow, widow of William Wynslowe, Thriplow release, c. 1432
1444	William Wynslowe's wife Agnes died 1444, Grey Friars
1444	Agnes Wynsley will, Mar 14, Comm. Court of London, 135,
1444	Winslow, Agnes, widow of William *Armiger*, mentioned 1444, Mar 23
1444	Agnes Wynslowe, widow of William *Armiger*, Wills, Grey Friars, London

Figure 3-17 Timeline for William Winslow Armiger and his family

William Winslow *Armiger* was born or christened in Cranworth, Norfolk on All Saints day, November 1 1387 or 1388. We know very little about the William's life and upbringing. There is no mention of William *Armiger* in the public records until 1410, when he was aged around thirteen, and by that time both his father John Winslow *Maunciple* and his mother Mary had died around 1399 and in 1406 respectively.

We know that after Mary remarried, Thomas Holgyll became William's stepfather. Gwilym Dodd identifies Holgyll as *chief of the accounts of the king's household*,[192] and maybe Holgyll facilitated William's subsequent marriage to the daughter of another member of the Royal Household, John de Tibbay. The Holgylls and Tibbays both probably originated from the Lake District, given that their home villages of *Tebay* and *Howgill* are located only seven miles apart.

After Mary Winslow's death in 1406, William Winslow *Armiger* eventually inherited Wood Hall, these days known as *Shore Hall*, and several other properties mentioned previously. It is noteworthy that the annual taxable value of the Wood Hall was more than three times greater than the family's original Crouchman estate in Hempstead, and that the family retained both properties when she died:[193]

> She held in her demesne as of fee: Hempstead, 1 tenement, of the earl of Oxford, a minor in the king's ward, service unknown, annual value 2s. Great Sampford, a capital messuage called 'Wodehall', of the same by knight service, annual value 6s.8d.

[192] Dodd G., Biggs D., *Reign of Henry IV Rebellion and Survival, 1403-1413*, Boydell & Brewer, York Medieval Press, 2008, p. 125
[193] *Cal. Inq. p.m., Henry iv, vol. 19, 1407-14*, entry C 137/76, no. 4., Entry 673

Edward Winslow's English Origins

She died on 25 Feb. 1406. Thomas Holgyll has held and taken the profits since her death by the king's grant [enrolment not found]. William Wyncelawe, her son by her former husband John Wyncelawe, is next heir. He was 21 on 1 Nov. 1409.

William's will also notes that by 1415 the Winslows still administered the manor of Ashdon near Hempstead.

William's father-in-law John Tibbay was latterly Chancellor to Queen Joan, second wife of King Henry IV, and stepmother to King Henry V. Multiple entries can be found under his name in the Patent and Close Rolls up to the year of his death. By February 21 1413 the Close Rolls are styling him as *Sir John Tibbay*.[194] Such were the circles into which young William Winslow *Armiger* was now connected through marriage.

Sir John was murdered by someone called *Nyauncer*. A fifteenth century MS held in the British Museum and published in 1827 records Sir John's murder: *Squire Nyauncer and his men slew Master John Tibbay as he passed through Lad Lane*:[195]

> *Neauser squyer, and his men, sclowen Maistre John Tybbay clerk, as he passed thorugh Ladlane; for the whiche deth the same John Nyauncer and iiij of his men fledden into seynt Annes chirche withinne Aldrichgate; and withinne the same chirche they were mured up, and men of diverses wardes watched them nyght and day. And the forsaid John Nyauncer and his men forsuoren the kynges lond, and passyd thorugh the citee of London toward Caleys in there schertes and breches, and ich of them a crosse in there hand.*

Before he finally expired, Sir John gave specific directions in his will:[196]

> *Archdeacon of Huntingdon and Chancellor of the Queen. To be buried in the Conventual Church of the Friars Minors, London. ..his will was made in the hall of the dwelling-place of Thomas Tykhull, in S. Lawrence Jewry..*

Cornish Lawyer and Chief Justice Robert Tresilian, executed under orders from the Merciless Parliament of 1388, already lay close to where Sir John Tibbay was finally interred. This same Tresilian was previously connected to both John Winslow *Maunciple* through the Justice Holt controversy in Cambridge, and to William Winslow *Pavilioner* for the Sandford Ferry. No evidence remains of the tomb these days; the Great Fire of 1666 consumed the Conventual Church of the Friars Minors in its path across London.

The evidence confirming that William Winslow *Armiger* married Sir John's daughter Agnes and not Agnes Poure can be deduced from the will of Agnes's mother Joan:[197]

> *1426. Joan de Tybbay. To be buried at the Friars Minors. Bequeathed two nobles to be distributed amongst the Friars on the day of her burial. Mentions her sons, Thomas—clerk, deceased—and John de Tybbay, and her daughter, Agnes Wynslaw.*

---

[194] *Cal. Close, Henry v, vol. 1, 1413-9, p. 93*
[195] *Chronicle of London, Sir N.H. Nicolas and Edward Tyrrell eds., Longmans 1827, p. 98-9*
[196] *P.C.C., 28 July, 1414. 29 Marche, p. 170*
[197] *Will dated (at London) 12 July, 1426. Proved 20 July, 1426. PCC 6 Luffenam*

This echoes the will of William Winslow *Armiger* drafted initially with Sir John, and later with Thomas Tibbay after Sir John's murder:

> *...if there remain anything beyond their maintenance, until £28 which I have from the supervisors and executors of Sir John de Tibbay, deceased, be fully repaid, and until my wife is in peaceful possession of all the lands and tenements which I have given her by declaration on oath before the said Sir John Tibbay...*

Agnes has lost her father to murder in 1414, her husband to sickness in August 1415, her mother in 1426, and eventually her daughter Joan, also in 1426.[198]

> *Joan died on the feast of St Margaret last past. [probably June 10]. Walter Huntyngdon is her kinsman and heir since she died without issue. He is the son of John Huntyngdon, son of Elizabeth, sister of William father of the said Mary, and is aged 24 years*

In her will dated 1444, Agnes expresses her final wishes:[199]

> *1444. Agnes Wynsley. To be buried in the Church of the Friars Minors within Newgate, 'juxta sepulturam matris mee.' [next to my mother's tomb]. Mentions her brother John Tybbay.*

It is unclear what provision had been made for Agnes Winslow in 1431 by the Huntingdons when they took over the Crouchmans' Hempstead estate following the death of Joan, her daughter with William Winslow *Armiger*. The Hempstead line descended through Elizabeth, sister of Mary Winslow's father William as per Mary's marriage settlement in 1375 covered earlier.

Sir John Tibbay, Selected Entries 1412-24

DC	ACTIVITY
1412	John de Tibbay clerk to Queen Joan. Quitclaim Nun Eton co. Warrewyk. London, Dec 2
1414	John Tibbay, father-in-law William Wynslowe, died 1414, probate July 28
1414	"...died of a murderous attack" Archdeacon of Huntingdon, Chancellor of the Queen
1424	Tibbay, John Tebeye, late rector of Wyncelogh, 1424, June 16

Figure 3-18 Lifespan of Sir John Tibbay

In May 1388 someone called *John de Tibbay,* described as *the king's clerk,* is being rewarded in Nottinghamshire:[200]

> *Grant to the king's clerk, John de Tibbay, of the prebend of South Muskham in the collegiate church of St. Mary, Suthwell, in the king's gift by reason of the temporalities of the archbishopric of York being in his hands.*

In 1393 John de Tibbay described as being *of Yorkshire* is acting as mainpernor after an arrest near Ripon.[201] By February 1393 John Tibbay is acting in a property transfer involving an estate in Hertfordshire and Cambridgeshire where he is

---

198 *Chancery Inq. P.M. 5 Henry vi, 1426-7, No. 7, File 27*
199 *Wills relating to Grey Friars, London: 1432-81, sole entry for 1444*
200 *Cal. Pat., Richard ii, vol. 3, 1385-89, p. 445*
201 *Cal. Close, Richard ii, vol. 5, 1392-6, p. 64*

described as *clerk*.[202] There are two further entries relating to this transaction in October 1394,[203] and another in November.[204] Evidently John Tibbay is now operating further south.

In March 1401 Thomas Tibbay *of Yorkshire* is acting as a mainpernor.[205] In July 1401 John Tybbey, *clerk*, is acting as one of several attorneys to Stephen Lescrope *Chivaler* who is accompanying the King's son Thomas of Lancaster to Ireland where he is acting as *Lieutenant*.[206] By December 1403 John de Tybbey *the younger* is acting for Richard Lescrope, taking him to the King's second wife Joanna of Navarre, known in England as *Queen Joan,* presumably after the death of his father Stephen Lescrope in May 1403, and *Queen Joan* is to have *custody of his lands with his marriage*.[207]

This John Tibbay is evidently William Winslow's future father-in-law. By February 1405, King Henry IV has confirmed that Queen Joan is to have income of 10,000 marks a year. John de Tybbay *the younger,* and Thomas Feriby *clerk* are now appointed to manage aspects of Queen Joan's finances.[208] In March the following year, *John Tybbay clerk* is still working for the Lescropes.[209] [210]

> *Stephen le Scrope knight to Dame Agnes who was wife of Robert de Plesyngton knight, Richard Norton, William Makenade, Thomas Knolles citizen and grocer of London, William Evelde and John Barton clerks. Confirmation of the estate which they have in the manor of Northwodeshepeye co. Kent, late of Roger de Northwode knight, and in all lands, rents, services, woods, marshes, reversions etc. in the Hundred of Melton and in Upchirche, Iwade, Bobbynge, Newenton, Northwode and Melton which the said Stephen with John Tybbay and Nigel Horlyngton clerks, and with William Periar deceased, had by feoffment of the said Roger, and made a charter of demise to Dame Agnes and the others, their heirs and assigns; and quitclaim with warranty of the said manor, lands etc. Dated 8 March 7 Henry IV [1406].*

The property transaction mentions the *Isle of Sheppey* situated on the North Kent foreshore. Another of the places mentioned is *Newington* in Kent, situated on the main road some twenty miles west from Canterbury and a place of interest for the next volume. John Tibbay's origins in Westmoreland are confirmed when he is working as a mainpernor in February 1408:[211]

---

202 *Cal. Close, Richard ii, vol. 5, 1392-6, p. 123*
203 *Cal. Close, Richard ii, vol. 5, 1392-6, pp. 373-5*
204 *Cal. Close, Richard ii, vol. 5, 1392-6, p. 377*
205 *Cal. Close, Henry iv, vol. 1, 1399-1402, p. 326*
206 *Cal. Pat., Henry iv, vol. 1,, 1399-1401, p. 507*
207 *Cal. Pat., Henry iv, vol. 2, 1401-5, p. 362*
208 *Cal. Pat., Henry iv, vol. 2, 1401-5, p. 454*
209 *Cal. Close, Henry iv, vol. 3, 1405-9, pp. 111-2*
210 *Cal. Close, Henry iv, vol. 3, 1405-9, p. 371*
211 *Cal. Close, Henry iv, vol. 3, 1405-9, p. 371*

Edward Winslow's English Origins

Order by mainprise of John de Tybbay of Westmerland, Adam Smyth of Westminster 'cordewaner,' William Baily of Derbyshire 'messangere' and John Cruce of Staffordshire 'taillour' to set free Nicholas Broun...

In July 1409 Tibbay is clearly still working both for Queen Joan and for the Lescropes. John de Tibbay in each case is *clerk,* and he remains the recorder and protector of the Queen's financial interests. There are entries in both the Patent[212] and Close Rolls[213] dated in the first week of July 1409, and her financial entitlement from the King is reconfirmed: *10,000 marks a year to her granted for life...*

The pattern continues in 1410. Tibbay remains bound up with the financial affairs of the royal court, and in July the dower is reconfirmed with *Kyngton* and *Tybbay* handling the administration of its collection and application:[214]

> *Order ... to pay to Queen Joan and to Master John Kyngton and John de Tybbay clerks, or to their attorney, £20 a year which by letters patent of 1 July last, among other things, the king has granted to the queen in full of her dower, to be deducted from 10,000 marks a year which at another time the king granted her for life.*

An entry from October 1410 refers to the *Lescropes* again, confirming that Stephen Lescrope is now archdeacon of Richmond in Yorkshire.[215] Reconfirmation of the Queen's entitlements appears in 1411, once more mentioning the names *Tibbay* and *Kington* as clerks.[216] By July 1412 Tibbay is acting as clerk in debt collection against John Giffard.[217] December 1412 is when Tibbay cedes the advowson of Nuneaton in southeastern Warwickshire:[218]

> *John de Tibbay clerk to Queen Joan. Quitclaim of the advowson of the vicarage of Nun Eton co. Warrewyk. Dated London, 2 December 14 Henry IV. Memorandum of acknowledgment, 12 December.*

Another Hertfordshire property transaction is found in December 1412.[219] By February 1413, an entry confirms that John de Tibbay has by now received a knighthood. A tripart letter of Attorney has been drafted in *Digoneswelle*, Digswell in Hertfordshire, dated 10 December 14 Henry IV [1412], whose contents refer to, among others, *Sir John Tybbay clerk.* The award is presumably for long-term services to Queen Joan rendered by Sir John.

Early in January 1413, Queen Joan's large annual entitlement from the King is again reaffirmed. It is stated that of the Queen's two serving clerks, John Kington has

---

212 *Cal. Pat., Henry iv, vol. 4, 1408-13, pp. 85-6*
213 *Cal. Close, Henry iv, vol. 3, 1405-9 p. 418*
214 *Cal. Close, Henry iv, vol. 4, 1409-13, pp. 44-45*
215 *Cal. Pat., Henry iv, vol. 4, 1408-13, 1410, pp. 259-60*
216 *Cal. Close, Henry iv, vol. 4, 1409-13, pp. 162-3*
217 *Cal. Pat., Henry iv, vol. 4, 1408-13, p. 342*
218 *Cal. Close, Henry iv, vol. 4, 1409-13, p. 410*
219 *Cal. Close, Henry iv, vol. 4, 1409-13, p. 418*

Edward Winslow's English Origins

chosen to adopt a religious life. Sir John's knighthood is not mentioned in this context:[220]

> Master John Kyngton, who has assumed the habit of religion in which he is professed, and John de Tibbay, clerks.

Sir John continues to work on Hertfordshire property transactions acknowledged on various dates.[221] A feature of the last several property transactions involving Tibbay is the increasing length of the narrative and their apparent complexity. They all involve Thomas Beaufort, a son of John of Gaunt and who became Earl of Dorset in 1412, and later Earl of Exeter under Henry V.

> Memorandum of acknowledgment by William Cheytwynt 8 June, by John Welsshe 12 June this year, both in chancery at Westminster, and by Thomas Cotere, Richard Horewode and John Northbury at Bedwelle on Monday before St. Matthew this year before the abbot of Waltham Holy Cross, by virtue of a dedimus potestatem which is on the chancery file for this year.

King Henry IV died on 20 March 1413 to be succeeded by his son and heir Henry V. Former Queen Joan has become Queen Consort, and Sir John continues to act for her. The first entry in the new reign from the Close Rolls is dated September 1413 concerning another property transaction involving *manors called Gobyons and Lauvares,* and several other properties in Hertfordshire, again connected with Thomas Beaufort, Earl of Dorset.[222] An entry from January 27 1414 confirms that Dowager Queen Joan is being granted a considerable property portfolio directed to herself and to her two clerks: Tibbay and Feriby, who has replaced John Kyngton.

The conclusion of the main entry notes that her annual entitlement has dropped from 10,000 marks to only 6,089 marks, and an addendum to the main entry identifies an entitlement to maybe another 3,500 marks.[223] Tibbay and Feriby are evidently safeguarding the former Queen's financial position.

An entry dated August 30 1414 confirms that Nyandesere has killed John Tybbay, clerk; and directs that Nyandesere's property and land be held by Sir Roger de Trumpington during the killer's lifetime to secure an income for Nyandesere's wife.[224] Trumpington of course has connections with the Winslows.

By July 1415 an entry confirms that Tibbay is now deceased.[225] The purpose of an obscure entry dated September 1415 directing that *John Tybbay* be arrested along with John Horne and Richard Altham is unclear.[226] Meanwhile, an entry in the Close

[220] Cal. Pat., Henry iv, vol. 4, 1408-13, p. 455
[221] Cal. Close, Henry iv, vol. 4, 1409-13, p. 427
[222] Cal. Close, Henry v, vol. 1, 1413-9, p. 92
[223] Cal. Pat., Henry v, vol. 1, 1413-6, pp. 164-7
[224] Cal. Pat., Henry v, vol. 1, 1413-6, p. 219
[225] Cal. Pat., Henry v, vol. 1, 1413-6, p. 368
[226] Cal. Pat., Henry v, vol. 1, 1413-6, p. 347

Rolls dated November 1414 – *now deceased, it is said* – seems sceptical or even incredulous about the news of Tibbay's death.[227]

What was the connection between Tibbay and the Winslows? The Winslows were in Hunsdon adjacent to Ware in Hertfordshire, and we have seen that John Tibbay was involved in property transactions in the area. The surprise here is that John Tibbay is elsewhere described as rector of *Wyncelogh*:[228]

> *Herts. C. 3388. Demise by Thomas Braghyng, William Castell, William Hert, Richard Huchon, John Woodeleef, and Richard Greteham, to John Hotoft, John Wodehows, John Feriby, esquires, John Snell, clerk, John Fray, and Thomas Knolles the younger, of all lands &c. in the towns and hamlets of Ware, Alcewyk, Leyston, and Hornmede Magna, and elsewhere in the same county, which they, together with the said John Hotoft, lately had of the gift of Richard atte Water of Ware, who, with John Tebeye, late rector of Wyncelogh, and others (named), had them of the gift of William atte Water, Richard's father. 16 June, 2 Henry VI. Two seals, imperfect.*

There is no other supporting material to explain the coincidence of Sir John Tibbay having a connection with Winslow, and no extant WMCB record exists to indicate the nature of any interest Tibbay may have had. We can only assume that the outreach of the Winslows was wider than contemporary documentary evidence discloses.

William Winslows located so far

WILLIAM WINSLOW	BORN	FIRST REF.	DIED
Patriarch	c. 1245-50	1278	After 1314, before 1327
Wodyam	c. 1300	1332	1349-1350
Candlewick	c. 1330	1370	1399-1400
Pavilioner	c. 1355	1381	1414
Armiger	1388-9	1406	1415
Chaplain	??	1397	c. 1414

Figure 3-19 Lifespans for William Winslows located to date

So far we have encountered several William Winslows, starting with William Winslow *Patriarch,* who died in 1314-27. Estimates for birth dates are guesswork at this stage.

William Winslows, *Chaplain,* Entries 1397-1414

By eliminating records for all the other William Winslows so far identified, the remainder probably relate to a single *William Winslow* with activities at first sight centred on ecclesiastical and legal affairs. Like two of his family namesakes, he dies around 1414 and is identified in this work as William Winslow *Chaplain.* Despite opinions to the contrary, this William was husband of *Agnes Poure* and father of

[227] *Cal. Close, Henry v, vol. 1, 1413-9, p. 153*
[228] *Descriptive Catalogue of Ancient Deeds: vol. 3, C. 3388, pp. 361*

Edward Winslow's English Origins

one of the two Thomas Winslows later called to Parliament, the historical record of whose life spans seventeen years. The next William separately identifiable after William *Chaplain* is William *Attorney*. He makes his first appearance in 1429, more than a decade after the last known reference to the lifetime of William Winslow *Chaplain*, by which time Agnes Poure, widow of William Winslow *Chaplain*, has remarried Robert Andrew as will be covered shortly. [229]

DATE	ACTIVITY
1397	William Wynselawe chaplain, Wiltshire, Jun 14
1401	William Wynslawe, chaplain, creditor Wilts, Jan 24
1403	William Wynselowe with Roger Poure, Jurors Oxford, 1403 Feb
1404	William Wynslawe, chaplain, creditor, Wilts, Feb 5
1406	Winslow, William Wynslawe, rector of church near New Sarum, quitclaim 1406
1407	William Wynselowe wife Agnes aged 28+, sister of Thomas, heir: Black Bourton etc. Sep 18
1407	William Wynselowe wife Agnes, seisin of Oxford/Berkshire, Chaucer Escheator, Oct 1407
1407	William Wynselowe wife Agnes aged 28+, subsequent inquest, Oct 3
1410	William Winslow, witness with John Blaket and Robert Andrew, Cricklade etc. Wilts, Feb 19
1410	Will. Wynslow *clericus* put in property possession, pay 200 marks. Nov 11.
1412	Winslow, William Wynselowe lands in Ramsbury, Wilts 1412
1413	Winslow, William Wynslowe Tax Collecting for Wilts, July 13, alive
1413	William Wynslowe, messuage & shops in Salisbury, Nov. 1
1414	William Wynselowe assumed death – no further record

Figure 3-20 Timeline for William Winslow Chaplain

A valid question to raise is whether this William Winslow might in fact be the amalgam of two separate individuals both called *William Winslow* active over the span of seventeen years from 1397 to 1414. We will consider such possibility at the end of this section in the light of other evidence.

The first entry for William Winslow *Chaplain* from 1397 connects him with Salisbury and Wiltshire. There has been a serious legal dispute involving one of William Winslow's clients, the late *John Bytterlegh* citizen of Salisbury, to whom William has acted as executor. This incident forms one of the extraordinary entries relating to any of the Winslows, so it is reproduced here in full:[230]

> *June 14. Westminster. To the sheriff of Wiltesir. Order to give notice to Thomas archbishop of Canterbury to be in chancery in the quinzaine of Michaelmas next, which day the king has given to William Wynselawe chaplain, executor of John Bytterlegh late citizen of New Sarum of the province of Canterbury who had goods in divers dioceses, in order to shew cause wherefore there ought not to be a stay pending the appeal, writ of supersedeas, and order by mainprise of John Carbenall of London 'goldsmyth' and John Tomelyn parson of*

---

[229] *See below, page 132.*
[230] *Cal. Close, Richard ii, vol. 6, 1396-99, p. 133*

Wyntreborne Monketon co. Dorset to set the said chaplain free if taken; as at the request of the archbishop, signifying that he was excommunicated for contumacy by authority of William late archbishop as ordinary, not willing to be justified by censure of the church, the king ordered the sheriff to justify the said chaplain by his body until he should content holy church for his contempt and wrongdoing; but he has appealed to the court of Rome and for protection of the court of Canterbury, as appears by a notarial instrument produced in chancery, and is minded effectually to prosecute his appeal, and such writ issues by favour of the king; and John Carbenall and John Tomelyn have mainperned in chancery to have him there at the day named.

The background to these events is that William Winslow is a *chaplain* or minor cleric, here acting as an executor during a turbulent political period. William's late client *John Bytterlegh* had lived in Salisbury under diocesan control of Canterbury where William Courtenay had served Archbishop until July 1396. Thomas Arundel, previously one of the King's opponents in the Merciless Parliament, had regained the King's favour and had become Archbishop of Canterbury on 25 September 1396 until, in a subsequent power-play, Arundel was exiled and replaced by Roger Walden in November 1397.

William Winslow has presumably displeased Archbishop Courtenay by refusing to accept his direction, possibly relating to an issue arising from his executorship; and the Archbishop has responded dramatically by excommunicating Winslow for *contumacy*, disobedience. Winslow refuses to let things rest. Astonishingly he escalates the issue over the heads of both the Archbishop of Canterbury and of King Richard direct to the Pope's court in Rome, an act of remarkable self-assurance for a provincial chaplain, and especially so when his actions are to protect the direction of his late client's interests rather than his own. To Winslow it is presumably a matter of principle, but it directly resonates with a previous incident where *Master Ambrose*, legal expert in St. Albans Abbey, had opted to take a similar course of action in 1158 AD.

All we know for sure is that William Winslow *Chaplain* is still working on the same *Butterlegh* legal matter four years later. There is a reference to a debtor, John Flortyn of Andover, *merchant of Hants* owing funds to John Butterleigh, described as a *merchant of Salisbury, Wilts deceased.*[231] The debt dates from January 1391 but it has taken until May 1399 to come before John Moner, Mayor of Salisbury and Ralph Tyle, Clerk in the Salisbury court.

On Jan 4 1401 William Wynslawe *chaplain* is pursuing Hugh Courtenay *chivaler* before the Justices of the Bench for recovery of 100s as executor of John Butterlegh's estate, *late citizen of Salisbury*, along with fellow executors Simon Tredenek and Stephen Edyngdon.[232] At the very least, the action will have enhanced his reputation as a lawyer. By 15 February 1403, William Wynselowe is

---

[231] *N. R. A., ref C 241/188/118*
[232] *Cal. Pat., Henry iv, vol. 1, 1399-1401, p. 492*

appearing with Roger Poure of Bletchingdon in Oxford as a juror in an inquest held in Oxford for the late *Amery De Sancto Amando, Knight* who had died in 13 June 1402. The full list of jurors is:[233]

> *Jurors: John Drayton chivaler; Peter Besyles chivaler; George Nowers chivaler; Roger Poure; William Wynselowe; Thomas Haryotes; William Mounford; Thomas Creyford; John Carsewell; John Yerman; John Gerard; and John Draper.*

Sir George Nowers is one of the three knighted jurors. Meanwhile William Winslow *Chaplain* continues his work on the same *Butterlegh* legal matter. This time William Wynslawe *chaplain* is pursuing *Ralph Ramsy of Yernemuth chivaler* before the Justices of the Bench in February 1404 for recovery of £20, and with the same fellow executors Simon Tredenek and Stephen Edyngdon.[234]

The next entry from 29 Sept 1406 places William Wynslawe as rector of the church of *Odestoke* near New Sarum Wiltshire, and involved in a quitclaim where he is moving out in favour of William Smyth of Edelsborough.[235] In September 1407 we find from another inquest[236] that Thomas Poure, brother of William Winslow's wife Agnes Poure and surviving heir of Sir Thomas Poure has died, leaving Agnes aged 28 as sole heir to her late father's estates in Berkshire and Oxfordshire. The first of these inquests gives the date of death for Agnes's brother Thomas as 27 August 1406, shortly before the quitclaim from Odstock on 29 September, and definitively confirming that William Winslow *Chaplain* is indeed Agnes's husband. Now they can afford to move to the properties she has just inherited.

A further report dated 3 October 1407 from the Close Rolls[237] establishes the outcome for William and Agnes. The Oxfordshire Escheator is Thomas Chaucer, and the Poure estate was held of Amery de Sancto Amando at whose inquest William Winslow was acting as a juror in February 1403 above.

> *To Thomas Chaucer escheator in Oxfordshire and Berkshire. Order to give William Wynselowe and Agnes his wife seisin of a toft, one carucate of land and 10 acres of meadow in Wendelby, and a messuage, one carucate of land and 6 acres of meadow in Charlton upon Ottemore co. Oxford, but to remove the king's hand and meddle no further with a messuage, two carucates of land, 30 acres of meadow and 100s. of rent in Bourton by Bampton, co. Oxford and a toft, half a carucate of land, 6 acres of meadow and 13s. of rent in Gareforde co. Berkshire, delivering to the said William and Agnes any issues taken of the premises in Bourton and Gareforde; as it is found by divers inquisitions, taken before the said escheator, that all were held by Thomas Poure knight, and came to the king's hands by his death and by reason of the nonage of Thomas his son and heir, who died within age in ward of the king, that the toft etc. in Wendelby are held by knight service of the heirs of Amery de Sancto Amando, the land etc. in Charlton of Warre priory rendering*

---

[233] *Cal. Inq. p.m., Henry iv, 18-801*

[234] *Cal. Pat., Henry iv, vol. 2, 1401-5, p. 340*

[235] *N. R. A., DE/HL/11881*

[236] *Cal. Inq. p.m., Henry iv, 19-226 & 19-227*

[237] *Cal. Close, Henry iv, vol. 3, 1405-9, p. 299*

to the priory and their successors (sic) 6d. a year rent, namely to their manor of Charlton, and suit of their court there every three weeks for all other services, and the other messuages, lands etc. of other lords, and that the said Agnes sister of Thomas the son is his next heir, and of full age; and the king lately granted the said priory to the queen, with the knights' fees and advowsons, and he has taken the fealty of the said William.

After this confirmation, the next entry appears three years later in July 1410, with *Thomas Canynges* acknowledging seisin to *Robert Alcestre now abbot of St. Mary Hayles co. Gloucestre* for a property in the same county. William is among five witnesses named:[238]

John Blaket esquire, William Wynslowe, Robert Androwas, Thomas Crykkelade, John Hynton. Dated 19 February 11 Henry IV.

John Blaket was connected with Woburn in Buckinghamshire in 1402,[239] and was *sheriff of Warrewyk and Leycester* by 1403.[240] The name *Blakette* is familiar from the misfortune involving John Winslow *Maunciple* in 1356-7. William Wynslowe is here acting as a witness in the company of the *Robert Androwas* or Andrews, the man unwittingly or not destined to marry William's widow Agnes after William's own death.

In its review of Robert Andrew, the *History of Parliament* incorrectly identifies the two William Winslows, *Pavilioner*, and *Chaplain*, as one person, and identifies William Winslow *Pavilioner* as husband to Agnes Poure:[241] This is one of the most frequent and recurrent misidentifications in the whole Winslow family history. We do know for sure that William Winslow *Pavilioner* and *Chaplain* both died around 1414, so the misidentification is understandable even when the underlying truth is so easy to establish.

The next reference comes from the *Tropenell Cartulary,*[242] a fifteenth century Wiltshire landowner's compilation of old manuscript materials written in Latin, and mentioning both William Winslow and Robert Andrew. The introduction to the Cartulary's two volumes contains a summary of content, with two references about William Winslow *Chaplain*:[243]

Final concord on certain tens. In New Sarum: R. Fawkener and Will. Wynslow &c. put in possession, and pay 200 marks of silver, 11 Nov. 1410

Will. Wynslowe to Hen. Harburgh and others, mess. and shops in Minster Street, S. Martin's Street, Frerenstrete, Drakehalstrete, and Melmongerstrete, 1 Nov. 1413

---

[238] *Cal. Close, Henry iv, vol. 4, 1409-13, p. 96*
[239] *Cal. Close, Henry iv, vol. 2, 1402-5, p. 133*
[240] *Cal. Close, Henry iv, vol. 2, 1402-5, p. 395*
[241] *Hist. Parl., 1386-1421, vol. 2, p. 36*
[242] *John Silvester Davies, ed., The Tropenell Cartulary: being the contents of an old Wiltshire Muniment chest, 2 vols., Wiltshire Archaeological and Natural History Society, 1908*
[243] *Tropenell, vol. 1, intro., p. 50, case notes pp. 223-5*

Edward Winslow's English Origins

The Latin text of the legal proceeding confirms the location of the hearing as London, in *the court of the Lord King* at Westminster. Richard Fawkener and William Wynslowe, clerk and some other representatives are acting for the purchasers, *concerning to certain tenements in New Sarum*. William Wynslowe is described here as *clerk* with the proceedings being heard before five judges:

> *Willelmo Thirnyng, Willelmo Hankeford, Johanne Cokayne, Johanne Culpepir, et Roberto Hill, justiciariis*

This is a very senior Bench of Westminster Justices indeed. *Thirning* was appointed Chief Justice under Richard II in 1396 and retained his post throughout the reign of Henry IV, and handled the request by John Winslow *Maunciple* and wife Mary to reassign the Justice Holt case to more senior justices earlier. *Hankford* was appointed a Justice of the King's Bench by Henry IV, and elevated to Chief Justice of the King's Bench under Henry V in 1413. *John Cokayne* was appointed Chief Baron of the Exchequer in 1400, and a Justice of the Common Pleas in 1405.

The History of Parliament notes Robert Hill's obscure family background, attributing his later prominence to his proficiency in Law.[244] In many respects the comment about Robert Hill's previous obscurity mirrors the recognition achieved by William Winslow *Chaplain* latterly and so quickly within the English legal system.

The second *Tropenell* manuscript is written in the first person. *William Winslow* is identifying the properties *in Minster Street, S. Martin's Street, Frerenstrete, Drakehalstrete, and Melmongerstrete*, confirming their geographical position with reference to existing occupants; and by studying a medieval map of the town, all of the street names remain identifiable today within Salisbury town centre.

The final section of his legal submission sees William Winslow summarising and confirming that he has discharged his legal duty. He invokes a list of twelve witnesses starting with the Bailiff of Salisbury *William Westbury*, and concluding with *Stephen Edyngton, clericus* whom we encountered as *Stephen Edyngdon* in the Salisbury *Butterlegh* executorship previously. The episode shows William Winslow combining local client work with proven competence to operate before the senior justices of the highest courts. This second manuscript is dated November 1, 1413.

The success of William's legal work is likely to have made him prosperous, evidenced by an entry in Feudal Aids in 1412 confirming his tenure of a property in Ramsbury, a village slightly west of Berkshire near its border with Wiltshire, and some forty five miles from London along the Bath Road.[245]

> *Willelmus Wynslowe habet terras etc. apud Remmesbury que valent etc. c.s*

By July 1413 we have an entry in the Fine Rolls indicating that William Winslow *Chaplain* is now collecting taxes in Wiltshire, suggesting that he has taken up

---

[244] *Hist. Parl., 1386-1421, vol. 3, p. 373*
[245] *Feudal. Aids, vol. 6, 1412, p. 533*

residence in Ramsbury.[246]   Apart from the reference above to William Winslow *Chaplain* in connection with the shops in Salisbury, that is the last record about him located for this study. We can assume that his death occurred around 1414.

William's death leaves two issues unresolved. Was William *Chaplain* the same person as William *Pavilioner*, as some have suggested? The first extant public record for William *Chaplain* dates from June 1397, placing him in Wiltshire after which he is seen operating as a successful lawyer at senior level. The other William was appointed *Pavilioner* in May 1395 and unfortunate enough to lose the pavilions and other equipment at sea in the winter of 1396. By October 1397, William *Pavilioner* and John Beaufitz were reported to be repairing them.

While William *Chaplain* was escalating his law case to the Pope, William *Pavilioner* is re-engaging for the Irish Campaign.[247]   It is therefore highly unlikely the *Pavilioner*'s work in military logistics demanding coordination between England and France could have been maintained alongside a parallel legal career in Salisbury, London and operating within the senior English law courts.   The probability is that these two William Winslows were separate individuals.

One unanswered question is about the year of birth of William *Chaplain*. We know that when Agnes Poure emerged as her brother's heir in 1407 she was aged 28, suggesting birth date around 1379. Husband William Winslow *Chaplain* was alive in 1414 conducting senior law cases at Westminster, but we also remember that he was someone already senior in legal affairs to be escalating his law case to the Pope in 1397. We can justifiably speculate that William Winslow *Chaplain* was much older than Agnes Poure, an unsurprising suggestion when we recall that Sir William Crouchman's wife Egidia was aged about 28 years when Sir William died in 1351 in his seventies, and John Winslow *Maunciple* was in his mid-forties when he married Mariota aged 9.

No will and testament have been found for William Winslow *Chaplain*. If he was in his fifties at death, that would suggest a birth date around 1365, or if in his seventies he was born around 1345. Their child Thomas Winslow *Alnwick* is considered later. Another unanswered question is how soon Robert Andrews married Agnes after the death of her first husband William Winslow *Chaplain*. All we know is that they were living in Ramsbury by 1416, and that Robert Andrews had died by 1437.[248]

> He died 13 April last. John Bourne, son of Agnes, sister of the said Robert, is his kinsman and heir, aged 40 years..

---

[246] *CFR, 1413, Henry v, vol. 1, p. 26*
[247] *Cal. Pat., Richard ii, vol. 6, 1396-9, p. 541*
[248] *Chancery Inq. P.M., 1436-7, 24 (File 80); also CFR, 1435-7, 1438, vol. 17, p. 30. Will is PCC 21, Luffenam*

Edward Winslow's English Origins

Richard Winslow, *Clacton, Entries 1375-1415*

Little is known about the next Winslow, the Richard Winslow mentioned in the 1415 will of his nephew, William Winslow *Armiger;* by which time Richard is presumably an elderly retired cleric. William Winslow *Armiger* implies that Richard is resident with the Winslow family in Hempstead, Essex, and we can only surmise that he had helped his nephew William Winslow *Armiger* following the death of both parents, Mary and John Winslow *Maunciple.* In his will which is reproduced in the first section of the Appendix below, William Winslow *Armiger* speaks warmly of *Richard Wynslowe, my very beloved uncle.*

DATE	ACTIVITY
1375	Richard Wynslowe, vicar of Great Claketon
1415	William Wynslowe's will mentions Uncle Richard W

Figure 3-21 Timeline for Richard Winslow Clacton

Around the time John Winslow *Maunciple* married Mariota in 1375 and moved to Hempstead, Richard was serving as a vicar in Clacton on the Essex Coast.[249]

> *1375. 1802. Mich., 48 Edward III., and Eas., 49 Edward III. Richard Wynslowe, vicar of Great Claketon, and John atte Rode, pl. Andrew Cray and Joan his wife, def. 42 acres of land and 2 acres of marsh in Thoryton. Pl. and the heirs of Richard to hold of the chief lords. Cons . 20 marks.*

Edmund Winslow *Kensington Entries 1411-1417*

DATE	ACTIVITY
1411	Edmund Wynselowe, mainpernor Middlesex, Jul 11
1411	Winslow, Edmund Wynselowe, Juror, Wimbysshe, 1411 Nov 30
1417	Winslow, Edmund Wynslowe. Juror re Earl of Oxford, Kensington, 1417

Figure 3-22 Timeline for Edward Winslow Kensington

Little has been discovered about this Edmund Winslow. What Edmund was doing here in July 1411 is unclear, but he was one of four involved in the mainprise with:[250]

> *John Hammynge, Edmund Wynselowe, Thomas Morys and John Bulle, all of Middlesex, in favour of Nicholas Kenan in regard to Thomas Everarde and Anne his wife.*

For the next two entries, Edmund is acting in Wimbish as a juror supporting Richard de Vere, Earl of Oxford, feudal lord of Hempstead and later a hero of Agincourt.

> *Jurors: Edmund Wynselowe; Robert Yonge; Stephen Wylkyn; William Bartlot; Adam Barbour; Thomas Totesham; John Asshley; Henry Cordwaner; Thomas Sherman; John Brystowe; John Lyoun; and John Mayhewe.*

---

[249] *Feet of Fines, Essex, vol. 3, 1326-1422, entry no. 1802, p. 175*
[250] *Cal. Close, Henry iv, vol. 4, 1409-13, p. 228*

Edward Winslow's English Origins

The king granted Richard de Veer that he should have livery of the manor of Kensington without proving his age, as above. He granted it to Philippa on 16 Jan. 1407 on the same condition as above. It is held of the king in chief as half a knight's fee, annual value £30.

Wimbish is located only two miles distant from Hempstead.[251] In the second entry dated 1417, also relating to Kensington Manor, the jurors are:[252]

Jurors: Edmund Wynslowe; John Spray; Nicholas Sherman; Thomas Grene; Thomas Carter; Nicholas Cumbe; John Theccher; John Wyght; Henry Norys; William Bartelot; William Robert; Richard Grene; John Thurston; and William Newman .

Perhaps Edmund was in Hempstead to support William Winslow *Armiger* after he had lost his parents, and it raises the possibility that several members of the extended Winslow family had taken up residence in Hempstead by this time.

John Winslow *Salop Entries 1419-1424*

DATE	ACTIVITY
1419	Joan, wife John Wynslowe, property: Gloucestershire, Oxon, Berks, Salop, May 1419

Figure 3-23 Timeline for John Winslow Salop

The name of another John Winslow separately identified appears in a document dating from 14 May 1419 in the Feet of Fines as a plea of covenant involving *Lewis Grevell* esquire and *Richard Mikelton'*, clerk as querents, and with *John Grevell* esquire and *Sibel* his wife as deforciants, and sets out the precedence of succession if she and her husband die without heirs of their own. *Sibel* was daughter of the MP for Shropshire Sir Robert Corbet, who died in 1417. The estate encompasses:[253]

The manor of Farnecote in the county of Gloucester and the manor of Stanlake in the county of Oxford and the manor of Tubbeney and the advowson of the church of the same manor in the county of Berkshire and the manors of Hadley and Hatton in the county of Shropshire.

Joan, the wife of John Wynslowe, is a potential beneficiary of a settlement together with *Margaret wife of Thomas More, Agnes, the wife of William Rokewode*, and *Elizabeth, the wife of Thomas Rothewell*. Sir Robert Corbet married three times, and it is hard to tell whether *Joan, the wife of John Wynslowe* is married to any of the other John Winslows active at this time, such as John Winslow *Chesham*, or to a John Winslow not recorded hitherto. For now, and pending the uncovering of further information, this new John Winslow is identified as *Salop* because of his wife's possible inheritance in the county of Shropshire.

---

[251] *Chancery IPM, 137/88/43, 1411*
[252] *CIPM, Henry v, vol. 20, C 138/23/53 mm. 7-8*
[253] *Feet of Fines CP 25/1/291/64, number 84*

Edward Winslow's English Origins

John Winslow, Yorks

DATE	ACTIVITY
1422	John Wynslowe of county of York, Rochester Castle, Kent Oct 10
1424	John Wenslawe witness Yorkshire 1424, Feb 3, Yorkshire Deeds: Volume 8 p.123

Figure 3-24 Timeline for John Winslow, Yorks

Two other entries from around the same time referring to a John Winslow from Yorkshire, probably unconnected to the Buckinghamshire Winslows, indicate that additional variants of the *Wenslawe* name were becoming more prevalent in the South of England by the 1420s. There are many other examples in Volume 2.

John Winslow, Soton, Entries 1415-1447

DATE	ACTIVITY
1404	John Wynslawe, Inquest Bucks 1404 Jan 2
1406	John Wynselowe of London, mainprise, Jan 16
1406	John Wynselowe of London with Hemyng Leget, Escheator Essex & Herts
1415	John Wynslawe, *clericus*, to pay shipmasters & owners by indenture, Apr 11
1416	John Wynslawe, *clericus*, Southampton, 1416 May 3
1416	John Wynslowe, arrest commission, Southampton 1416 July 25
1416	John Wynslawe mustering ships in Bristol and Dover, 1416 Aug 5
1418	Johannis Wynslowe, campaign Rouen, Pont de L' Arche, 1418 Jun 9

Figure 3-25 Timeline for John Winslow Soton

John Winslow acts as a juror at an inquest into Richard de la Pole held in Buckingham in January 1404 , son of the Michael de la Pole, first Earl of Suffolk, Chancellor of England, and formerly close adviser to King Richard II. The connection is unsurprising: de la Pole held property in Mursley, only 4 miles east of Winslow in Buckinghamshire. We also encountered a *de la Pole* in connection with Robert Winslow *bercarius* in Sydenham, Oxfordshire in the 1280s, and an *Atte Pole* in connection with Trumpington Manor.

Marsh is only 9 miles from Winslow to the west. The Poure family who would later intermarry with the Winslows also owned land in Mursley in the second half of the thirteenth century, and it presumably their property referred to below as *Powereslond.* Here is the record of his inquest:[254]

> Jurors: John Peyntour; Roger Faucus; William Wodeward; John Chastiloun; William Barker; John Smyth; John Wynslawe; John Grafton; William Sprygenell; William Taylour of Moreton; William Evesham; and Richard Carpunter of Buckingham.

> He [Richard de la Pole] held the manor of Marsh in his demesne in fee tail of the king in chief by the grant of Michael de la Pole his father by the fine of 1384. It is held by knight service, annual value 20 marks. He also held 11s. 4d. rent from a tenement called

---

[254] Cal. Inq. p.m., Henry iv, vol. 18, entry 981

Edward Winslow's English Origins

'Gracielord' and land called 'Powereslond' in Mursley to himself and his heirs and assigns, of the king in chief by knight service. Altogether the manor and rent constitute a fifth part of a knight's fee.

He died on 27 Dec. last without heirs male of his body. Thomas is his heir under the fine and aged 26 years and more. Michael earl of Suffolk is heir to the rent of 11s. 4d., being next heir in blood, and aged 30 years and more.

Mursley lies only three miles' distant from the town of Winslow, Buckinghamshire as shown on the map on page 41 above, adjacent to Swanbourne. From the proximity we can speculate that the two men were acquainted. The beneficiary of Richard de la Pole's estate is his second brother, Thomas de la Pole.

There is another coincidence involving the de la Poles. Richard's elder brother Michael, the second Earl of Suffolk, commanded the siege at Harfleur in 1415 where he died on September 17 following an outbreak of dysentery that Sumption reckons destroyed half the English army.[255] A fortnight or so earlier the same outbreak claimed the life of *Chesham's* relative, William Winslow *Armiger*, who would ultimately have been fighting under Michael de la Pole's command.

The first entry presents *John Wynselowe of London* as a mainpernor:[256]

To the sheriff of Essex. Writ of supersedeas, and order by mainprise of William Coggeshale knight, Helmyng Leget of Essex, John Wynselowe of London and William Senclere of Sussex to set free Thomas Steel of Bristol, if taken at suit of the king and Joan countess of Hereforde for leaving her service at Racheforde contrary to the ordinance of King Edward III and his council.

Of the three others, we have already encountered *Helmyng Leget*. On the list of Sheriffs of Herts and Essex, Leget was in office in 1402 and 1407. In 1402 Leget, described as *Escheator of Essex and Hertfordshire*,[257] is granted special commissions by the king,[258] and called to parliament in 1406[259] and later becomes a deputy for the ports of Ipswich and Colchester.[260] Coincidentally it was the same Leget who was acting as clerk in the City court when Thomas Winslow *Homicide* borrowed £20 in 1375, as discussed above.

A similar coincidence concerns *Sir William Coggeshall,* son of a previous *Sir William Coggeshall,* whose daughter was the *Joan Welle* from whom the Crouchmans and later the Winslows were renting property in Sampford, as disclosed by several inquests already mentioned. *Coggeshall* is also described as someone *whose family*

---

[255] So Sumption, The Hundred Years War, vol. 4, Faber and Faber, London, 1990 and ongoing, pp. 440
[256] Cal. Close, Henry iv, vol. 3, 1405-9, p. 87
[257] Cal. Close, Henry iv, vol. 2, 1403-5, p. 17
[258] Cal. Close, Henry iv, vol. 3, 1405-9, p. 191
[259] Cal. Close, Henry iv, vol. 3, 1405-9, p. 282
[260] Cal. Pat. Henry iv, vol. 3, 1405-8, p. 372

was of high standing in *Essex*,[261] and he was called to Parliament no fewer than nine times. Sir William Crouchman had previously worked with the Coggeshalls.[262]

The *Sencleres* or *St. Clers* mentioned in the same document are described[263] as *probably the most important tenant of the duchy of Lancaster in Sussex,* but not much information has been found about this *William Senclere*. What is starting to emerge here is a picture of the significant overlap and interconnections between Winslow family branches and within the broader strata of prominent English society of the time, the full scale of which becomes apparent in Chapter 4.

Based on the evidence below, John Winslow *Soton* was initially a cleric operating from Southampton or *Soton,* and associated with naval supply and administration of ports. Later we find him on the French Campaign under Henry V in 1418. A later reference to a John Winslow from 1447 is assumed to relate to a separate John Winslow due to the extended intervening time interval.

John's description in 1415 as a *clerk* implies that he has received education and, from the entries above, some operational experience in military logistics and administration. Date references to John Winslow end abruptly in 1418, so it is feasible that John Winslow *Soton* died around this time, or that he returned to England and moved to a new location and out of sight of the public records, a topic reconsidered in Chapter 4.

John Winslow, *Junior, Entry 1423*

Another John Winslow separately identifiable is the son mentioned in the will of John Winslow *Chesham* in connection with the son's daughter Agnes, apparently born out of wedlock. Grandfather John Winslow *Chesham* is making provision for his granddaughter's wedding in his will which is reproduced in Appendix 6.1.

DATE	ACTIVITY
1423	John Wynslow, father of bastard daughter Agnes Wynslow, 1423 Nov 3

Figure 3-26 Timeline for John Winslow, Junior

This is apparently the only reference found for this John whose subsequent activities have not yet been determined.

---

[261] See *Hist. Parl., vol. 2, 1386-1421, pp. 616-8*
[262] See *index for details*
[263] See *Hist. Parl., vol. 4, 1386-1421, pp. 277-8*

Thomas Winslow, *Saddler, Entries 1400-1422*

To be described in the City of London as a saddler, Thomas must have served an apprenticeship. In 1404 he is found in Cordwainer, the compact Ward at the heart of the City of London. For several hundred years, the gild of Saddlers had operated out of Gutter Lane off Cheapside, and close to St Paul's Cathedral, as it does even today. The proximity of dates and the absence of other Thomas Winslows in London at this time suggest that these five entries relate to the same individual, and separately from Thomas Winslow *Homicide*.

DATE	ACTIVITY
1396	Thomas Wyncelowe, mainprise, London, 1396, Aug 14
1400	Thomas Wyneslowe, London, surety for defendant, Herflete, saddler, Michaelmas,
1404	Thomas Wynselowe, London, of Cordwainer, surety Nov 25, Common Plea
1407	Thomas Wyncelowe, mainpernor re "each of London Sadeler", May 10
1422	Thomas Wynselow citizen and 'sadeler' of London, debtors prison, £40, 1422 March 26

Figure 3-27 Timeline for Thomas Winslow Saddler

In the first entry Thomas acts as a mainpernor for Sir Geoffrey Brokhole of Essex.[264]

> To the sheriffs of London. Writ of supersedeas, by mainprise of John Gernoun of Gloucestershire, Thomas Wyncelowe and John Lecchelade 'barbour' of London and Henry Rolves of Essex, in favour of Geoffrey Brokhole of Essex knight at suit of Thomas Somerton 'draper' and Clemence his wife, executrix of Robert Boxforde late citizen and draper of London, for render of 15l.

Sir Geoffrey was High Sheriff of Essex in 1385 and lived in Great Sampford as an immediate neighbour of John Winslow *Maunciple* in Hempstead. Two properties adjacent to Hempstead in Radwinter and Finchingfield bearing the *Brockhold* name survive today, both registered as scheduled monuments.[265]

The 1400 event takes place in the court of Common Pleas where Thomas Winslow is one of four men providing surety in a preliminary hearing for defendant John Herflete in 1400. There has been a dispute relating to John Herflete's apprenticeship as a saddler, and Thomas is progressing the legal process with the plaintiff William Charnels representing himself. The interim verdict is that the next hearing will be before a jury.[266] There is no mention of Thomas being a saddler.

The 1404 entry for Trinity Term is based in the Court of Common Pleas.[267] Again, Thomas acts as surety in a dispute about a debt bond allegedly raised in St Mary Aldermary in the Cordwainer Street Ward, the area from which John Winslow

---

[264] Cal. Close, Richard ii, vol. 6, 1396-99, p. 56
[265] Great Brockholds moated site and fishpond, Radwinter; Brockhold Farm moated site, Finchingfield
[266] Court of Common Pleas, CP 40/559, rot. 107
[267] Court of Common Pleas, CP 40/574, rot. 420d

Edward Winslow's English Origins

Maunciple had been summoned for the inauguration of Sir Nicholas Brembre in 1384.

Thomas next appears in a writ of *supersedeas* from 1407 when he acts support from four saddlers as mainpernor for John Chirche of Staplehurst in Kent. Thomas has evidently developed an appetite for litigation. It is unclear whether Thomas Winslow occupies a position of authority within the gild of saddlers whose members he is supporting.[268]

The final entry in 1422 shows that Thomas is evidently receiving support:[269]

> *March 26. Westminster. To the sheriffs of London. Order by mainprise of William Sutton 'armurer,' Richard Valdrean 'sadeler,' Thomas Wynell 'sadeler,' Stephen Cleauer 'brewer,' Henry Nobyll 'brewer,' John Reynolde 'lorymer,' John Horsle 'sergeant' and Thomas Leget 'sargeant,' all of London, to set free Thomas Wynselow citizen and 'sadeler' of London of the parish of St. Faith under the 'Northdore' rood...*

The connection between Thomas Winslow and the sheriff of Essex who lived by the Winslows in Hempstead suggests that Thomas is related to the Essex Winslows, and this is further explored in Chapters 4 and 5.

Thomas Winslow *Alnwick*, Entries 1437-1461

Thomas Winslow, son of Agnes Poure and William Winslow *Chaplain,* had a long and illustrious career in matters of law and public office before his own call to attend Parliament as a member for Worcestershire. Fradd takes the view that Thomas Winslow *Alnwick* was not a blood relative of the Kempsey Winslows.

DATE	ACTIVITY
1437	Thomas Wynslowe, attorney acting for Agnes Poure, re Wantyng Bryan Sep 29
1439	Winslow, Thomas Wynslowe, lead juror inquest re Countess of Warwick, Worcs. 1439
1440	Thomas Wynslowe appointed escheator for Glos, Nov 4
1441	Thomas Wynslow and wife Agnes, property Wantage Bryants Berks, Xmas 1441
1441	Thomas Wynslowe & Agnes, demise from John Throckmorton, Wantage Berks, Xmas
1443	Thomas Wynneslowe of Causlaunde, Worcs, assault with Throckmorton, 1443 no day
1444	Thomas Wynslow & Musgros quitclaim & Throckmorton, 1444 Apr 9, following in 1454
1444	Thomas Wynslowe, Commission of Peace in Worcester, 1444 Dec 18
1446	Thomas Wynslowe, Commission of Peace in Worcester, 1446 Feb 18
1447	Thomas Wynslawe, justice gaol Worcester 1447 May 1
1448	Thomas Wynslawe, gaol commission Worcs 1448 May 1
1449-50	Thomas Wynslawe, MP for Worcestershire
1450	Thomas Wynslow, Worcester, lawyer, son-in-law of Throckmorton married Agnes T
1450	Thomas Wynslowe esq. re Rebels in Wilts, 1450 Sep 20

---

[268] *Cal. Close, Henry iv, vol. 3, 1405-9, p. 255*
[269] *Cal. Close, Henry v, vol. 2, 1419-22, p. 237*

Edward Winslow's English Origins

DATE	ACTIVITY
1451	Thomas Knight and his wife Agnes Throckmorton, Worcs 1451, no day
1451	Thomas Wynslowe esquire and Agnes his wife, Hill Court, Worcester 1451 Feb. 9
1451	Thomas Wynslowe, wife Agnes & Thomas & John Throgmerton, Worcs. Feb.
1451	Thomas Wynslawe, Commission of Peace for Worcs, 1451, Nov 11
1454	Thomas Winslow, Commission of Peace, Worcs 1454, Apr 22
1454	Thomas Wynslow, land Chaddesley, Castle Morton & Longedon Worcs, 1454-5 Nov 29
1454	Thomas Wynslow Esq, Worcs estate, from Richard Musgros, 1454 Nov 29
1455-6	MP for Wiltshire 1455-6, Aldermen in Parliament
1456	Thomas Wynslowe, Esq, & wife Agnes, disposal 40 messuages, Ramsbury, 1456 Easter
1456	Winslow, Thomas Wynslowe, Agnes, disposal Wantynge Bryan, 1456, May & Jun
1456	Thomas Wynslowe, esq., sale to John Roger, Wantage estate, Berks, 1456 Dec 1
1457	Thomas Wynslowe, Coroner in Worcestershire 1457
1457	Thomas Wynslawe Commissioner, supply of soldiers Worcester, 1457 , 17 Dec
1458	Thomas Wynslawe, Worcester Commissioner of the peace 1458, Jul 8
1458	Thomas Winslow's daughter Elizabeth married John Terumber (Towker), 1458, no date
1458	Thomas Winslow's chantry gift to James Terumber, father-in-law, 1458, Feb 17 et seq.
1458	Thomas Winslow's gift of lands in Wilts to John Terumber, son -in-law, 1458, Feb 18
1458	Thomas Winslow's further gifts to Terumbers, 1458 June 16
1458	Thomas Winslow's mandates further Throckmorton gifts to Terumbers, 1458 June 166
1458	Thomas Winslow's triangular deal with Throckmortons & Terumbers, 1458 June 28
1460	Thomas Wynslaw late Remysbury Wilts Esq, to Thomas Throkmarton, gift of all, Mar 27
1461	Thomas Wynslowe, gift of all goods to Thos, Throckmorton, 1461 Dec 1
1461-3	Thomas Wynslowe died between Dec. 1461 and 1463, final relief of siege, see *Anneys*
1463	Thomas Wynsselowe, esq, decd., Wilts property 1463 Mar 31
1501	Winslow, Thomas Wynslowe estate, Oxford, Worcs inc. Olvedon, 1501 no day

Figure 3-28 Timeline for Thomas Winslow Alnwick

The timeline of references for Thomas Winslow *Alnwick* is extensive, running from 1437 to his death at Alnwick around 1461-3, and then onward to 1501 following estate complications after his death.

The main purpose for this study has always been to establish as far as possible the accurate lineal ancestry of Governor Edward Winslow. Fradd was correct in asserting that Governor Edward Winslow did not directly descend from Thomas Winslow *Alnwick*; so we do not need to examine the timeline evidence in this volume to establish possible linkages, unlike other Winslows explored so far.

Edward Winslow's English Origins

In summary, Thomas Winslow *Alnwick* was drawn to Worcestershire through the opportunities generated by his stepfather, Robert Andrew, the implications of whose exploits documented in the History of Parliament[270] are considered later.

---

[270] *Hist. Parl, 1386-1421, vol. 2, p. 36*

4   The Road to Kempsey

The previous chapter looked at individuals in the Winslow family line. Using further secondary evidence we will now explore linkages between Winslow family members and the broader social milieu in which they operated, identify their expertise and sponsors, and propose reasons why the Winslows emerged in Kempsey, Worcestershire around 1430. The action reads like a series of unlikely coincidences, but taken together its evidence explains with a high degree of probability how and why the Winslow family opted to move to Worcestershire before 1432.

The evidence presented in Chapter 3 has confirmed that the Winslows from the South of England were a well-regarded family with connections and linkages documented from the 1250s onwards. Initially based in Buckinghamshire, the Winslows by the fourteenth century had expanded geographically into Oxfordshire, St. Albans, Rutland, London and elsewhere; socially into a broader network of prominent Anglo-Norman families; and commercially into property, the military, ecclesiastical activities, London gilds and provision of professional services under patronage.

Fradd rejects Moriarty's view that the family could have originated from anywhere other than Shropshire, and mainly on the basis of his perception about *a considerable gap in class* between the Winslows of Worcestershire and their namesakes in Oxfordshire and Wiltshire.[1] Now that some obvious inconsistencies in Winslow family tradition have been corrected, we will merge the primary evidence from Chapters 1 to 3 with circumstantial secondary material, and we start by assessing the significance of Holton's *Walter Winslow*.

Walter Winslow *Muster*

Walter Winslow *Muster* was evidently a prominent member of Winslow Manor with overlapping property interests in Swanbourne. We have established that Walter is son of William Winslow *Patriarch* whose origins probably date back to the 1240-50. The only mention of Walter himself in WMCB is the record of his death in 1346.

The extant WMCB record starting in 1327 does not mention the death of Walter's wife. Maybe her death was the trigger for Walter's decision to join the priesthood and to move to Aldingbourne, home to the Bishops of Chichester. We can place

---

[1] *Fradd, pp. 50-51*

Edward Winslow's English Origins

Walter in Swanbourne in March 1329 and we can presume that Walter's 1334 appointment was approved by the elderly incumbent Bishop John Langton who on his death in 1337 was succeeded by Bishop Robert de Stratford. Walter remained in this post for a decade or so until shortly before he died in 1346.

What is striking about the two bishops is their significant seniority in English political circles. Bishop John Langton was originally a clerk in the Royal Chancery, and later rose to prominence as the first ever Master of the Rolls, advancing to become Chancellor of England in 1292.[2] As both a Chancellor and a bishop, John Langton combined several leading roles including keeper of the Great Seal, chief Royal chaplain and general adviser in matters of state and spirituality to the King, and after his appointment to the Bishopric of Chichester in 1305 he remained in office until his death in 1337.

Winslow lies nearly ninety miles due north of Chichester, so there is no question of Walter simply applying to fill a local vacancy. The appointment of *Sir Walter Winslow priest* must have been made on Bishop's direction or with his full approval, suggesting that Walter was summoned to take the post based on personal attributes recognised by one of the King's closest former advisers, just as Walter had been summoned previously by the King for military service in Scotland in 1322.

Langton's successor Bishop Robert de Stratford also held important offices of state and other public positions. He served as Chancellor of the Exchequer from 1331 to 1334, and as Lord Chancellor from March to July 1338. He was also Archdeacon of Canterbury from 1334–7 as well as Chancellor of the University of Oxford from 1335 to 1338. His consecration as Bishop of Chichester occurred on 30 November 1337. Bishop Robert embraced the Sussex manor of Aldingbourne as his home; in his later years it was the place where he drafted his will and eventually died, 9 April 1362.

Walter's standing and capability must have justified his appointment in the first place, and once appointed chaplain would presumably have enjoyed proximity both to Bishop John and three years later to his successor Bishop Robert. As their priest during his residence in Aldingbourne in Sussex, Walter would have operated as confessor, counsellor and *confidante* for two former statesmen of eminence.

The Aldingbourne events interlock sequentially with the WMCB record. Walter's summons to the Scottish campaign in 1322 and his return to Winslow by 1329 is interspersed with a gap in both the WMBC and Feudal Aids from 1334 up to his death in 1346. His name does not appear in WMCB during that period simply because he was living away, an absence confirmed by Bishop Stratford's Register which records Walter's appointment by 1334 and his resignation from Aldingbourne in 1345. Holton's military man, the Swanbourne landowner and

---

[2] *For general information on both Bishops, see D. N. B, 1885-1900, vol. 55, online*

latterly the priest are likely to have been the same individual. From the evidence available, Walter Winslow *Muster* was a man of significant standing operating in senior medieval social and political circles.

Robert Winslow *Bercarius*

The earlier undated reference to Robert Winslow *Bercarius* noted that Robert's patron Isabel, widow of Adam Franchum, had sold Robert part of her house in Sydenham, Oxfordshire. We speculated that Robert was operating in the profitable medieval sheep farming sector. The other party mentioned was *Peter de la Pole of Sideham and Emma his wife* to whom the right to Robert de Winslow's annual payment of ½d was being assigned. A similar reference about a grant by *John Osebern of Ocle* to *Peter de la Pole of Sydenham*[3] is also undated, but a third reference to *Peter de la Pole* carries the date Michaelmas 14 Edward I, September 29, 1286.[4] The *de la Pole* family, also known as *Atte Pole,* originated from Hull in the East Riding of Yorkshire and would swiftly advance within a single generation to become one of the most successful commercial entrepreneurs in the English sheep trade. Later they became the Earls of Suffolk and were highly influential in both politics and warfare.

Exactly what office Robert Winslow *Bercarius* was occupying around 1286 cannot be determined. Maybe Robert he was indeed acting as a steward or *reeve* rather than as someone tending the sheep in the fields, but from his surname and close proximity of Sydenham to Winslow, we can be reasonably certain that he derived from the Buckinghamshire Winslows. From the date of 1286, we can speculate that Peter was a younger brother of William Winslow *Patriarch* working for a local patron, implying that as a son outside the direct line of inheritance, he is reduced to operating in a subsidiary profession while the heirs of his Winslow family are arranging advantageous marriages to other privileged families such as the Godards.

This sharp contrast between the first-born and the rest of the male branch of the medieval family did not imply a difference in *class* as Fradd would see it, but rather a difference in levels of perceived advantage and *affluence* even within a single family generation due to the medieval conventions relating to inheritance. The loss of an heir would have damaging consequences even for those only peripherally involved, as we will discover shortly.

---

[3] *Descriptive Catalogue of Ancient Deeds: vol. 6, entry C. 5645*
[4] *Descriptive Catalogue of Ancient Deeds: vol. 3, Entry C. 3456*

Edward Winslow's English Origins

Richard Winslow, *Barrowden*

The bare facts about Richard Winslow presented earlier have offered little context to his true identity. The Rutland Lay Subsidy notes the relatively modest taxable value of the dwelling that Richard Winslow was occupying, but the fact that he was the owner at all indicates some level of relative prosperity. Examination of secondary evidence about his neighbours in Barrowden and residents of the surrounding villages is informative. We can confirm

Figure 4-1 Barrowden in Rutland

immediately not only that Richard Winslow is part of the mainstream Winslow family from Buckinghamshire, but that he is a key connection to a number of notable families encountered earlier as well as involved with the St. Albans Abbey law courts in cooperation with an opponent of the agenda promoted by the Abbey.

In their study of the 1296 Lay Subsidy for Rutland,[5] David Postles and Karen Harris have listed the individuals living in each Rutland town, including Barrowden. The highest tax assessment applies to *William de Bello Campo*, better known as William de Beauchamp, 9th Earl of Warwick, alive between 1238 and 1298, eldest of the eight children of William de Beauchamp and his wife Isabel de Mauduit. Descent of the estate passed through Maud, first wife of Henry I, to Michael de Hanslope, and onward to Michael's grandson William Mauduit, King's Chamberlain who inherited in July 1163. The Mauduits originated from Hanslope in Buckinghamshire, each roughly fifteen miles from Winslow and Swanbourne, as we saw earlier.

The five highest personal assessments for the Barrowden are presented in the Table below. The right-hand column show the broad percentage of the total, with Richard's assessment at the bottom.

BARROWDEN RESIDENT	VALUE	% OF TOTAL
WILLIAM DE BELLO CAMPO	14s/0¾d	9%
LAURENCE DE HAMPTON	12s/6¼d	8%
PETER DE WAKERL'	10s/11d	7%
RICHARD HOUTELAWE	9s/8½d	6%
BENEDICT DE BLAKENHAM	8s/8½d	5%
RICHARD DE WINSLOW	2s/4½d	1.4%

Figure 4-2 Barrowden Taxpayers 1296 ranked by Assessment

William de Beauchamp, later 9th Earl of Warwick inherited the Warwick estate including Barrowden when the Mauduit line died out in 1268.[6] A title dispute with

---

[5] Postles, Dr David, *Rutland Lay Subsidy of 1296*, found online
[6] Cal. Inq. p.m., Hen. iii, vol. 1, no. 679

Edmund, Earl of Cornwall was resolved in William's favour.[7] These Beauchamps operated from Elmley Castle in southern Worcestershire. William de Beauchamp had enjoyed a long and cordial friendship with King Edward I, supporting him in wars against the Welsh and the Scots. Already an elderly man by the time of the taxation in 1296, William de Beauchamp died two years later, to be succeeded by his son Guy.

As for the other names in figure 4.2, *Peter de Wakerl'* is evidently a local public administrator who is granted a commission of *oyer et terminer* in the area in January 1297,[8] appointed a tax collector in 1297,[9] and the earl had granted him Rutland property.[10] Perhaps Richard Winslow at this point was playing a role similar to *Peter de Wakerl'*. *Lawrence de Hampton* and *Richard Houtelawe* are names otherwise unknown in this context. A *Benedict de Blakenham* is granted £20 a year in 1271 as steward of Queen Eleanor, *so long as he stands in that office*,[11] and someone of the same name leaves property to his son and heir in 1297.[12]

We can speculate that the Earl of Warwick would have required a sizeable household entourage to administer his new inheritance and safeguard its orderly transition to an eventual successor, and maybe Richard was working here in such a capacity. With no other Winslows in this Rutland Lay subsidy, we can assume that Richard Winslow *Barrowden* is not a local, but it is evident that Richard Winslow possessed or had formed connections in the area. From the evidence of the Lay Subsidy, Earl William's inheritance included four villages adjacent to Barrowden, one of which is Seaton, home to Mabel, daughter of Sir Ralph de Beaufeu of Seaton. Mabel Beaufeu married *John de Trumpington,* and her new husband settled 100 acres of the Trumpington estate:[13]

65 Ralph de Bella Fago v John fil Walter de Tru'peton in Trumppeton

This holding passed in turn to their son William; and by 1302 the estate was known as *Beaufo,* and later as *Crochemans* and *Beaufuse* as we found earlier. This builds a connection back in the world of the Crouchmans and reconnects with Essex and Cambridgeshire. After William's death the manor was leased from Beaufu's widow Sarah, and eventually purchased in 1336 from Beaufu's son Roger by the Crouchman family.[14]

12. William Crocheman v. Roger Beaufo' in Trumpington.

---

[7] *Placitorum in domo capitulari Westmonasteriensi asservatorum abbreviation, Record Commission, 1811, p. 234*
[8] *Cal. Pat., Edward I, vol. 3, 1292-1301, pp. 259, 382, 630*
[9] *Cal. Pat., Edward I, vol. 3, 1292-1301, p. 297*
[10] *Cal. Inq. p.m., Henry iii, no. 679. p. 214*
[11] *Cal. Pat., Henry III, vol. 6, 1266-1272, p. 604*
[12] *Cal. Close, Edward I, vol. 4, 1296-1302, p. 13*
[13] *Ex. e Rot. Fin. (Rec. Com.), ii, 411*
[14] *Fines Relating to the County of Cambridge, Walter Rye, CAS, 1891, entry 12, p. 101*

Edward Winslow's English Origins

In fact there is much more to know about Ralph de Beaufeu found in an informative article by Anthony Musson.[15] Musson talks about the pressure on the English legal system at the end of the thirteenth century. Wrongdoings, reported from such sources as coroners, were duly considered and presented to a pre-trial or *presentment* jury, and if this presentment jury considered that the case should be pursued and that charges were warranted, then the matter was passed to a trial jury, often composed of members of the nobility, bailiffs, coroners and constables.[16] Musson mentions that *constables and bailiffs represented the nexus at which royal and manorial justice met and intermeshed.[17]*

The names of jurors involved were frequently omitted from court records, but Musson's article specifically refers to legal records surviving from 1296 concerning hearings held in Oakham, Rutland. Musson notes that two names stand out among the jurors because of their relatively enormous caseload. One of these is a man called *John Hotot*, and his was the sole name recorded against seventeen of the cases. The other person mentioned was *Ralph Beaufeu*, and his was the sole name recorded for a further eighteen cases. Most remarkable of all, their names were jointly recorded against a further twenty-one sessions. They must both have played a significant role in the local legal process and general administration of justice.

We have established a connection between Roger Beaufeu and the Crouchmans in the 1320s; can we establish a link between the Beaufeu and Richard Winslow? It is time to revisit the Handmills case based on the evidence found in Volume 2 of *Gesta*.

This first report of the Handmills dispute in 1274 occupies no fewer than fourteen pages of the *Gesta*.[18] In a second dispute around 1330-32, the initial legal finding is that no collusion had occurred in the St. Albans townsfolk's refusal to use the Abbey mills, but that they will be obliged to use them in future.[19] The individual leading the opposition is St. Albans resident John Baldewyne. In the next iteration, Richard Winslow is introduced as one of thirteen tenants who are listed in the first column of table 2.4 below.[20] Richard is reported by the chronicler as John Baldewyne's tenant.

TENANT	PROPERTY OWNER	WEALTH
Willelmus Bolun	*Alexandrus Goldston	5/3½
*Thomas Atte Delle	Sancta Maria de Sopwelle	
Willelmus de Tydenhangre	*Nicolaus filius Andrew, in Halywellestrat	

---

[15] Musson, *Twelve Good Men and True? The Character of Early Fourteenth-Century Juries.* Anthony Musson, *Law and History Review, Vol. 15, No. 1, Spring 1997 (1997), pp. 115-144.*
[16] Musson p. 127
[17] Musson p. 128
[18] Gesta, vol. 1, pp. 410-23
[19] Gesta, vol. 2, pp. 237-43
[20] Gesta, vol. 2, pp. 246-53

TENANT	PROPERTY OWNER	WEALTH
*Gilbertus Cok, de Hertforde	*Thomas Prest "now passed to Abbot"	6/9½
*Magister Johannes Schepherde	*Willelmus Heroun *(terra)*, 13d	15/3
*Ricardus de Wynslowe	Johannes Baldewyne, 2/4	
Rogerus Thangtone	Abbas	
*Robertus Atte Halle	Robertus Atte Halle	
Willelmus, filius Willelmi Marchal	*Frimbaldus Mercer	20d
*Johanna Poleyn (Codicote?), witness	*Ada Medici in Vico Francorum	5/2½
*Thomas Petyt	Abbas in Dagenhale	
Ivo Perceval	*Butelerus in Dagenhale	
*Emma Modi	*Modi in Bonegate	18d

Table 4-3 –Litigants and Tenants in the Handmills case

Where relevant, the value of the claimant's wealth drawn from the 1307 Lay Subsidy for St. Albans is shown. Claimants and tenants prefaced with * are mentioned in *Gesta* vol. 2 exclusively in connection with the dispute, including Richard Winslow. The chronicler provides no clues about the personal circumstances of claimants, so it is difficult to assess or qualify with certainty the underlying rationale or merit of each legal challenge.

Ricardus de Wynslowe is tenant of *Johannes Baldewyne* from St. Albans, and Baldwyn is the richer of the two claimants recorded as wealthy enough to be taxable in 1307. Furthermore Baldwyn has already been involved in the second episode in the series of handmills legal actions, consistently addressed by the honorific title *Magister* or Master, suggesting a personage of especial legal importance. From a July 1329 reference we deduce his year of birth as 1271.[21] By 1332 John is in trouble: acting as coroner for the County of Essex, he has upset some residents, including the former sheriff for Hertfordshire and Essex:[22]

> *1332 January 28. Westminster. To the sheriff of Essex. Order to cause a coroner for that county to be elected in place of John Baldewyne, who does not dwell in that county and is so occupied with the affairs of divers magnates, whose steward he is, that he cannot attend to the duties of the office. By testimony of Richard Perers and several others of the said county.*

Evidently Baldewyne, an administrator busy with the affairs of *divers magnates, whose steward he is,* has been promoted to the role of county coroner, indicating that he possesses legal expertise or has persuasive patrons, or both. What is being challenged is not his competence, but rather his application to the task. John is mentioned in a number of Essex property and legal transactions including 1310,[23]

---

[21] *Cal. Inq. p.m., Edward iii, vol. 7, entry 245*
[22] *Cal. Close, Edward iii, vol. 2, 1330-1333, p. 433*
[23] *Cal. Pat., Edward ii, vol. 1, 1307-1313, p. 276*

Edward Winslow's English Origins

1318[24] and 1324,[25] and *John Baudewyne* is recorded with no fewer than ten entries in the Lay Subsidy for Essex in 1327[26] in addition to any property he still owns in Hertfordshire.

Within a month of the entry above, Baldwyne, hitherto consistently addressed in *Gesta* as *Magister* or Master, is now addressed with the additional title *chaplain*, as William Winslow would be addressed later:[27]

> *Master John Baldwyne of St. Albans, chaplain, acknowledges that he owes to Roger de Clare, citizen of London, £20; to be levied, in default of payment, of his lands and chattels in co. Hertford.*

Meanwhile in April the same year, the third iteration of the handmills case has been progressing and has clearly upset the townsfolk, who clearly feel frustrated. The names marked in bold below have also been reported in the description of proceedings in *Gesta*, confirming the authenticity of both narratives:[28]

> *Memorandum, that on 13 April, Adam le Ussher, John de Neubury, Peter atte Cunduit,* **Robert de Thwangton**, *the younger,* **Ivo Perceval**, *John de Brockele, John de Hereford,* **William son of John le Mareschal**, *Richard Amy, Henry de Drayton,* **Robert atte Halle**, *Henry Angelberd, John le Barber,* **Master John Baldewyne**, *Walter de Bylindon, John le Coupere, Robert le Goldsmyth, Thomas le Goldsmyth, Adam de Pountfreyt, Geoffrey Bolum, Benedict Spichfat,* **William Bolum**, *Roger Reysoun, Simon Dode, John son of Andrew le Tannere,* **William de Tydenhangre**, *Nicholas de Bydewell, William le Longe, William de Langeforde, Richard de Paxton, and Geoffrey Hereward, men of St. Albans, came into chancery, for themselves and other men of that town, and brought there a certain royal charter of confirmation of certain liberties granted to them by the deed of Hugh, late abbot of St. Albans, and of the convent there, and sought that the charter might be condemned....*

By July 1333 John Baldewyne is under renewed pressure to give up his role as coroner for Essex.[29] At this point he emerges as overall leader of the group opposed to the Abbey, as another statement dated July 4 1334 makes clear:[30]

> *To the justices of the Bench. Order to proceed to render judgment in a plea between the abbot of St. Albans and Master John Baldewyne and other of his tenants in the town of St. Albans for making suit as they ought and were wont to do at the abbot's mill of that town, notwithstanding that such suit was not deraigned previously, as the abbot has shown the king by his petition before him and his council that whereas he has impleaded John and the other tenants before those justices for the said cause, and although John and the others pleading before the justices did not deny that they ought and were wont to make suit at the mill of the abbot for baking all corn and for brewing, on those messuages which they*

---

[24] *Cal. Pat., Edward ii, vol. 3, 1317-1321, p. 225*
[25] Cal. Close, Edward ii, vol. 4, 1323-1327, p. 531
[26] *Jennifer C. Ward, The Medieval Essex Community, The Lay Subsidy of 1327, Essex Record Office Publication No. 88, 1983, p. 127*
[27] *Cal. Close, Edward iii, vol. 2, 1330-1333, p. 536*
[28] *Cal. Close, Edward iii, vol. 2, 1330-1333, p. 558*
[29] *Cal. Close, Edward iii, vol. 3, 1333-37, p. 66*
[30] *Cal. Close, Edward iii, vol. 3, 1333-37, p. 231*

hold in that town, yet the justices delayed to proceed to render judgment in that plea according to the process held before them because it was not shown to them that the exaction of such suit in past times was deraigned unless by reason of arable lands where corn is grown, wherefore the abbot has besought the king to provide a remedy. By pet.

The last two references to Baldewyne in the Close Rolls relate to witnessing a property transaction in Chelmsford Essex in October 1334[31] and to a rent roll in September in 1337.[32] Judgement in the *Suit of Multure* has gone against them, and nothing further is heard of Richard Winslow. Why did Baldewyne include Winslow so prominently in the handmills case, marking Winslow as the tenant of his own property? Possibly because Winslow was well-known in the St. Albans court in his own right, and because of professional links to Baldwyne, and because of overlapping client interests.

This returns us back to the question of the connections between the Beaufeus, the Crouchmans and Richard Winslow. In 1332 the St. Albans townsfolk are rejecting the Abbot's charter of liberties while in 1336 the Crouchmans will take over Beaufo Manor. We have seen that in 1332 William Crouchman was in Santiago as a pilgrim, and that John Grigge died in December 1332. William meantime has also married Egidia, John Grigge's nine-year-old daughter and heir. The transfer of the Hempstead property after John Grigge's death provides the biggest surprise of all, as the Essex Feet of Fines show:[33]

234. Trinity and Michaelmas. John son of Henry Grigge and Margaret his wife, plaintiffs, Ralph de Pokethorp and John Baldewyne, chaplain, deforciants. 2 messuages, 1 mill, 700 acres of land, 30 acres of meadow, 8 acres of pasture, 36 acres of wood and 40s. rent in Hampstede, Fynchyngfeld and Great Sampford. Pl. and the heirs of their bodies to hold of the chief lords, with remainder to the right heirs of John son of Henry.

The plaintiffs are Margaret and the late John Grigge, parents of Egidia Grigge, future wife of Sir William Crouchman who will be future grandfather of John Winslow's wife Mariota. The deforciants, presumably acting as trustees, are *Ralph de Pokethorp* and *Magister John Baldewyne*, chaplain, lawyer and sometime Coroner for Essex, resident of St. Albans; and nominally the landlord of Richard Winslow in the Handmills case. Suddenly connections can be established between the Beaufeu, Crouchman, Grigge and Winslow families through associations with Trumpington and John Baldewyne.

This begs some questions. As the legally trained leader of the opposition to the Abbot's milling policies, John Baldewyne would maximise his likelihood of success in court by presenting the most prestigious and credible candidate to bring his case, and he selects Richard Winslow. And If Baldewyne is described as a steward *of the affairs of divers magnates*, does this indicate that Richard Winslow's credibility

---

[31] *Cal. Close, Edward iii, vol. 3, 1333-37, p. 231*
[32] *Cal. Close, Edward iii, vol. 3, 1333-37, p. 261*
[33] *Feet of Fines for Essex vol. 3, p. 24*

Edward Winslow's English Origins

arose through operating in the same sector, and that Baldewyne was familiar with his professional work? Was Richard Winslow working within the process of administration of justice? If that were the case then Richard Winslow and Ralph Beaufeu are very likely to have been working together in Rutland.

We have already made a speculative assumption that Richard Winslow *Barrowden* moved to the small village of Rutland, perhaps to act as a young steward for a local magnate, in this case the Earl of Warwick. We found Robert Winslow *Bercarius* earlier, although his role in Sydenham was not especially exalted. But in the case of the Winslow connection with Rutland we have been able to uncover the existence of a network of individuals who all feature in the future history of the Winslow family. Are there other clues in the locality that we are overlooking?

If Richard's appearance in the lay subsidy of 1296 marked him in his early twenties, then we can place his birthdate around 1270-75, and his subsequent appearance in the Handmills case around 1332 would place him in his early sixties. We saw above that John Baldewyne was born in 1271.[34] In the light of what we have found, there is a reasonable likelihood not only that Richard Winslow *Barrowden* is the same individual as Richard Winslow *Handmills*, but also that at the end of his professional service in Rutland he had returned to his home base of St. Albans.

The second factor to consider is the existence in St. Albans of other Winslows living away from the home base in Buckinghamshire. Who else do we find in St. Albans around this time? The answer is the John Winslow *Bailiff* acting as the Abbot's legal enforcer in 1340. John Winslow *Bailiff* is also working for the judiciary. The *Bailiff's* son was John Winslow, acting in St. Albans Abbey as *Maunciple*. And Brother William *Cellarer* would be working as recorder for Winslow Manor Court in 1340 as successor to Brother Walter Mare, later to become Abbot. The reason for the moves to Rutland and back to St. Albans could be explained by Richard Winslow's status as younger brother to heir Walter de Winslow *Muster*.

Richard Winslow was in Rutland alongside the Beaufeus who intermarry with the Trumpingtons, and who settle in Trumpington, changing the manor name to *Beaufuse*. John Baldwyne has later been working with his associate from St. Albans Richard Winslow, and at the same time with a prosperous Hempstead family, the Grigges. The Grigges' daughter Egidia will become future wife of Sir William Crouchman of Trumpington, and later grandmother to Mary Crouchman of Hempstead who marries John Winslow *Maunciple* in 1375. And what did Sir William Crouchman do? As we saw earlier, Sir William was a leading member of the judiciary as well.

The sojourn in Rutland alongside the Beaufeus carried some other consequences. The two John Winslows had previously been resident alongside John Beaufeu in

---

[34] *See footnote 18 above*

Edward Winslow's English Origins

Little Horwood, as we saw in WMCB, strengthening the supposition that the two Johns are probably Richard Winslow's grandsons. John Beaufeu will serve as Yeoman of the Chamber alongside William Winslow *Pavilioner*, and later become his deputy when William is promoted to *Pavilioner*. The jigsaw pieces are starting to interlock.

There are valid grounds for supposing that Richard Winslow was an associate of Sir Ralph Beaufeu and worked with him on managing the heavy legal workload, possibly as a functionary within the legal process. That would also explain how and why his Richard's son John Winslow *Bailiff* is found to be fulfilling a similar role in St. Albans later a generation later: we can extrapolate that Richard Winslow *Barrowden* had a reputation in local legal circles, and that in turn would explain his connection to *Magister John Baldewyne*. We cannot be completely certain because, as Musson has indicated, the quality of documentation relating of the administration of local justice is imperfect. But the evident breadth of Richard Winslow's social circle is striking.

William Winslow *Wodyam*

William Winslow *Wodyam* was the heir of Walter Winslow *Muster*, and if the hypothesis about Richard Winslow's lineage is accepted, then *Wodyam* would be Richard's nephew; and the future direction of William's career would be following a family pattern.

A reference in the 1332 Warwickshire Lay Subsidy Rolls places a William Winslow in the village of Barston next to Berkswell in Warwickshire. The family of the Earls of Warwick had held property there continuously since the Norman Conquest. V.C.H. notes that *...the count's lands passed to his brother Henry de Newburgh, Earl of Warwick, and the overlordship of the manor continued with the earls.*[35] *Newburgh* in this context is the modern Normandy town of *Le Neubourg*, where remnants of the Earl's Norman castle are still visible. Barston is located about ten miles away from Oakham where the Rutland court sessions were held, and Barston is about the same distance from the Warwickshire courts.

An inquisition from 1401 identifies the Earl's Warwickshire estate spanning seven adjoining manors: Warwick, Brailes, Claverdon, Tanworth, Sutton Coldfield, Berkswell and Lighthorne,[36] valuing the Warwickshire estate in 1401 above £217:

Warwick	Brailes	Berkswell	Lighthorne	S. Coldfield	Claverdon	Tanworth
£66 7s 2d	£48 3s 4d	£33 0s 0d	£25 0s 0d	£17 5s 0d	£14 8s 2d	£12 15s 0d

Table 4-4 Relative values of Earl's Warwickshire income valuation, 1401

Berkswell is centrally positioned between them, with Sutton Coldfield 15 miles to the North, Lighthorne 18 miles and Brailes 30 miles to the South respectively.

---

[35] *Berkswell, History of the County of Warwick: vol. 4, Styles P., London 1945, p. 28*
[36] *Cal. Inq. p.m. Henry iv, vol. 18 Entry 509, Warwick, 12 April 1401*

Edward Winslow's English Origins

Claverdon and Warwick some 10 miles to the South, and Tanworth some 14 miles to the South West. If William Winslow *Wodyam* was also operating in the judicial or legal profession, then he would be well placed to reach the law courts in Warwick. If he was working on the affairs of the Earl of Warwick, then Berkswell would be a logical choice thanks to its central location. As a single manor, Berkswell is valued at more than £33:

> *Berkswell, site of the manor, nil; 200 a. arable, 26s.8d.; 20 a. meadow, 20s.; a park, beyond the keeping of the game 13s.4d.; underwood, 20s.; and assize rents, £29, payable as above.*

As was the case with Richard in Rutland, William's commitment to Barston he would leave him habitually away from Winslow even though he still held Winslow family land. The extant WMCB record post 1327 makes no further mention of William Winslow *Wodyam* beyond his inheritance in 1346, and his death as reported in 1350. His father Walter *Muster,* who would also have been habitually absent in Aldingbourne until shortly before his death in 1346, received equally scant coverage in WMCB.

Mortality rates recorded in WMCB between 1348 and 1349 at the height of the Black Death pandemic are especially revealing

COURT SESSION	MONTHS' INTERVAL	REPORTED DEATHS	MONTHLY DEATH RATE
October 1347	6	5	<1
June 1348	8	5	<1
April 1349	10	105	>10.0
October 1349	6	50+	>8.0
May 1350	8	3	<0.5
Jan 1351	8	1	<0.2

Table 4-5 Mortality figures in Winslow 1348-51 including Black Death victims

WMCB give a full account of individual fatalities which by a perverse twist of fate would have produced a bonanza of tax revenue for the Abbey. The table above records the death rate between 1347 and 1351, omitting Alice and *Wodyam*. The peak of the reported death rate occurred during 1349.

By the time the deaths of *Wodyam* and his wife are reported in WMCB in 1350, the pandemic was effectively over. Most likely Wodyam and his wife had died the previous year when the pandemic was at its height, and news of their death was slow to be conveyed to Winslow for inclusion in the manor records. It is less likely that both died of unrelated causes during that same period. Had they been based around Winslow, news of their deaths would be relatively common knowledge. If instead they were based in Warwickshire, Thomas Winslow *Homicide* would presumably have conveyed the sad news, but quite likely he was campaigning in

France or apprenticed in London at the time, in either case remote from Warwickshire. That would explain delays in news reaching WMCB.

There are other factors to consider in judging see how swiftly *Wodyam* reacted in relation to his father's death. *Wodyam* is only ever mentioned twice in WMCB: once about his right to inheritance after Walter's death, and once for not undertaking the *due and accustomed services,* something of a trivial formality for anyone residing in the immediate vicinity: [37]

> *..it was ordered to distrain the heir of Walter of Wynselowe to do the outstanding relief and fealty etc.*

The sequence of events in WMCB suggests that William *Wodyam,* like Richard *Barrowden,* was absent from Buckinghamshire. *Wodyam* had bigger priorities than interrupting his Barston work schedule for a relatively pointless two-way trip to kiss hands, or whatever the protocol. By comparison, John Winslow *Maunciple* is mentioned in WMCB no fewer than eleven times in his five year residence in Little Horwood from 1352-57, but not beforehand, and never again.

Firm evidence to place Wodyam in the legal profession operating out of Warwickshire is not forthcoming, but we do know his family lineage and we can deduce that he worked away from home.

John Winslow *Bailiff*

We saw in Chapter 3 that John *Bailiff* is first recorded as enforcer for the Abbot in the 1340s, and the section on Richard Winslow above suggests the he was John's father. If Richard was born around 1270-75 as has been suggested, then John Bailiff may have been born around 1300-5. John's two sons are identified as John *Maunciple* and John *Hunsdon*, and we have also suggested that John *Maunciple* was born around 1330. The idea of father and both sons sharing the same forename *John* seems implausible, but so far no evidence has been found to disprove it.

Year	Suffix	Activity
1350	Homicide	William & Alice Wynselowe both dead, Thomas inherits May 24
1351	Homicide	Winslow, Thomas de Wynselowe, Swanbourn, May 1351, Black Princes Register
1352	Bailiff	John Wynselowe, "then" St. Albans Bailiff, witness, Sopwell Lane, Sept
1352	Bailiff	Winslow, John Wynselowe, alienate land to the abbot, 1352
1352	Bailiff	John Wyncelowe of St. Albans & Andrew Mentemore, St Albans property, Dec
1352	Homicide	Thomas Winslow surrender Swanbourne estate to Thomas Williams, 1352
1353	Bailiff	John de Wyncelowe of Honesdon, Oliver de Bohun funding, 20 marks, Jan 21
1353	Bailiff	John Wynselowe and Thomas Morteyn, their bailiffs re saddlers, July
1360	Homicide	Pardon to Thomas de Hundesden alias Wynselowe, John Turk apprentice, Jul 1

Figure 4-6: Thomas Winslow Homicide and interactions with John Winslow Bailiff, 1350-60

---

[37] WMCB, vol. 1, p. 185

Edward Winslow's English Origins

The report of Thomas's parents' deaths reaches Winslow in 1350; by which time Thomas *Homicide* may already be committed to the French campaign, or serving an apprenticeship in London. Around 1352 John Winslow *Bailiff* ceases to operate in St. Albans, and Thomas has surrendered his inheritance in the Swanbourne property.

There are two other possible factors here. One is the likelihood that Richard Winslow *Barrowden* died around this time – his elder brother Walter had died in 1346, so the suggestion is not implausible. Perhaps the St. Albans Baldwyne residence occupied by Richard during the Handmills trial was no longer available, and eventually the family chose to move 1352-3.

It is impossible to assess the scale of family upheaval caused by these events. Hunsdon is some sixteen miles from St. Albans, while Winslow is about forty, and if access to its apprenticeships is a priority then Winslow was located the wrong side of the City of London. An important document has been sighted; although the reference will require revalidation, *Hunsdon Local History and Preservation Society* has issued a pamphlet mentioning medieval property units in the heart of the village, originally an extended double dwelling: *Winslows alias Legates, and the coach house Cote House alias Cottles alias the Gatehouse:*

> *The house most likely to have been the Cote House is number 53 High Street with the archway, and the house on the west called Wynslowes Legates would be the one called White Horses.*

> *Wynslowes. These two houses have certainly stood together for centuries; possibly parts of both date back to the 16th century.*

> *According to a title deed of 1528 William Lawrence, a husbandman and Laurent Leister, Rector of Hunsdon sold a freehold house called the Cote House to William Bereman yeoman of Waltham Cross and his son Thomas Bereman for the use of Thomas Bereman . In the Manor Court Roll of 1532 Thomas Bereman, a yeoman was said to hold a freehold house in Hunsdon.*

The name *Winslows alias Legates* suggests that these several properties were where the Winslows settled after the two family branches reunited in Hunsdon sometime after 1350. No link with Helmyng Leget has been established.

Walter and Emma Winslow, *Kimpton*

Kimpton is a Hertfordshire village eight miles north of St. Albans, nineteen miles from Hunsdon and about thirty miles from Winslow. The Feet of Fines for 1368 mention disposal of property and rights in Luton and Kimpton comprising *1 messuage, 100 acres of land, 1 acre of wood and 16 pence of rent in Luyton' and Kympton'*, between:[38]

---

[38] Feet of Fines, 1368, Bedfordshire, CP 25/1/5/64, no. 2

Edward Winslow's English Origins

Edward Plummer of Kympton', querent, and Walter Wynselowe and Emma, his wife, deforciants.

Kimpton is only a few miles away from St. Albans where both Richard *Handmills* and John *Bailiff* were operating. This Walter Winslow *Kimpton* may be a son of William Winslow *Wodyam,* sharing his forename with his grandfather Walter Winslow *Muster.* If so, then presumably this Walter Winslow *Kimpton* was brought up in Barston and away from Winslow, explaining why there is no record of him nor of his wife in WMCB.

From the reported scale of their estate, Walter and Emma are evidently a prosperous couple. Is he a lawyer working for the Abbey? We cannot tell.

Thomas Winslow *Homicide*

WMCB informs us about the death of Thomas's father *Wodyam* in 1350; and because Thomas is old enough to inherit, we can assume that his year of birth predates 1329. After mentioning his inheritance, WMCB never alludes to Thomas again. We know from other sources that Thomas acted as a witness in 1383 in the company of Sir Robert Turk, heir of the family with whom Thomas had served his apprenticeship in London. So by the time of Turk's visit, Thomas was living in Hunsdon.

The sequence of events for Thomas in the decade following 1350-60 is as follows:

YEAR	ACTIVITY
1350	Thomas inherits May 24 1350, WMCB
1351	Thomas de Wynselowe, Swanbourn, May, Black Prince's Register
1352	Likely date for surrender of Swanbourne property
1356	Battle of Poitiers, 19 September 1356
1360	Peace through Treaty of Brétigny, 8 May 1360
1360	Pardon: Thomas de Hundesden alias Wynselowe, Jul 1

Figure 4-7 Thomas Winslow Homicide Decade 1350-60

If we assume that Thomas *Homicide* had spent his formative years living with his parents, he was presumably sent to London maybe in his teens to serve the apprenticeship with the John Turk cited in his pardon in 1360. We can speculate that his apprenticeship began perhaps around 1340, and we cannot be sure whether Thomas's apprenticeship was completed by 1350. The gild of fishmongers was a well-regulated *mistery*, with clear governance about attendance:[39]

> The Fishmongers in 1278-9 say that no one shall take more than two or three apprentices at most, and then only if he is able to support them, nor shall he take an apprentice for less than seven years. The master and apprentice must bring the covenant to be enrolled at Guildhall, and at the end of his term the apprentice shall be presented again by his master,

---

[39] *Calendar of Plea and Memoranda Rolls, vol. 2, 1364-1381, Thomas A.H. ed., 1926 Intro., pp. xxxi*

Edward Winslow's English Origins

or if his master be dead, by four reputable men of the mistery, after which he may be allowed to engage in trade.

Thomas's appearance in the Black Prince's Register suggests involvement in military activities in 1351, and by 1352 he had probably surrendered the property in Swanbourne. In his 1360 pardon he is styled *Thomas de Hundesden alias Wynselowe*, so perhaps the Hunsdon property was acquired earlier when the Swanbourne property was first vacated.

William de Bohun, 1st Earl of Northampton, in whose company Thomas was serving up to 1360 when the pardon was issued, died later that same year. Thomas was presumably involved in the latter phase of hostilities brought to a close through the Treaty of Brétigny, also in 1360. The phrasing of Thomas's pardon mentioned above indicates that Thomas had acquitted himself favourably on campaign.

Based on the reasonable assumption from his inheritance that Thomas *Homicide* was born sometime around 1325-8, the last reference located for him from 1383 would place him by then about 55-60 years old. We have no verifiable date of death. Maybe his death occurred as late as 1400.

Among the Winslow family heirs, Thomas's lifetime marks the transition away from the tradition of military service based on feudal landholding into a commercial and professional lifestyle accessible through apprenticeship within the City of London gilds, an option less readily available to earlier family members like Walter Winslow *Muster*. Walter combined his military obligations with a subsequent ecclesiastical life, and he was largely absent from both Winslow and Swanbourne. Such absence probably equally applied to William Winslow *Wodyam* and to Thomas *Homicide*, and by Thomas's time the incentive to return to Winslow must have been low.

Thomas's bigger objective as lineal heir seems to have been stabilising the Winslow family fortunes, an endeavour successful from 1352 until 1375. Thereafter the Hempstead branch of the Winslow achieved significant success, affluence and expansion that evidently attracted other family members.

John Winslow *Maunciple*

We know from *Gesta* that John was punished under Abbot Thomas de la Mare with a substantial fine of £20 in 1357. We can only speculate why he chose to position himself within the jurisdiction of Winslow Manor Court by moving into Little Horwood aged perhaps around 22 in 1352, accompanied by his brother John Winslow *Hunsdon*. That relocation to Horwood coincides with John Winslow *Bailiff* moving to Hunsdon with the two brothers who only followed him after the significant fine incurred by John *Maunciple* in 1356-7.

John Winslow *Maunciple* settled his Hunsdon interest on his brother John Winslow *Hunsdon* in 1375 presumably after the death of their father John Winslow *Bailiff*.

Whereas John moved to Hempstead to join his new bride, there is no evidence that John Winslow *Hunsdon* ever subsequently changed his residence.

It was debated in Chapter 3 whether the reference to John Winslow *Hostytter* from 1365 could be identified with John Winslow *Maunciple*. The conclusion was there was no primary evidence that John Winslow ever had any interest in a catering establishment, lodging or Inn. But reference to the incident is also found in a footnote to an entry in the Plea Rolls, where editor A. H. Thomas describes *Hostytter* as *a word of several meanings, probably denoting here an innkeeper or lodging-house keeper.*[40]

> John Wynselowe, hostytter, and Alice his wife, executrix of the will of Henry Sket, were committed to prison till they paid the sum of £24 due to Joan and Anne, the testator's daughters. Afterwards they were mainprised by William Whetele, cordwainer.

However, in a section of his book covering the gild of the Spicers, Gwyn Williams identifies one of the important members of the Spicers gild at the end of the thirteenth century as a prominent *Cahorsin* named *William Servat* who came to England as the head a company of merchants trading in wool and spices, settling as a citizen by 1292. His volumes of trade in the City between 1311 and 1313 were enormous: £518 for cloth and £600 for wine.

Gwyn Williams reports that Servat had been personally responsible around 1311 for the establishment of an Inn for the Spicers in Cordwainer Ward where John would be based half a century later in 1365,[41] circumstantial evidence that John, already a spicer, can also be identified as the *Hostytter* with reasonable certainty. Such evidence would imply that John Winslow *Maunciple* was already committed to his apprenticeship between 1352 and 1357 when he held the tenancy in his own name in Little Horwood, and possibly explaining his frequent amercements for absence, as well as his early eagerness to pass the Horwood tenancy to his brother John Winslow *Hunsdon*.

What was the event or negotiation that facilitated John's marriage to Mariota Crouchman? The detailed analysis of the Crouchman family earlier has disclosed the crisis that the Crouchmans had reached. The accepted version of events records the death of Mary's father William as 1391, but now we know that William C4's death occurred twenty years earlier in 1371 when as a minor he was too young to inherit from his brother John, also a minor too young to hold the family estate inherited from their father, *Sir William Crouchman*. William C4 presumably had no influence on the outcome.

Mariota was barely five years old when her father William died; and presumably Mariota Crouchman was married off as a nine-year-old to John Winslow, by that time in his mid-forties, and possibly previously married. Perhaps the arrangement

---

[40] *AH Thomas, membrane 14, entry 16 June 1365, footnote 21*
[41] *Gwyn Williams, pp. 142-3*

Edward Winslow's English Origins

was negotiated by the Huntingdons. Mariota's only other known surviving Crouchman relatives were her mother Matilda and her paternal aunt Elizabeth, by now also married to one of the Huntingdons. It is uncertain whether her grandmother Egidia, born around 1323, was still alive. The Crouchman estate was extensive and valuable, and it says much about John Winslow that he was selected to become Mariota's husband. The families had already known each other for two generations; but what was at risk was retention of the extensive Crouchman family estate in the event of Mariota's premature death without an heir. Mariota's father had died in 1371, and it was four years before her later betrothal to John Winslow.

William Winslow *Pavilioner*

It is relatively easy to connect the *Pavilioner* with the rest of the Winslow family. One of the royal gifts offered to William Winslow *Pavilioner* is the office of parker of *Stondon* in Hertfordshire, situated only some six miles away from Hunsdon where the two Winslow family branches had settled since the 1350s. On the basis of probability, this finding supports the theory that William *Pavilioner* is the son of Thomas *Homicide* and grandson of Walter *Muster*, and that Hunsdon had been the place of his upbringing. As landowners, Walter and Thomas performed their due military service, and William Winslow *Pavilioner* was the Winslow family member to follow their lead.

One important item requiring clarification is the statement in V.C.H. for Cambridge[42] that *Mary, daughter of William Beaufeu's son John, married William Winslow.* The cited source of this reference is MS Gough.[43] Examination of the relevant entry held in the Bodleian in Oxford indicates that the text has been misinterpreted; what the narrative is presenting is the sequential descent of Trumpington Manor, later known as *Beaufo*, through the various generations. First reported holder is Sir William Crouchman; later it passes to the father of Mary Crouchman, erroneously identified in MS Gough as *John* instead of *William Crouchman*, and eventually to Mary's son William, known to us by the suffix *Armiger*. The confusion reflects a more general misinterpretation of the Crouchman descent covered in Chapter 1.

The identity of the *Pavilioner's* wife for now therefore remains unknown. The close connection between several successive Beaufeu and Winslow generations continued. William Winslow *Pavilioner* worked alongside John Beaufeu, confirming the depth and validity of friendship stretching through both branches of the Winslow family back at least far as Barrowden in 1296 when we find Ralph Beaufeu working the Rutland courts.

Lang indicates that William *Pavilioner* must have enjoyed high social status to have warranted inclusion in John Bradmore's medical treatise, *The Philomena*. In her

---

[42] Caldecote, *History of the County of Cambridge and the Isle of Ely: vol. 5 (1973)*, p. 20
[43] Bodl. MS. Gough Camb. 19, f. 19

view, Bradmore enjoyed emphasising the social importance of his patients and the apparent hopelessness of their medical condition where he alone had the expertise to remediate. The events following Richard II's deposition in 1399, William's early dismissal from Royal Service in 1399 followed by swift restoration of royal privileges by the incoming King Henry IV, suggest that William himself was a personage held in high royal esteem.

William Winslow *Armiger*

A possible pointer to the Winslows' longer-term ambitions and aspirations for their estates in Essex is found in a related event concerning a property acquisition by a member of the Beaufeu family, this time Thomas and his wife Katherine in the autumn of 1414.[44]

> *18. Mich. Thomas Beaufitz and Katharine his wife, pl. John Stykker and Alice his wife, def. The manor of Monehalle. Def. quitclaimed to pl. and the heirs of Thomas . Cons. 100 marks.*

By 1414 William Winslow had emerged as sole heir to an estate larger than his mother Mary's ample Crouchman inheritance thanks to the acquisition of Wood Hall. When William aged in his mid-twenties makes his will in 1415, he is already recorded as *Armiger,* a title that not assumed by his father John *Maunciple* nor his uncle William *Pavilioner* until they were twice his age. Recognising the ultimate entitlement of John Huntingdon to the residue of the Crouchman estate in the event of the Winslow line dying out, William makes the following bequest to his wife:

> *I bequeath also and give to Agnes my very beloved wife all my lands and tenements, which I have in the vill and fields of Thriplowe in the county of Cambridge with all their appurtenances whatsoever, and all other my lands and tenements whatsoever, which I have in fee simple in the county of Essex or elsewhere wheresoever.*

Later in his will he gives direction about the Ashdon Manor holding and refers to the Huntingdons:

> *I also further ask and request by these presents that my abovesaid very beloved kinsman John Huntyngdon, my next heir after the heirs of my body lawfully begotten, both in making a favourable gift to my said wife in the manors of Thriplowe, abovesaid, and also in the manor of Assheton, in which I similarly have my estate, by the payments of all my debts, and also in fulfilling a happy conclusion upon the declarations of my last will...*

The preliminary draft of William's will had been prepared the previous autumn by his highly-connected father-in-law, Sir John Tibbay, Exchequer to dowager queen Joan, King Henry V's stepmother.

> *which I disposed of according to an oath, taken by me to my said lord John de Tibbay, in a certain declaration of my last will to my abovesaid wife*

---

[44] *Essex Feet of Fines vol. 3, 1414, p. 262, entry 18*

Edward Winslow's English Origins

For William, following the early loss of both his parents, Sir John was possibly an important stabilising force. William's preliminary will was drafted presumably on Sir John's professional advice in anticipation of William's planned expedition to the French Campaign in Normandy the following year.

But then disaster strikes. Sir John is murdered: *Squire Nyauncer and his men slew Master John Tibbay as he passed through Lad Lane.* William's published will was eventually handled by Sir John's son, Thomas:

> *I appoint as executors lord Thomas de Tibbay, clerk, and the aforesaid Agnes my very beloved wife, whom I ask to expend favour to the aforesaid Richard, my uncle, as regards his maintenance, and love equally. ...in testimony of which matter, to these presents I have affixed my seal. Dated at London on the 6th day of July in the year of the lord 1415 in the third year of the reign of our lord king, abovesaid.*

So what is the significance of the Beaufeus' acquisition of *Monehalle* in Stambourne? These days Moone Hall still exists. As for Stambourne's location, the village is situated about three miles from the extensive Winslow residence of Wood Hall acquired by John Winslow in 1399. Wood Hall, now *Shore Hall*, is a statement both of achievement and of aspiration, a supplementary trophy house for an ambitious Winslow family about embark on their next stage of their social advancement following a successful commercial and military career. We have already seen that at least one other Winslow in addition to William's *uncle Richard* had developed social interactions within the area, with Edmund Winslow acting as a juror in the enquiry held on Richard de Vere, Earl of Oxford, at nearby Wimbish in 1411. We also saw that Walter Crouchman had earlier been active in the area while Sir William held the manor.

Can we therefore speculate that the Beaufeus are preparing to move into the area in the autumn of 1414 to help with the administration of the Winslow estate ahead of William's planned departure for the French campaign? Perhaps so; after all, the Winslows and Beaufeus had been close friends, neighbours and colleagues for more than a century, and *Thomas Beaufitz and Katharine his wife* are paying the considerable sum of 100 marks for the Stambourne property.

But then disaster strikes again. *Dated at London on the 6th day of July in the year of the lord 1415...* The ink on William's last will and testament is barely dry before William Winslow Armiger dies on August 31st from the infection sweeping though the English military camp in Harfleur. Worse follows for William's wife Agnes; the stipulations of William's will are challenged, and perhaps justifiably.[45] A subsequent document, also undated, *enfeoffed Sir William de la Pole, knight, William Alynton, Esq., John Burgoyn, William Godrede the younger, Nicholas*

---

[45] *Early Chancery Proceedings, B 7/48, 15 Richard II-10 Henry VI.*

Calcote and John Huntyngton to perform his will, namely, to enfeoff Agnes of the manor for life,[46] but evidently Caldecote refused to comply.

In view of the tortuous sequence of legal events following the death of Sir William Crouchman in 1351, the death of William must also have set alarm bells ringing. William's ultimate heir was his daughter Agnes; but she was a minor with interests requiring protection in law. Her status was bound to lead to legal complications, and it duly did so.

Thomas Beaufitz and Katharine his wife evidently heard the bad news about their kinsman's death. How did they react? With considerable haste. Around the time that the news of William's death reached England in late summer or early autumn in 1415, Thomas and Katherine were planning the disposal of their new acquisition, Moone Hall.

> 47. *Trin. and Mich . William Edsale, Thomas Clerk and Robert Portman, pl. Thomas Beaufitz and Katharine his wife, def. The manor of Monehalle. Def. quitclaimed to pl. and the heirs of Robert. Cons. 100 marks.*

The timing of the Beaufitz property sale so soon after its acquisition points strongly to a perception that no benefit would accrue from their remaining in place with the likely ensuing turmoil. Their judgment was probably correct: the events that followed included a disputed will, the eventual pronouncement of the legal status in 1420, and unsubtle attempts to deprive widow Agnes Winslow of an entitlement.

On the Crouchman side of the family, Joan's grandmother Mariota had survived to inherit, but died in her middle years aged around 40. Mariota's son William died prematurely in his mid-twenties. William's grandfather William C4 had survived long enough to become heir but died still a minor, just like his brother John C2 before him. John's natural son and heir William C3 barely survived beyond the death of his father, dying little older than an infant, and without the inheritance to which he was entitled. A premature death for young Joan was predictable.

The Beaufeu family, close and enduring friends of both the Crouchmans and the Winslows, may have been aware of both families' histories. Their decision to move away was vindicated by what happened next. Joan's interests in Wincelowe Hall and Wood Hall were protected by taking both properties into the King's hands thanks to the intervention of deputy Treasurer William Kynwolmershhe, as set out on page 19 above. Later in 1426 after the death of Joan, a new order is delivered.

> *The king has taken fealty of John Huntyngdon the son of Elizabeth the sister of William [C4] the father of the aforesaid Mary, and John Huntyngdon is of full age. Seisin of the Crouchman family acres and properties comprising Wood Hall in Finchingfield and Great Sampford, the tenement called Crouchmans in Hampstede, and the wood called Spains Wood also in Finchingfield therefore passes irrevocably to John Huntyngdon.*

---

[46] *Early Chancery Proceedings, B 7/49, 15 Richard II-10 Henry VI.*

Edward Winslow's English Origins

Any ambition that the Beaufitz family may have held to support their kinsman William Winslow *Armiger* has been extinguished, and the sizeable Winslow family fortune centred on Hempstead that John Winslow *Maunciple* had laboured so hard to develop and retain has been swept away.

William Winslow, Chaplain, Entries 1397-1414

William Winslow *Chaplain,* husband to *Agnes Poure* probably died in 1414. His year of birth cannot be determined with certainty, but the location and nature of his work offer helpful pointers.

William had acted as executor in the *Bytterlegh* case and displeased Archbishop Courtenay in doing so. The Archbishop responded by excommunicating Winslow for *contumacy.* Winslow retaliated by escalating the matter over the heads of Archbishop and the King direct to the Pope's court in Rome in 1397.[47] We characterised William's action as demonstrating *remarkable self-assurance for a provincial chaplain,* an observation suggesting that he was already a mature and experienced lawyer.

One of William's two mainpernors in the *Bytterlegh* controversy had been *John Carbenall of London 'goldsmyth'.* By 1397 the Carbonels were evidently a wealthy and successful family with extensive property interests centred on London and Norfolk. But like the Winslows they had also been Buckinghamshire landowners from early times, with two adjacent manors located barely three miles from the town of Winslow: Addington since at least 1198, and North Marston since 1284. This timespan coincides with the period of the Winslow family's residency in Buckinghamshire.

Evidently the Carbonels had other connections similar to the Winslows. We also saw earlier that William Winslow *Chaplain* was involved in a substantial property acquisition *concerning to certain tenements in New Sarum.* On examination it turns out that John Carbonel had been investing in adjacent property at the heart of Salisbury town located in close proximity, as this report from 1406 confirms:[48]

> John Houton to John Chitterne clerk, his heirs and assigns. Charter of a corner tenement in the city of New Sarum called 'Canevasserescorner' with two cottages on the west side thereof, situate between the churchyard stile of St. Thomas on the west and a tenement of Richard Oward on the south, the grantor with John Carbonel and John Gilberd, both now deceased.. Dated New Sarum, 4 January 7 Henry IV.

First we have John Carbonel acting as William's mainpernor, then we find that they share ancestral roots going back at least a hundred years, and also enjoy overlapping commercial interests. On the balance of evidence, William Winslow's ancestral descent is more likely to have originated within the Buckinghamshire

---

[47] *Cal. Close, Richard ii, vol. 6, 1396-99, p. 133*
[48] *Cal. Close, Henry iv, vol. 3, 1405-1409, p. 87*

Winslows rather than through any other ancestry such as the Wensleys of Yorkshire.

Robert Andrew

William Winslow *Chaplain* had been working with fellow lawyer Robert Andrew from February 1410 until William's death in 1414-15. After William's death, Robert Andrew married William's widow Agnes Poure, and so became stepfather to Thomas Winslow *Alnwick*. The Tropenell Cartulary depicts Robert Andrew as exploitative, describing him as *acting with great malice* in his dealings with a William Rous.[49] Was Andrew seeking to discredit the Winslow family after the death of William Winslow *Chaplain,* cementing his own reputation at the late William's expense? Robert Andrew serves in an enquiry about concealments in 1415:[50]

> *February 8 Westminster. Commission to William Beauchamp of Poywyk, 'Chevaler', John Russell, Robert Andrewe, John Wyke and John Derehurst to enquire into the report that divers land, rents, services and other possessions in the county of Gloucester and wards, marriages, reliefs and escheats which should pertain to Henry IV and Queen Joan of England in his lifetime have been concealed from them and from her and the king.*

The financial adviser and custodian of Queen Joan's assets at the time of this controversy had of course been Sir John Tibbay, father-in-law of William Winslow *Armiger*, and Sir John had recently been murdered in the streets in London. Was Andrew trying to undermine Sir John Tibbay's reputation? This Sir Walter Beauchamp fronting the commission would serve three terms as a justice of the peace for Wiltshire between 1410 and his eventual death in 1430,[51] and he collaborated with Wiltshire-based Robert Andrew as witness on Wiltshire property transactions, the first in Bewley on 28 November 1415,[52] and the other in *Hulle Deverell co. Wiltesir* in May 1417, but formally reported only in 1421.[53]

The initiator of this enquiry is not identified. A further commission involving both men is reported in June 1416 relating to dilapidations in Wiltshire.[54] Andrew appears alone in an estate enquiry in Hampshire in January 1415,[55] but acts as a witness in the company of Walter Beauchamp in Wiltshire in October 1415.[56]

With Sir Walter absent on campaign in France, Robert Andrew's focus was mainly on Wiltshire, with an enquiry concerning John Oldcastle in February 1418,[57] a

---

[49] So Tropenell Cartulary, vol. 1, pp. 406-7, 294-5,317-8
[50] Cal. Pat., Henry v, vol. 1, 1413-16, p. 224
[51] Hist. Parl, vol. 2, pp. 158-160
[52] Cal. Close, Henry v, vol. 1, 1413-9, p. 292
[53] Cal. Close, Henry v, vol. 3, 14219-22, p. 129
[54] Cal. Pat., Henry v, 1416-22, p. 76
[55] Cal. Close, Henry v, vol. 1, 1413-9, p. 151
[56] Cal. Close, Henry v, vol. 1, 1413-9, p. 292
[57] Cal. Pat., Henry v, vol. 2, 1416-22, p. 322

property transaction in Wiltshire in March 1418[58] followed by nomination to a commission of array relating to defence against potential invasion in March and November 1419.[59] The Oldcastle controversy also touched the Winslows because William Winslow *Armiger* on his death in 1415 was renting property from Oldcastle in Little Radwinter.

The same month an inquisition takes place about a property in Wiltshire.[60] Andrew joins a commission in June 1420 to reopen the Gloucester concealment enquiry,[61] reconvened in April 1421.[62]

November 1421 sees Andrew and his wife Agnes Poure describe as *of Wiltshire* in a quitclaim.[63] Andrew is created a Commissioner of the Peace for Wiltshire in February and June 1422.[64] By May 1421, and after the return to England of Walter Beauchamp, both men are witnesses to a quitclaim in Hulle Deverell, Wiltshire.[65] Again Andrew does not follow the Beauchamps to France.

Robert Andrew's name is missing from the 1423 settlement of the Earl's property spanning Buckinghamshire, Staffordshire, Northamptonshire and Worcestershire. The name of *John Throkmarton* appears alongside *John Barton* as deforciants. The scale of the Earl's interests in areas like salt production is evidently considerable:[66]

> *14 salt-works, 37 salt-pans and salt-vats, a certain brine-pit, salt-pan and salt-vat called Shirreuesputte*

The names of Robert Andrew and Sir Walter Beauchamp appear again together in 1425 in the document settling into trust Richard Earl of Warwick's considerable estate straddling eight counties. This time the names of the Earl's principal legal team, Throckmorton, Andrew and Wollashill, are prominent. Sir Walter is presumably included because of his trusted status and seniority within the extended Beauchamp family following the death of Walter's elder brother Sir William in 1421.[67]

> *Henry, bishop of Winchester, Thomas, bishop of Durham, Philip, bishop of Worcester, John, bishop of Bath and Wells, William Babyngton', Walter Beauchamp', knight, William Mountfort, knight, John Baysham, clerk, John Verney, clerk, John Thomas, clerk, Robert Andrewe, John Throkmarton' and William Wollashill', querents, and Richard, earl of Warwick, deforciant.*

---

[58] *Cal. Close, Henry v, vol. 1, 1413-9, p. 458*
[59] *Cal. Pat., Henry v, vol. 2, 1416-22, pp. 209, 251*
[60] *Cal. Pat., Henry v, vol. 2, 1416-22, p. 273*
[61] *Cal. Pat., Henry v, vol. 2, 1416-22, p. 320*
[62] *Cal. Pat., Henry v, vol. 2, 1416-22, p. 384*
[63] *Cal. Close, Henry v, vol. 2, 1419-22, pp. 195-6*
[64] *Cal. Pat., Henry v, vol. 2, 1416-22, p. 461*
[65] *Cal. Close, Henry v. vol. 2, 1419-22, p. 129*
[66] *Feet of Fines, CP 25/1/291/65, no. 15*
[67] *Feet of Fines CP 25/1/291/65, number 44*

The manor of *Beroughdon* or Barrowden where Richard Winslow was operating in the 1290s is included, whereas the Earldom's Warwickshire manor of Berkeswell where William Winslow *Wodyam* was based between 1330 and 1348-9 appears in the subsequent, more wide-ranging settlement of the Earldom's properties in 1450-60.[68]

We can speculate that the Winslows as a family had been associated with the Earls of Warwick since at least the thirteenth century. From the evidence as reported in *Gesta*, the Abbey's relationship with the Warwicks was one of relative indifference, with a single reference to the Beauchamp family found in the first two volumes of *Gesta* when *Simon de Bello Campo* is acknowledged as a benefactor of St Julian's leper hospital under Abbot Geoffrey between 1119 and 1146.[69] By contrast, Volume 3 has eight entries from Abbot Thomas's time between 1349 and 1396, signalling a change maintained in Thomas Walsingham's follow-up work after *Gesta*, his *Chronicon*.[70]

After the election of Abbot John of Wheathampstead in 1420 reported in *Chronicon,* the Earl of Warwick is received with honour on his return from campaign in Paris in 1428.[71] At the start of May the same year, Richard Earl of Warwick and his wife Isabella are admitted to the Fraternity of St. Albans. Even Henry de Bello Campo, *son and heir of the Earl of Warwick* is admitted, barely three years old.[72] Included in a large throng of associates, *aliis quamplurimis*, are some *illustrious men and women devoted to the monastery.*

The History of Parliament records the admission as taking place in 1425, and reports that the entourage included both John Throckmorton and Robert Andrew, but without citing its sources. *Chronicon* contains no specific reference to either man.[73] Whatever the truth, it can be demonstrated that the circle comprising John Throckmorton and Robert Andrew was ingratiating itself with the Earls of Warwick.

Meanwhile Robert Andrew is again involved in the Gloucester concealments enquiry, but by now its scope has expanded to cover Wiltshire and Somerset.[74] By 1424 Andrew is appointed keeper of a forest in Wiltshire,[75] and in 1426 he is raising funds for the King as appointee for Wiltshire.[76] In 1429 Andrew is working on a commission with the Earl of Warwick about the theft of grain from a ship on the river Severn.[77] Andrew is again created a Commissioner of the Peace for Wiltshire

---

[68] *Feet of Fines CP/25/1/294/74 no. 41*
[69] *Gesta v. 1, p. 77*
[70] *Chronicon Rerum Gestarum in Monasterio Sancti Albani, vol. 1, 1422-31, Ed. Riley, Longmans Green, 1870*
[71] *Chronicon, vol. 1, p. 20*
[72] *Chronicon, vol. 1, p. 67*
[73] *Chronicon, vol. 1, p. 67*
[74] *Cal. Pat., Henry vi, vol. 1,1422-9, p. 36*
[75] *Cal. Pat., Henry vi, vol. 1, 1422-9, p. 213*
[76] *Cal. Pat., Henry vi, vol. 1, 1422-9, p. 354*
[77] *Cal. Pat., Henry vi, vol. 1,1422-9, p. 551*

Edward Winslow's English Origins

in all five sessions between 1423 and 1428,[78] presumably with support from the Earl.

From the evidence located, Sir Walter and Sir William Beauchamp are initially seen functioning alongside Robert Andrew in their judicial capacity, but he is not acting as their legal representative because the focus of his attention is his work for the Earls of Warwick through Throckmorton.

Eventually Robert Andrew dies on April 13 1437.[79] His will mentions his wife Agnes as one of his executors, but without specific reference to his stepson Thomas Winslow. Thomas first appears that September as administrator of his mother's interest in Wantyng Bryan.[80] Thomas Winslow *Alnwick* would later marry one of Throckmorton's daughters.

Walter and William Beauchamp

The Beauchamps are a family interesting for a study of the Winslows. Sir Walter Beauchamp in Rouen was second son of Sir John Beauchamp who died around 1389. After the successful siege of Rouen, Sir Walter Beauchamp was appointed *bailli* of the town where he resided there until January 1421.[81] He reappeared in England as a witness to a Wiltshire quitclaim in May 1421 with Robert Andrew,[82] and in a Wiltshire enquiry dated July the same year.[83] Thereafter his career in Royal circles in England advanced rapidly, and by April 1429 Sir Walter was appointed Master of the King's Horse. He died shortly afterwards in 1430.

Sir William Beauchamp, Walter's elder brother, was also campaigning in Normandy and received a commission from the King while based in Evreux.[84] William's son John Beauchamp was appointed joint administrator of the extensive inheritance from Richard de Beauchamp, 13th Earl of Warwick and the estate eventually passed to Henry de Beauchamp, 1st Duke of Warwick, after Earl Richard's death in May 1439.[85]

John Beauchamp, well rewarded for his work,[86] and he was also made Master of the King's Horse, and later in 1445 a Knight of the Garter. He had already served in a number of public offices including Commissioner of the Peace six times between November 1439 and July 1441,[87] and again in February 1446.[88] 1446 marked the death of Duke Henry de Beauchamp aged barely 21, leaving his daughter Anne a

---

[78] *Cal. Pat., Henry v, vol. 2, 1416-22, p. 571-2*
[79] *Nat. Archives online, PCC ref. PROB 11/3/409*
[80] *Nat. Archives online, ref. C 146/5530*
[81] *J.S. Roskell, Three Wilts. Speakers, Wilts. Arch. Mag. lvi. 342-58.*
[82] *Cal. Close, Henry v, vol. 2, 1419-22, p. 129*
[83] *Cal. Pat., Henry v, vol. 2 1416-22, p. 389*
[84] *Rymer's, April 1419, vol. 9, pp.591-99 QQQ*
[85] *Cal. Pat., Henry vi, vol. 3, 1436-41, p. 279*
[86] *Cal. Pat., Henry vi, vol. 3, 1436-41, p. 284, p. 435, p. 516*
[87] *Cal. Pat., Henry vi, vol. 3, 1436-41, p. 583*
[88] *Cal. Pat., Henry vi, vol. 4, 1441-46, pp. 480-1*

## Edward Winslow's English Origins

two-year-old infant. In April 1448 John is addressed as *John Beauchamp knight lord of Powyk*,[89] while a reference in a quitclaim from July 1453 provides Lord John Beauchamp's ancestry:[90]

> *John Beauchamp lord Beauchamp knight, son of William son of John son of Giles Beauchamp, his heirs and assigns. Quitclaim.. Dated 25 June 31 Henry VI.*

In 1462 Sir John Beauchamp is permanently excused future public service:[91]

> *Exemption for life of John Beauchamp, Knight, Lord of Beauchamp, on account of his old age and debility, from attendance in council or Parliament, and from being made collector, assessor or taxer of tenths, fifteenths or other subsidy, Commissioner, Justice of the peace, constable, Bailiff or minister of the king, or trier, arrayer, musterer or all leader men at arms, archers or hobelers.*

Despite this exemption, John Beauchamp was appointed to commissions of peace and array five times between 1462 and 1464.[92] Lord Beauchamp lived on until 1475 and survived the political turmoil of the War of the Roses. On his death he was succeeded by Richard Beauchamp, 2nd Baron Beauchamp of Powick, who died in January 1503. Richard's son Sir John Beauchamp had already predeceased him, leaving his three daughters as co-heirs of his estate.

This extract from the inquest indicates that Richard died in debt to the king:[93]

> *861. Richard Beauchamp, Knight, Lord of Beauchamp. Writ of mandamus, 14th of October, Inquisition 21 November, 20 Henry seventh*
>
> *He was seised of the undermentioned moiety of a manor and alternate presentation to the church thereof, and, being so seised, by charter gave them to Richard Pole and Giles Bregges, Knight, to hold to them and their heirs, by virtue of which they were seised thereof in fee, and being so seised, by charter gave them to John Mordaunt, since deceased, and Thomas Lovell, James Hobart, Richard Empson, knights, and Thomas Lucas, esquire, who survive, to hold to them and their heirs for security of a certain sum to be paid to the king, for the debt of the said Richard Beauchamp, from the issues and profits of the said moiety to the king's use to be received. The said Thomas, John, James, Richard and Thomas, were seised thereof accordingly in form aforesaid; and afterwards the said Richard Beauchamp died, and afterwards the said John Mordaunt died and the others continued their possession and are still seised thereof by survivorship.*

Notable in this 1504 list is the name *John Mordaunt*, *since deceased* whose family later intermarried with the Huntingdons, successors to the Crouchmans and Winslows in Hempstead. The *Mordaunt* family would eventually take over the Crouchman / Winslow Hall and the Wood Hall estates of John Winslow *Maunciple*, reasserting the circularity of the Winslow world.

---

[89] *Cal. Close, Henry vi, vol. 5, 1447-54, p. 51*
[90] *Cal. Close Henry vi, vol. 5, 1447-54, p. 445*
[91] *Cal. Pat., Edward iv, vol. 1, 1461-67, p. 213*
[92] *Cal. Pat., Edward iv, 1461-67, p. 564*
[93] *Cal. Inq. p.m. Henry vii, vol. 2, 1503, p. 551*

Edward Winslow's English Origins

The reasons for covering Walter and William Beauchamp in detail here will become apparent in Chapter 5 and will continue in the next volume.

Thomas Winslow *Alnwick*

Chapter 3 noted Robert Hill's swift rise to recognition from virtual obscurity, and similar success was achieved by Thomas Winslow *Alnwick*, son of William Winslow *Chaplain*. Thomas's rise to prominence is in some ways is even more remarkable than his father's, and is covered in the next volume. Meanwhile, we have another John Winslow, this time the John Winslow emerging to prominence in Southampton.

John Winslow *Soton*

The first reference located for John Winslow *Soton* in Chapter 3 describes him as a *clerk*, suggesting that John has received a sound education. It took until 1410 for William Winslow to advance to the style of *clericus*. Maybe this indicates that John is already a senior and proficient administrator, and explains his commission in April 1415 organising payments on behalf of the crown ahead of the planned invasion of France.[94]

> *April 11 Westminster. Commission to John Wynslawe, clerk, to make payments to all masters and owners of ships another vessels seized by Nicholas Mauduyt, Serjeant at Arms, by indentures testifying the payments and the place and day.*

The same day, another entry records *Serjeant at Arms* Nicholas Mauduyt's activities:

> *April 11. The K. orders Nicholas Mauduyt and Robert Spellowe, sergeants-at-arms, to arrest ships of 20 tons and upwards, and bring them to Winchelsea, London, or Sandwich*

Evidently this John Winslow occupies a position of authority. The last Winslow connected with the maritime industry and military logistics had been William Winslow *Pavilioner,* exonerated from blame after the loss of the king's military equipment in the storm off Calais in 1396. The naval and military activities here strongly suggest a connection, and we can assume with reasonable certainty that John Winslow *Soton* is the son of William Winslow *Pavilioner.*

The following year John is found on the South Coast of England at Southampton operating as paymaster to both the military and the navy:[95]

> *May 3 1416, Westminster. Commission to John Wynslawe, clerk, and Henry Bromley, Serjeant at arms, to supervise the muster at Southampton at the King's kinsman John, Earl of Huntingdon, and other men at arms and archers of his retinue and the master mariners of the ships and other vessels in his company going on the King's service to sea, and to certify thereon to the King and Council, and to the said John to make payment of the wages*

---

[94] *Cal. Pat., Henry v, vol. 1, 1413-6, p. 342*
[95] *Cal. Pat., Henry v, vol. 2, 1416-22, p. 71*

of the masters and mariners of the ships and vessels seized in the said port for the shipment of the Earl and his retinue the 47 days with reward for six weeks.

A subsequent entry from May 1 authorises *John Wynslowe* to provide additional funding, and in July 1416 the king issues further instructions out of Southampton:[96]

Commission to the King's kinsman Ralph, earl of Westmoreland, William Darell, esquire, John Wynslowe, and Henry Maunsell to arrest John Langton, esquire, Thomas Shepherd of Heslyngton and John Shepherd of Heslington without delay and bring them before the king in Chancery.

By August 5 John Winslow and John Knyght receive instructions to assemble all available boats and to head with haste to Dover.[97] John Winslow is emerging as a trusted member of the royal household like the *Pavilioner* before him.

Rymer's Foedera provides the next references to John Winslow who by now has transferred to the French mainland. A sizeable English expeditionary force estimated by Jonathan Sumption to number as many as ten thousand troops[98] is assembling around Pont de L'Arche ahead of the planned siege of Rouen in 1419. An announcement is addressed to the *King's dearest uncle, the Earl of Exeter* and to the *Chancellor of the Dukedom of Normandy, Master Philip Morgan*. A report from in June 1418[99] places John Winslow with Sir Walter Beauchamp, who had signed up for military service on 8 Feb. 1417.[100]

Pro Waltero Beauchamp & Roberto Whitgrene. Ad Capiendum ut supra, Johannis Rothenale, Roberti Babthorp, Radulphi Rocheford, Rogeri Fenys, Johannis Styward, Lodowici Robessard, Militum, Ac Johannis Cheyne, Nicholai Merbury, Willielmi Swynborn, Ricardi Wodevyle, Johannis Pyrent, et Johannis Wynslowe.

John's name appears in this list alongside several distinguished names. Is John acting for the two Beauchamp brothers William and Walter as some sort of retainer? John Winslow *Soton* is clearly proficient in military logistics, but he is also *clericus,* someone with a level of legal recognition only attained by his relative William Winslow *Chaplain* in his closing years.

Why is the significance of the Powick Estate? There is a strong likelihood that the Winslows moved to Worcester from the South of England in order to work for the Beauchamp family of Powick. Styled *clericus* and having previously appeared in the public record as a military administrator, we know that John Winslow *Soton* had been campaigning around Rouen in 1418 and that Winslow had been serving with Walter Beauchamp. William Beauchamp was involved in the same campaign. But what is the significance of Powick for the Winslows?

---

[96] *Cal. Pat., Henry v, vol. 2, 1416-22, p. 81*
[97] *Cal. Pat., Henry v, vol. 2, 1416-22, p. 79*
[98] *Sumption, Hundred Years War vol. 4, p. 562*
[99] *Rymer's Foedera, vol. 9, June 1418 pp. 596*
[100] *PRO, E101/70/1/579*

Edward Winslow's English Origins

Here is the area immediately north of Kempsey in Worcestershire, with the three circled areas located about a mile apart. At the bottom of the map on the left stands Beauchamp Court, seat of the Beauchamps of Powick, which is found above Beauchamp Court. Just across the river Severn, about a mile to the North East, stands Clerkenleap, the Winslows'

Figure 4-8 Clerkenleap, a mile from Beauchamp Court

eventual home in Worcestershire. About two miles to the south down the A38 we find the parish of Kempsey. And on whose land did their house stand? Fradd correctly attributes it to the Bishops of Worcester. And who was Bishop of Worcester in 1420? It was Master Philip Morgan, Chancellor of the Dukedom of Normandy, the same person with whom John Winslow and the Beauchamps of Powick had been campaigning in 1417-21.

There is strong evidence to support the view that the connection between Kempsey and the wider Winslow family originated through John Winslow *Soton*.

Edward Winslow's English Origins

5 Conclusion

By tracing the Winslow lineage back as far as the extant records allow, the Winslows emerge as a prosperous and respected family of status in Buckinghamshire, and their English origins stretch back presumably to the time before the Norman Conquest. Their close association with the Abbey of St. Albans suggests that they were literate and numerate from early generations. Brother William *Cellarer* and Walter *Muster* join the church, and both progress to important levels of seniority.

A thread that runs through the family and its social connections is expertise in matters of the Law. We find William Winslow *Patriarch* in 1313 assisting his neighbours the Doygnels with their property transaction in Wiltshire, and Richard Winslow *Barrowden* associated with legal matters in Rutland. Richard's associate John Baldwyn *Magister* is a coroner active in property transactions throughout Hertfordshire and Essex. Richard's son John *Bailiff* works in law enforcement in St. Albans, and later we find that he too is involved in administration of property transactions. John *Maunciple*, son of John *Bailiff*, falls foul of the Abbot of St. Albans over the controversy with the *Blakette* property transfer, and later he is also personally involved in property transactions initially around Cambridge but later more extensively in Essex, and challenging the legal authority of senior Justice Holt.

The grandfather of his wife Mary, Sir William Crouchman C1, has been a senior member of the judiciary. William Winslow *Chaplain* is clearly skilled in legal matters; we have seen his audacity following his excommunication, but then we also see him working with some of the most senior judges in the Royal Courts. Latterly he becomes son-in-law of another member of the judiciary, Sir Thomas Poure. This thread of legal connection is present in the family line from the earliest records examined. John Winslow *Soton* is a later member of the family described in 1415 as *clericus*.

Meantime Richard Winslow *Barrowden* from Rutland may latterly have been living in St. Albans with his son John *Bailiff* and grandson John *Maunciple* born around 1330, roughly the time when Richard himself was involved in the St. Albans Handmills dispute. It is unclear which if any Winslow family members remained in Swanbourne at this stage, because we can project that William *Wodyam* was probably moving his family to Barston around the same time as his father Walter *Muster* was contemplating his ecclesiastical vocation in Aldingbourne.

The difficulties start to emerge when Walter resigns his living in Sussex shortly before his death in 1346. His son William *Wodyam* has barely inherited his father's

Edward Winslow's English Origins

estate before he, his wife and perhaps other members of his family succumb to the Black Death in 1348-9. This can probably be seen as a most difficult episode for all the Winslows. Of the Winslow adults, we know that Thomas *Homicide* survives the pandemic along with the three Johns. If Wodyam's wife Alice was still of child-bearing age when she died, we can speculate she may have left young offspring who may not yet have even reached their adolescence, and they would have been Thomas's brothers and sisters.

We have no information about what happened to Geoffrey Winslow *Galfrid;* and we have three other Winslow offspring whose parentage we are so far unable to establish with certainty: Walter Winslow *Kimpton* with a single reference in 1368, William Winslow *Candlewick* active 1370-1400, and William Winslow *Chaplain,* active 1397-1414.

From his name we can speculate that Walter Winslow *Kimpton* may have been a younger son of Walter Winslow *Muster,* but we have no proof. With a normal 70 year lifespan we could expect William Winslow *Candlewick* to have been born around 1330, and he evidently served an apprentice before joining the gild of Tailors and taking up residence in London where he died in 1400. If he were only 60 years old when he died, his year of birth would have been around 1340. On the same basis we can argue that William Winslow *Chaplain* was born around 1345 if he lived a full lifespan; again we cannot be certain, although we pointed out that the senior workload he was carrying in 1396 when he appealed to the Pope suggests that by that date he was already accepted as a mature lawyer, possibly middle-aged.

These dates of birth become significant when we consider the impact of the Black Death in 1348-49, leading to the deaths of both William *Wodyam* and his wife, Alice; and leaving surviving offspring as orphans. This would explain why two subsequent events occur: John *Bailiff* and Thomas *Homicide* take the momentous decision to move together to the three dwellings in Hunsdon collectively known as *Winslows* and *Cott* around 1352, and the same year the two Johns move away to Little Horwood near Winslow. Perhaps the two John were freeing up accommodation for their younger relatives. After all, John *Bailiff* and Thomas *Homicide* would have been the surviving uncles to children otherwise homeless, in 1349 William Winslow *Candlewick* may have been serving his apprenticeship in London and in no position to offer practical assistance.

This leaves the broader Winslow family reunited in Hunsdon around Thomas *Homicide* and John *Bailiff* by 1352. John Winslow *Maunciple* may already have been committed to an apprenticeship in Cordwainer Ward in his quest to become a pepperer, explaining why he was so often fined for absence in the Winslow Manor Court. If this general principle of adoption is accepted, it may explain why the supposed two sons of John Winslow *Bailiff* shared the name *John;* perhaps they

Edward Winslow's English Origins

were actually cousins. John *Maunciple* emerges as heir to John Winslow *Bailiff* in 1375, and John *Hunsdon* may have been the child effectively adopted, perhaps descended from *Wodyam* or *Galfrid* or a different unidentified Winslow parent. The exact lineage is somewhat academic since the extended Winslow family was by now behaving as a single entity and residing in three conjoined Hunsdon family units. It is significant that in challenging times these Winslows chose to stick together, a presage of what was to come after 1620.

On the same principle of identical forenames applied to John *Maunciple* and John *Hunsdon*, the two William Winslows *Candlewick* and *Chaplain* probably did not share the same paternity. Given his legal career and the descent of the senior male line, William Winslow *Chaplain* may have been the son of *Wodyam;* while William Winslow *Candlewick* could have been the son of *Galfrid*. It is unlikely that *Candlewick* was son of Thomas Winslow *Homicide* because we are placing Thomas's birth around 1325, and William Winslow *Candlewick*'s around 1330.

We know that John Winslow *Bailiff* lives on in Hunsdon until his death, presumably in the run-up to 1375, placing him by that time in his late sixties or early seventies. 1375 is the year when John *Maunciple* moves to Hempstead, leaving John *Hunsdon* still in residence with Thomas *Homicide,* by now probably in his fifties.

Thomas's son William Winslow *Pavilioner* is still operating as a *Yeoman of the Chamber* and later as *Serjeant of the King's Pavilions,* and so we can assume he is based wherever royal service dictates. We also know that Thomas *Homicide* and John *Hunsdon* are still residing together in 1383 in the town of Hunsdon because Sir Robert Turk had dropped by to pay them a visit, and both are mentioned by name. We can guess that Thomas Winslow *Homicide* was dead by 1400. Based on the timings of some subsequent events discussed below, we can assume that after the attempt to take his own life with a *baselard* and his subsequent retirement, William Winslow *Pavilioner* possibly moved back to Hunsdon. Based on the progression of his military and naval career and timing of subsequent events we can also now propose with some certainty that John Winslow *Soton* is son of William Winslow *Pavilioner*.

Meanwhile John Winslow *Maunciple* has been extending the family estate in Hempstead with the additional space of the considerably larger Wood Hall, and has given up his commercial City life to join the military. Succession has been assured through the birth of John's son and heir, William Winslow *Armiger*. We also know that the extended Winslow family is operating in the vicinity of Crouchman and Wood Halls; Edmund Winslow appears as a juror in the enquiry on Richard de Vere, Earl of Oxford at nearby Wimbish in 1411, and Uncle Richard was evidently still living in Wood Hall while William Winslow *Armiger* was drawing up his will in 1415.

By now the Hempstead estate is taking on greater significance. We can deduce this from the fact that 1414 brings the sad news that William Winslow *Pavilioner* has died, and we can assume that William *Pavilioner* was heir to his father Thomas Winslow *Homicide* more than a decade earlier. From the *clericus* title applied to him in public records, we can assume that John *Soton* has inherited the broader Winslow intellectual gifts as well as the descent of the Winslow family heritage stretching back to Buckinghamshire.

By this time John Winslow *Soton* is following family tradition and involving himself in the imminent invasion of France as mentioned at the end of Chapter 4. A further connection can be made between John Winslow *Soton* and William Winslow *Pavilioner* based on the timing of a property disposal in Hunsdon in February 1416, shortly after the *Pavilioner* has died.[1] Of the Winslows' house comprising three units, this disposal related to *a third part of one messuage in Honesdon*. The transaction is dated *one week from the Purification of the Blessed Mary, 3 Henry [V]* [9 February 1416] and is likely the disposal of the Pavilioner's house there. The buyers are *John Goldyngton, esquire, and William Rokesburgh*, the same *John Goldyngton* who had been beneficiary of the transaction witnessed by John and Thomas Winslow in the company of Sir Robert Turk as far back as 1383.

John Winslow *Hunsdon* has been resident with Thomas *Homicide* and his brother John Winslow *Maunciple*, so the disposal of the Hunsdon property in 1416 probably also marks the conclusion of the family's links with the village. The timing of the disposal within two years of the *Pavilioner's* death and John Winslow *Soton's* preparation for the campaign in France from 1415 adds credibility to the proposition that by breaking the Hunsdon links, John Winslow *Soton* is planning a new life elsewhere. But the loss of Hunsdon also means that the only two centres for the Winslow family remaining in the South of England are the City of London and the ample Essex estate with its two large houses comprising Crouchmans and Wood Hall and their considerable landholding.

Everything seems set fair for the Winslow succession. William Winslow *Armiger* has lost his parents, gained a stepfather, lost a father-in-law to murder; but the Hempstead, Ashdon and Thriplow estates remain in good order. Elderly uncle Richard Winslow is in attendance as family support. From the text of his will written in July William Winslow *Armiger* evidently loves his wife and speaks warmly of his children, even though the evidence suggests that at this stage only a single child Joan is alive.

But then disaster strikes. At the end of August, William Winslow's premature death is reported, and everything starts to unravel with the inevitable sequence of legal disputes and controversy. The December 1419 conclusion of an inquest held in Saffron Walden reconfirms Joan's status as heiress:[2]

---

[1] *Feet of Fines CP/25/1/91/108 no. 20*
[2] *National Archives. 7 Henry V (1419-20), C 138/38/43*

The custody of the said 36 acres, etc., ought, by reason of Oldcastell's forfeiture for high treason and by reason of the minority of Joan, daughter and heir of William, to belong to the king, together with her custody and marriage. William Wynslowe died 31 Aug 3 Henry V (1415). Joan his daughter is his heir, aged 6 years on the feast of St. Barnabas Apostle last..

A follow-up in January 1420 talking of the various properties makes it clear that Joan remains heiress:[3]

[the 2 properties] ...came into the hands of the said king by the death of Mary and by reason of the minority of William Wynslowe her son and heir, likewise deceased, and are now in the king's hands, to hold during the minority of Joan the daughter and heiress of William, with her marriage without disparagement and so from heir to heir, paying 40l. in hand for the keeping and marriage if they be adjudged to the king, finding a competent maintenance for the heir, maintaining all houses, enclosures and buildings and supporting all other charges. By bill of William Kynwolmersshe, deputy treasurer

The inquests rumble on until we jump to 1426: now it is even worse. Joan Winslow has died as well, and without successors.

Writ 3 August 1426, on the death of Joan (a minor in the King's custody), daughter and heir of William Wynslowe, son and heir of Mary, who was wife of Thomas Holgill, deceased, who held of the heir of Aubrey de Veer, late Earl of Oxford, late within age and in the custody of the late King Henry IV, by knight's service, which William lately while he was within age and in the custody of Henry V, died, and which land, by the death of Mary and by reason of the minority of the said William, came into the hands of Henry IV.

Walter Huntyngdon is her kinsman and heir since she died without issue. He is the son of John Huntyngdon, son of Elizabeth, sister of William father of the said Mary, and is aged 24 years

Under the terms of her grandmother's marriage settlement of 1375, the estate will pass out of Winslow hands through Elizabeth Huntingdon, sister to William C4, Joan's great-grandfather, the Huntingdons, leaving the Huntingdons in charge.[4]

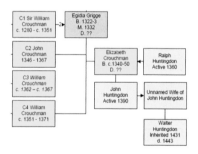

While all this has been playing out and after the disposal of the Hunsdon property in 1416, John Winslow *Soton* has followed the Beauchamps to the campaign in Rouen where they would reside until January 1421.

Figure 5-1 Decent to the Huntingdons

We know from Chapter 4 that Sir William Beauchamp, Walter's elder brother died in 1421, whereas Walter Beauchamp goes on to play a leading role as steward of the queen's household by March 1422, and later in managing the sequence of

---

[3] *Cal. Pat., Henry v., vol. 2, 1416-22, p. 254*
[4] *Chancery Inq. P.M. 5 Henry vi, 1426-7, No. 7, File 27*

Edward Winslow's English Origins

events following the sickness and death of King Henry V. The Beauchamps were already heavily committed to public duties. Little wonder that they would need help from someone they could trust.

Walter Beauchamp was next appointed an executor of the King's will and put in charge of the dower lands of the late King's widow Katherine, a role similar to the role filled a decade previously by Sir John Tibbay, father-in-law of John Winslow's cousin William *Armiger*. This was a period of intense administrative activity for Walter Beauchamp and we can justifiably speculate that as an acknowledged *clericus* John Winslow *Soton* may have been assisting him in some capacity.

Such an arrangement would have been mutually beneficial because by 1431 the Winslows previously of Essex and Hertfordshire were effectively homeless. Where does a large family group with no established domicile go next? The answer is *elsewhere*. By now, John Winslow *Soton* was connected with Walter Beauchamp of Powick, and the village adjacent to Powick is where Fradd independently places the Winslows by 1432. This cannot have been an accident. There is additional compelling evidence to be explored in Volume 2 further supporting the probability that the Winslows of Kempsey were the continuation of the Essex and Hertfordshire Winslow families of 1415.

Volume 2 will further explore the many other family relationships such as between the Essex Winslows and their cousin Edward Winslow *Alnwick,* and the interactions the Throckmorton and Robert Andrew, the Beauchamps and the Earls of Warwick, set to become Dukes of Warwick. Within thirty years the Houses of Lancaster and York will be at war. It is a tumultuous time in English History during which we can understand why the Winslows went to Worcestershire and explore the circumstances that eventually caused Edward Winslow to leave Droitwich and move back South. There are other strange Winslow coincidences to explore, such as parallels in Clifton fields names reminiscent of the Kerswell / Careswell practice.

The overall conclusion for this first volume is that John Winslow *Soton* entered the service of the Beauchamps of Powick following his satisfactory service ahead of the French campaign in 1415, and later in Rouen. The next volume of this work covering the events after 1432. A more extended Winslow family chart will be presented taking account of Thomas Winslow *Alnwick's* namesake, Thomas Winslow *LondonMP*, and track the parallel activities of the Winslow family in Worcestershire and London to explain why Edward Winslow Sr. of Droitwich chose to marry Magdalene Oliver so far away from Worcestershire in St Brides Church, London in 1594.

The one certainty about the Winslows' story is that it is much easier to understand when the primary historical records have been verified and corrected; and their fascinating history is never dull. What a remarkable family indeed...

6   Appendices

6.1   Two Winslow Wills: William W Armiger, John W Chesham

Will of William Wynslowe, Esquire, PROB 11/2B/94. Proved March 1416.

This translation from the Latin original does not reflect possible manual deletions or corrections in the face of the will, and the impact of these has not been quantified. The copy was obtained from the Public Record Office / National Archives. The cover sheet reference is given as *Catalogue reference:prob/11/2B* with *image reference 66*. The note in the margin specifies *Willm Wynslowe armiger*.

In the name of God, Amen, I, William Wynslowe, esquire, at present on a voyage of the most excellent leader and our lord king Henry V towards the parts of France or elsewhere at his pleasure, being about to cross to the lord duke, make my testament in this manner. Namely, first of all, I subject my body and soul to the disposition and mercy of omnipotent God, in whose hands at every moment is the death and life of all living things. Secondly, in case God the most high arranges that I die on the same voyage, I will and bequeath to the fabric fund of the church of Hempstede 20s, once my debts have been first of all paid. I bequeath also and give to Agnes my very beloved wife all my lands and tenements, which I have in the vill and fields of Thriplowe in the county of Cambridge with all their appurtenances whatsoever, and all other my lands and tenements whatsoever, which I have in fee simple in the county of Essex or elsewhere wheresoever. To have and to hold to my same wife all the aforesaid lands and tenements, which I so have in fee simple, wherever they lie, during the life of the same Agnes my wife, and after her decease to remain to my right heirs. Item, I bequeath to my same wife one red and white bed of scattered worsted, containing a canopy of an entire tester, with curtains, one mattress, two blankets, one fine 'quilepoint'. Item, I bequeath to Richard Wynslowe, my uncle, in part of his maintenance 40s. The rest, indeed, of my goods, my debts having been paid in full, as is aforesaid, is to be disposed of more salubriously for the salvation of my soul according to the discretion of my executors. Moreover, of this my testament I appoint as executors lord Thomas de Tibbay, clerk, and the aforesaid Agnes my very beloved wife, whom I ask to expend favour to the aforesaid Richard, my uncle, as regards his maintenance, and love equally. In testimony of which matter, to these presents I have affixed my seal. Dated at London on the 6th day of July in the year of the lord 1415 in the third year of the reign of our lord king, abovesaid.

In addition, I, the within written William Wynslowe, on account of the deep love, which I bear to the within named Agnes my wife, ask and request that any feoffees in the manor of Thriplowe and especially John Huntyngton, my very beloved kinsman, that, notwithstanding the cancellation of the gift of the same manor made in the present

Edward Winslow's English Origins

testament, they permit my same wife to have and enjoy all and singular the rents and profits thereupon issuing after the date of this testament, both for her maintenance and that of my children, being in her governance, and also for my paying my debts, if any remain beyond this maintenance, until £28, which I had in exchange from the overseers and executors of lord John de Tibbay, deceased, be fully paid to the same men, and until my same wife will be peacefully in possession of all the lands and tenements, which I disposed of according to an oath, taken by me to my said lord John de Tibbay, in a certain declaration of my last will to my abovesaid wife. Also I will and request the aforesaid feoffees and especially the aforesaid John Huntyngdon, that, after my debts are paid and my last will completed, just as in the aforesaid declaration is more fully contained, Richard Wynslowe, my very beloved uncle, shall have for his life per annum, if it can be so done, and otherwise during the minority of my heir, 40s in maintenance of his estate, but in such a way that he lives with my said wife as along as she is unmarried after my decease, if it happens me to decease on the present voyage at the disposition of God. I also further ask and request by these presents that my abovesaid very beloved kinsman John Huntyngdon, my next heir after the heirs of my body lawfully begotten, both in making a favourable gift to my said wife in the manors of Thriplowe, abovesaid, and also in the manor of Assheton, in which I similarly have my estate, by the payments of all my debts, and also in fulfilling a happy conclusion upon the declarations of my last will, just as he wants to answer before the highest judge in judgment, that he does not impede or cause anyone to impede any of my feoffees with him to impede my executors to fulfil my last will, because to that end and intention they had estate in the abovesaid manors, and God does not know otherwise.

The testament and codicil, above written, were proved before Master Jo: S., commissary, etc., on the 23rd day of the month of May in the year of the lord 1416, and there was committed the administration to the executors, named in the same will, etc., a bodily oath having been first of all taken by the same, etc. He paid nothing for a fine, because he owed, etc.

Will & Codicil of John Wynselowe, PROB 11/3/31, Proved November 1423

In the name of God Amen. I, John Wynselowe, citizen and Draper of London, (of) sound mind, and in good memory being, (on) the Twelfth day of the month of July (in) the Year of (our) Lord the One Thousandth 400th (&) twenty-third, and (in) the Year of the Reign of King Henry the Sixth, after the conquest, the first, compose, make, and appoint my testament in this manner: Firstly, I bequeath and commend my soul (to) god almighty, my creator and saviour, and (to) the blessed virgin Mary, his mother, and (to) all saints, and my body to be buried where God will dispose; Likewise, I bequeath (to) the fabric of the church of Chesham 40 shillings; Likewise, I bequeath (to) that church where my body will happen to be buried, 6 shillings 8 pence; the Residue, truly, of all of the goods and chattels, and debts, wheresoever being, I give and bequeath wholly (to) my Executors below-written, towards paying all and singular debts which (to) anyone by law I am held or owe, towards safeguarding and furnishing (to) Philippa, my wife, for her entire life, who now lies sick & weak, nourishment, clothing, & all other sustenance of the same Philippa, in all, duly and honourably, and her sustenance aforesaid, what is needed according to exigency of her condition; of this, moreover, my testament, I make, ordain, and appoint John Gamelyngey, vicar of the church of Chesham, John Sudbury, Grocer, and Walter Frebarn, Draper, citizens of London, my Executors, toward all & singular in my present testament contained executing, Willing that whoever of my Executors aforesaid should have and should reasonably gain for his labour according to what Office or Ordinance before any (plural) my present testament will happen to be approved, according to their good discretion, they will wish to appoint or decide; of which thing In testimony, (to) this my present testament my seal I have affixed; Given (at) London (on) the day (&) in the Year above-said.

Proved was the present testament before master J. Lyndefeld, the Commissary, etc., (on) the 3rd day of the month of November, & Granted was administration of the goods, etc., (to) the executors in the same named, & subsequently the same executors have been discharged.

CODICIL OF THE SAME JOHN

Likewise, where at my Manor of Cheshamboys in the County of Buckingham, in which diverse persons at my denomination, from assurance, are feoffees, the will of myself, the aforesaid John Wynselow, is such, to wit, firstly I will that my Executors above-said, as quickly as (it) better can be done after my death, should sell from the woods and under-woods growing in the outer part of the wood of the same manor, to the value of 100 marks of sterling, and that my said feoffees from this sale should make sufficient standing (to) that or (to) those who (singular) or who (plural) the said sale should be made when, thereupon, the debts [/what is owed] should have been required by my said Executors for the said wood & under-wood, to the value of the said sum of 100 marks, knocked over, cut down, and from there carried; And the entire provision of this sale issued and received, I bequeath, to wit, firstly (to) Agnes, the bastard daughter of John Wynselow, my son, towards her marriage 10 marks of sterling; And if the same Agnes under lawful age or unmarried will die, then I bequeath the aforesaid 10 marks to be distributed between the same (male, plural) and the same (female, plural) who (male) or who (female) are the nearest of my family, according to the good discretion of my Executors, willing that the said 10 marks should be and should remain in the keeping of my said Executors until the same Agnes will come to lawful age or will have been married; Likewise, from the money coming from the sale aforesaid, I bequeath (to) Emma, wife of the said Walter Frebarn, my kinswoman, 10 marks; Likewise, (to) Thomas Legeard of Anleby in the County of York, & (to) his children, 10 marks of sterling; Likewise, (to) John, son of Peter Legeard, if he will be alive after me, 40 shillings; The Residue, truly, of all the aforesaid money coming from the sale aforesaid, I bequeath towards paying all & singular debts which, any whatever, by law I am held or owe, and towards the doing, disposing, & distributing by my Executors aforesaid for my soul & the souls of my peoples, and all (by) whom I am supported, & all the faithful departed, in works of mercy among poor men, & especially between them who are of my family, just as my aforesaid Executors by their good discretion will consider better to give pleasure (to) god & to give profit (to) the salvation of my soul; Likewise, I will that my said feoffees make standing (to) the said Philippa, my wife, of & in the entire aforesaid Manor, with its appurtenances, to have and to hold (to) the aforesaid Philippa for her entire life, to remain thereupon after her decease (to) the said John Wynselow, my son, and (to) the heirs of his body lawfully begotten, and for defect of lawful issue or heir of his body begotten, to be returned and to remain thereupon (to) my feoffees, or (to) others whom the same and my Executors will wish to name (to) that purpose, towards the sale thereupon made, & the money thereupon issuing justly & faithfully to dispose and distribute for my soul, and the other souls aforesaid, by my Executors, or the Executors of the same, in pious uses, just as the same should hope better to give pleasure (to) god & (to) the salvation of my soul to give profit, in the case that (it) will befall the aforesaid John, my son, without heirs of his body lawfully begotten, as is before-offered, to die, provided always that after the sale, cutting down, & carrying away of the woods & under-woods aforesaid, to the value of the sum aforesaid, as is before-offered, done, I will that my said feoffees should acquire the standing of all the Manor aforesaid, with appurtenances, (in) manner & form by me before-appointed (regarding) the profits, truly, of the entire Manor aforesaid, with appurtenances, (to) the said Philippa, my wife, (in) the mean time reserved; Proved was the present testament & codicil before Master John Lyndefeld, the Commissary, etc., (on) the 3rd day of the month of November (in) the Year of (our) Lord above-said, (to) John Gamelyngey and Walter Frebarn, the Executors, etc., (with) power Reserved, etc., & they have the discharge (in writing), etc.

Edward Winslow's English Origins

6.2   Chronology

Year	Individual	Suffix	Activity	Source
1278-9	Winslow, William	*Patriarch*	Fee in Swanbourne to Godard's heir, later married to William Winslow Patriarch	VCH Hist Bucks
1284-6	Winslow, William de	*Patriarch*	Godard Fee in Swanbourne held by Willelmus de Wineslowe, Thomas de Walda	Feudal Aids
1296	Beaufeu, Richard		Bella Fago family in Seyton near Barrowden, home of Beauchamps and Richard W 1296	LaySub
1296	Winslow, Richard	*Barrowden*	Barrowden, Rutland, Richard Winslow taxed on Barrowden property	LaySub
1302-3	Winslow, William de	*Patriarch*	Willelmus de Winslawe, jury duty for 6, Honour of Berkhamsted	Feudal Aids
1302-3	Winslow, William de	*Patriarch*	Fee in Swanbourne	Feudal Aids
1313	Winslow, William	*Patriarch*	Property transaction for Doygnel, W. Tockenham, Wilts, 1313	FF Wilts
1322	Winslow, Walter	*Muster*	Walter de Wynslaive ex Buckinghamshire muster at Newcastle	Holton
1325	Baldwin, John	*Baldwyn*	Baldwin, John Baldewyne, Essex Funding 1325	CCR
1326-35	Winslow, Bro Will	*Cellarer*	Brother William de Wynslowe Coquinarius fined	Gesta
1326-35	Beaufeu, John		Beaufeu, John Beaufitz Taxed By Abbot re Redbourne, 1326-35	Gesta
1327	Winslow, Geoffrey	*Galfrid*	Geoffrey de Wynselowe, son of William & Alice W moves dwelling New Winslow	WMCB
1329	Winslow, Walter	*Muster*	Walter de Wynselawe of Swanbourne witness March 20	CCR
1332	Winslow, Richard	*Handmills*	Richard de Wynslowe re handmills in St. Albans	Gesta
1332	Baldwin, John		John Baldewyne, eviction attempt as coroner, January	CCR
1332	Baldwin, John		John Baldewyne, chaplain £20 loan, January	CCR
1332	Baldwin, John		John Baldewyne, rejection of St. Albans Liberties, April 1332	CCR
1332	Baldwin, John		John Baldewyne, rejection as coroner, July, insufficiently qualified	CCR
1332	Winslow, William	*Wodyam*	William de Wynselowe, *Bernaston*, Barston 2/7d, (Barlichway Hundred), Warks 1332	Warks Lay Subsidy
1332	Grigge, John		Grigge, John of Hempstead, father of Egidia aged 9, Dec 1332	IpM
1334	Baldwin, John		Order for Judgment re St. Albans Handmills	CCR

Edward Winslow's English Origins

Year	Individual	Suffix	Activity	Source
1337	Winslow, John	Wynslou	John Wynslou, Ireland, Tipperary	Inq PM
1340	Winslow, John	Bailiff	Legal enforcer houses of Benedictine monks	Monks
1340-44	Winslow, Bro Will	Cellarer	Brother William of Wynselow is St Albans Cellarer, Winslow Manor	WMCB
1340	Winslow, John	Bailiff	John Wynselowe & Andrew Mentemore re apostate monk, 1340	RP
1334	Winslow, Walter	Muster	Walter de Wynselowe, Rev., honoured, Sussex, Cleric, 1334	Stratford
1345	Winslow, Walter	Muster	ix Kal. Jun. (24 May). 1345. Resignation of Sir Walter de Wynselowe	Stratford
1346	Winslow, Walter	Muster	Waltero de Wynselowe, Swanbourne property previously of William de Winslow	Feudal Aids
1346	Winslow, Walter	Muster	Walter Wynselowe dies May 1346, son William is heir	WMCB
1346	Winslow, William	Wodyam	William Wynselowe, heir of Walter of Wynselowe fealty 1346	WMCB
1347	Winslow, John	Bailiff	John de Wyneslowe, bailiff of St. Albans, May 1347-1348	Deeds
1349	De la Mare, Abbot		Thomas de le Mare Abbot of St. Albans, 1349-96, elected April 1349	Gesta
1350	Winslow, William	Wodyam	William & Alice Wynselowe both dead, Thomas inherits May 24	WMCB
1350	Winslow, Thomas	Homicide	William & Alice Wynselowe both dead, Thomas inherits May 24	WMCB
1351	Winslow, Thomas	Homicide	Winslow, Thomas de Wynselowe of Swanbourn, May 1351, Black Princes Register	BPR
1351	Wyneslegh, Roger de		Apostate monk of Evesham, not a Winslow.	VCH?
1352	Winslow, John	Maunciple	Transfer of John le Irmonger's Horwood property to John de Wynselowe, January 1352	WMCB
1352	Winslow, John	Bailiff	John Wynselowe Bailiff of St. Albans, witness re Sopwell Lane St. Albans, Feb 1352	Deeds
1352	Winslow, John	Bailiff	John Wynselowe, "then" Bailiff of St. Albans, witness re Sopwell Lane St. Albans, Sept 1352	Deeds
1352	Winslow, John	Bailiff	Winslow, John Wynselowe, alienate land to the abbot, 1352	Nat Arch
1352	Winslow, John	Bailiff	John Wyncelowe of St. Albans & Andrew Mentemore, St Albans property, Dec 9	RP
1352	Winslow, Thomas	Homicide	Thomas Winslow Swanbourne family estate to Thomas Williams, 1352	CR
1353	Winslow, John	Bailiff	John de Wyncelowe of Honesdon, De Bohun funding, 20 marks, January	CR
1353	Winslow, John	Maunciple	John de Wynselowe placed in Thomas Atte Dode's tithing, Horwood May 1353	WMCB

Edward Winslow's English Origins

Year	Individual	Suffix	Activity	Source
1353	Winslow, John	Bailiff	John Wynselowe and Thomas Morteyn, their bailiffs re saddlers, July	Cal Letter Books
1353	Winslow, John, John	Maunciple	John Wynselowe Maunciple, demised land to brother John; amerced 6d, December	WMCB
1353	Winslow, John	Hunsdon	John Wynselowe Maunciple, demised land to brother John; amerced 6d, December	WMCB
1354	Winslow, John	Maunciple	John Wynselowe (6d), committed default, amerced May 20	WMCB
1355	Winslow, John	Maunciple	John Wynselowe (3d), amerced, January	WMCB
1355	Winslow, John	Maunciple	John Wynselowe (3d), amerced, June	WMCB
1355	Winslow, John	Maunciple	John Wynselowe (3d), amerced, October	WMCB
1356	Winslow, John	Maunciple	John Wynselowe, amerced 6p, May Horwood	WMCB
1356	Beaufeu, John		John Beaufitz (3d), amerced, Horwood, May	WMCB
1356	Beaufeu, John		John Beaufitz Horwood acquires 2 acres, May	WMCB
1356	Winslow, John	Maunciple	John Wynselowe default twice, John Beaufiz once	WMCB
1356	Winslow, John	Maunciple	John Wynselowe (3d), amerced, November	WMCB
1356	Winslow, John	Maunciple	John Wynslowe £20 fine per 1340 County of Hertford re Blakettes	Gesta
1357	Winslow, John	Maunciple	John Wynselowe surrenders the Horwood property, May, heriot 10s.	WMCB
1360	Winslow, Thomas	Homicide	Pardon to Thomas de Hundesden alias Wynselowe apprentice of John Turk, July	RP
1365	Winslow, John	Hostytter	John Wynselowe, hostytter & wife Alice executrix, evidence against them	RP
1365	Winslow, John	Hostytter	John Wynselowe, hostytter & wife Alice executrix, gaoled	RP
1366	Winslow, John	Maunciple	John Wyncelowe of Hunsdon, ship 400 Q of wheat, "make his profit"	RP
1368	Winslow, Walter	Kimpton	Walter Wynselowe and Emma, his wife, deforciants, Luton & Kimpton	FF Herts
1369	Beauchamp, Thomas		Sir Thomas "11th Earl of Warwick, Marshal of England" de Beauchamp KG, will 1369	
1369	Beauchamp, Thomas		Thomas Beauchamp Earl of Warwick. Presented to Earls Croome 1369	BHO
1370	Winslow, William	Candlewick	William de Wyncelowe, citizen & tailor of London, wife Joan his wife, property deal 1370	FF Essex
1371	Winslow, William	Candlewick	William de Wyncelowe, citizen & tailor of London, wife Joan his wife, property deal 1371	FF Essex

Edward Winslow's English Origins

Year	Individual	Suffix	Activity	Source
1371	Winslow, William	Candlewick	William Winslow, citizen and tailor of London, Creditor Jul 25	N. R. A.
1372	Winslow, William	Candlewick	William de Wyncelowe, citizen & tailor of London, wife Joan his wife, property deal 1372	FF Essex
1373	Winslow, John	Maunciple	John Winslow {Wyncelowe}, citizen and pepperer of London, Creditor, October	N. R. A.
1374	Winslow, William	Candlewick	William Wynselowe, citizen & merchant tailor and wife Joan, St Katherine's June	RP
1374	Winslow, Bro Will	Cellarer	William of Winslow elected Prior of Beaulieu 1374	Benedictine
1374	Winslow, John	Maunciple	Not named in Cordwainer St. donors' list November	Letter Books
1375	Winslow, John	Maunciple	Marriage of Mariota and John Wynselowe	RP
1375	Winslow, John, John	Maunciple	John Wyneslowe of Honysdon elder quitclaim to younger brother John Wynselowe, October, Hunsdon	CR
1375	Winslow, John, John	Maunciple	Quitclaim by John W, property sometime of his father John Wynselowe, October, Hunsdon	CR
1375	Winslow, Thomas	Homicide	Thomas Winslow of Hunsdon [Herts] £20 debt December	N. R. A.
1375	Winslow, Richard	Clacton	Richard Wynslowe, vicar of Great Claketon	FF Essex
1375	Winslow, John	Bailiff	John Winslow *Bailiff* deceased by this date	RP
1376	Winslow, William	Candlewick	William Wynselowe, City of London, Mainprise Garton's Somerset property, September	FR
1376	Winslow, William	Candlewick	William Wyndeslowe, Mainprise Garton's Soton and Kent property, September	FR
1376	Winslow, William	Candlewick	William Wynselowe, St Katherine's, Sherborne Lane property, September	RP
1377	Winslow, William	Candlewick	Winslow, William Wenselowe, of City of London re Whitley Surrey, December	FR
1377	Poure, Agnes		Year of birth of Agnes Poure	
1378	Winslow, William	Candlewick	William de Wynslowe, house in Candelwyk Strete London, February	CR
1380	Winslow		1½ acre of 'Wynseloweslonde' in 'Chirchefeld', Acton, Middx, W London, February	CR
1381	Winslow, William	Pavilioner	Grant of Mildenhale land to William Wynselowe, March	RP
1382	Winslow, William	Pavilioner	Grant of Stondon Park to William Wynselowe February, Standon near Hunsdon	RP
1382	Winslow, William	Pavilioner	Grant of Kayo to William Wynselowe May	RP

Edward Winslow's English Origins

Year	Individual	Suffix	Activity	Source
1382	Winslow, William	Pavilioner	Grant of Standon Park, update to William Wynselowe September	RP
1382	Winslow, William	Pavilioner	Mewes to William Wynselowe September	RP
1383	Winslow, John	Maunciple	Legal challenge re fitness of justices on bench in Cambs	N. R. A.
1383	Winslow, John	Maunciple	Legal challenge re fitness of justices on bench in Cambridge, December	N. R. A.
1383	Winslow, John	Hunsdon	John Wynselowe with Sir Robert Turk & Thomas W, witness Hunsdon 1383	CR
1383	Winslow, Thomas	Homicide	John Wynselowe Younger with Sir Robert Turk & Thomas W, witness Hunsdon 1383	CR
1384	Winslow, William	Pavilioner	William Wynslowe, re Mildenhale incl. Tresilian February	CR
1384	Winslow, John	Maunciple	John Wyncelowe Cordwainer ward re mayoral election Nicholas Brembre, undated	Cal
1384	Winslow, John	Maunciple	John Wynslowe of London, mainprise for Edmund Fraunceys of London June	CR
1384	Winslow, John	Maunciple	John Wyncelowe, Cordwaner Stret, re Mayor Brembre, July	Cal. Letter
1384	Winslow, John	Maunciple	John Wyncelowe Cordwainer Street: Common Council, October	Cal. Plea
1384	Winslow, John	Maunciple	John Wyncelowe, Debtor re Harlow £100, Oct 1384 October, 3 sources	CR etc.
1385	Winslow, John	Maunciple	John Wynslowe of London & Culham, recognisance re £400 loan January	CR
1385	Winslow, John	Maunciple	Crochemans estate Hempstead etc. to Wynselowes, undated	FF Essex
1385	Winslow, William	Pavilioner	William Wyncelowe re Mildenhale, Feb 4	RP
1385	Winslow, William	Pavilioner	William Wyncelowe cedes Mildenhale, Feb 24	RP
1385	Winslow, William	Pavilioner	William Wyncelowe, St John Colchester gift March	CR
1385	Winslow, John	Maunciple	Citizen and grocer of London, Debtor June, Chancery: Extents for Debts, Series I June	Nat Arch
1385-90	Winslow, John	Maunciple	Multiple property transactions in Cambs	FF Camb
1386	Winslow, John	Maunciple	John Wynselowe of London, mainpernor with Fraunceys, £170, February	CR
1386	Winslow, William	Candlewick	William Winslow, citizen and tailor of London, Creditor: £278, February	Nat Arch
1386	Winslow, William	Pavilioner	William Wyncelowe, yeomen chamber, Chilternelange parker, April	RP
1386	Winslow, John	Maunciple	John Wyncelowe citizen and pepperer of London, debtor £100, May, not actioned	Nat Arch

Year	Individual	Suffix	Activity	Source
1386	Winslow, John	*Maunciple*	Ref to John Wynselowe "of Norffolk" re £500 mainprise re Carthusians, July	CR
1386	Winslow, William	*Pavilioner*	William Wyncelowe Accepts Post of Parker Of Chilterne Langele with a swap, August	RP
1386	Winslow, William	*Pavilioner*	William Wyncelowe, yeoman chamber, king's stannary, Cornwall, December	RP
1387	Winslow, John	*Maunciple*	John Wynselowe, Newnham property, Cambridge, April	CCCC
1387	Winslow, William	*Pavilioner*	William Wyncelowe accepts post of parker of Chilterne Langele swap, April	RP
1387	Winslow, John	*Maunciple*	John Wynslowe is to be again sought and imprisoned (for £400 debt), July	Nat Arch
1387	Winslow, John	*Maunciple*	John Wynslowe is to be again sought and imprisoned (for £400 debt), August	Nat Arch
1387	Winslow, William	*Pavilioner*	William Wyncelowe payment for post of parker of Chilterne Langele park, October	CR
1387	Winslow, William	*Pavilioner*	William Wynslawe to receive 10 marks a year from Preston estate, Sussex, October	RP
1387	Winslow, John	*Maunciple*	John Wynslowe £400 debt, John Walcote to hold property until recovery, November	Nat Arch
1388	Winslow, William	*Pavilioner*	William Wynslawe, Preston Sussex benefit, case heard in Cambridge, September	CR
1387	Winslow, William	*Armiger*	William Wynselow, son of John & Mary born Cranworth, Norfolk, November 1387 (or 1388)	Inq pm
1389	Winslow, William	*Pavilioner*	William Wyncelowe king's yeoman Pershore Abbey, Worcester, August	CR
1389	Winslow, William	*Pavilioner*	William Wyncelowe and post of parker of Chilterne Langele park again October	RP
1390	Winslow, William	*Pavilioner*	William Wyncelowe, Chilternlangley, January	RP
1390	Winslow, William	*Pavilioner*	Winslow, William Wyncelowe, Chilternlangley back pay, October	CR
1390	Winslow, William	*Pavilioner*	William Wenselawe, woodwardships Dyntheleyne & Iscorvay, co. Carnarvon, November	RP
1391	Winslow, William	*Pavilioner*	William W takes Sandford Ferry, surrenders Chilternlangley, January	RP
1391	Winslow, William	*Pavilioner*	William Wyncelowe, YoC, former under-parker of Chilternelangley park, May	RP
1391	Winslow, William	*Pavilioner*	William Wynselowe, takes Sandford fair, July	RP
1391	Winslow, William	*Pavilioner*	William Wynselowe cedes Chilternlangley, July	RP

Edward Winslow's English Origins

Year	Individual	Suffix	Activity	Source
1392	Winslow, John	*Chesham*	John Winslow with wife Philippa, Chesham Bois post 1365, son John, d. 1423	Bucks
1392	Winslow, John	*Maunciple*	John Wynselowe, pardon for non-appearance re £140 debt, London, June	RP
1392	Winslow, John	*Maunciple*	John Wynselowe, witness in Hempstead September3	Private MS
1392	Winslow, John	*Chesham*	John W presented to church at Chesham Bois	Hist Bucks
1393	Winslow, John	*Maunciple*	John Wyncelowe and wife Mary, heiress of William Crocheman, inherits, January	CR
1393	Winslow, John	*Maunciple*	John Wyncelowe, trespass in Hempstead family property, Spring 1393	Coram Rege
1393	Winslow, John	*Chesham*	John Wynselowe, London citizen & draper, mainpernor, March	CR
1393	Winslow, William	*Pavilioner*	William Wyncelowe, Kings serjeant, surrenders Pershore, Worcs, June	CR
1394	Winslow, William	*Pavilioner*	William Wyncelowe, gift Evyonyth N Wales, (Eifionydd) commote, Caernarvonshire, Wales, February	RP
1394	Winslow, John	*Maunciple*	John Wynslowe, landlord Trumpington re inquest, March	Inq PM
1394	Winslow, John	*Maunciple*	Hist of Parliament confusion, 1387-94 re Maunciple	HoP
1394	Winslow, John	*Maunciple*	John Wynselowe citizen and grocer, prison and debt pardon, May	RP
1394	Winslow, William	*Pavilioner*	William Wyncelowe military service Ireland, September	RP
1394	Winslow, John	*Maunciple*	John Wynselowe of Hempstede, co. Essex, Irish Campaign with William W, September	RP
1395	Winslow, William	*Pavilioner*	William W takes office of the king's Pavilioner, May	RP
1396	Winslow, John	*Maunciple*	John Wyncelowe, esq., Irish Campaign with Roger, Earl of March, January	RP
1396	Winslow, Thomas	*Saddler*	Thomas Wyncelowe, mainprise, London, 1396, August	CR
1398	Winslow, John	*Chesham*	John+ Winslow, citizen and draper of London, Creditor v John Prendergast, Kt 1398 January	CR
1396	De la Mare, Abbot		Thomas de le Mare Abbot of St. Albans, 1349-96, died 1396 September	Gesta
1396	Winslow, Bro Will	*Cellarer*	William Wynslowe Prior of Hertford, October	Gesta
1396	Winslow, William	*Pavilioner*	William Wyncelowe, King's Esquire and Pavilioner, pardon for loss of pavilions at Calais, December	RP
1396	Winslow, John	*Maunciple*	Winslow, John Wyncelowe, esquire, tarrying in England, July	RP

Edward Winslow's English Origins

Year	Individual	Suffix	Activity	Source
1397	Winslow, John	*Maunciple*	John Wyncelowe esquire £100 debt, Essex, February	CR
1397	Winslow, William	*Chaplain*	William Wynselawe chaplain, Wiltshire, June	CR
1397	Winslow, John	*Maunciple*	John Wynselowe, Esq, protection with Roger Earl of March, Lieutenant of Ireland, October	RP
1397	Winslow, William	*Pavilioner*	William Wynselowe pavilioner, and John Beaufitz, pavilions repair October	RP
1397	Beaufeu, John	*BeaufeuJ2*	William Wynselowe pavilioner, and John Beaufitz, pavilions repair, October	RP
1398	Winslow, John	*Chesham*	Winslow, John, citizen and draper of London, Creditor, January	Nat Arch
1398	Winslow, John	*Maunciple*	John Wynselowe property, Newnham, Cambridge Cokking Yard, September	CCCC
1399	Winslow, John	*Chesham*	John Wynslowe, Attorney to Richard Brevvos, Ireland, April	RP
1399	Winslow, John	*Maunciple*	John Wynslowe, of Cambridge, alias of Essex, protection to Ireland, April	RP
1399	Winslow, William	*Pavilioner*	William Wyncelowe, nominating Gaunstede and Pygot attorneys, April	RP
1399	Winslow, William	*Candlewick*	William Wynslowe, Candlewyck St. London citizen & tailor dies	Comm Lon
1399	Winslow, William	*Candlewick*	Will. Candlewyck St. connection places him with Thomas London MP, May	Comm Lon
1399	Winslow, John	*Maunciple*	John and Mary Wyneslowe, bought Wood Hall, Finchingfield, Michaelmas	Comm Pleas
1399	Winslow, John	*Maunciple*	Approximate date of death for John Winslow Maunciple, 1399-1400	
1399	Richard II		Richard II deposed Sep 29/ Oct 1	History
1399	Winslow, William	*Pavilioner*	William Wynselowe loses office of the Pavilioner, October	RP
1399	Winslow, William	*Pavilioner*	Probable year for Pavilioner's attempted suicide	
1399	Winslow, William	*Pavilioner*	William Wynselowe, Wenslawe, Wyncelowe, royal grants, November	RP
1400	Winslow, William	*Candlewick*	William Wynslowe, reference to Will, Memorials Guild Merchant Taylors, August	MT
1400	Bradmore, John		John Bradmore citizen of London to Richard Roos citizen and mercer, August	CR
1400	Winslow, Thomas	*Saddler*	Thomas Wyneslowe, London, surety for defendant, Herflete, saddler, Michaelmas	CCP
1401	Winslow, William	*Chaplain*	William Wynslawe, chaplain, creditor Wilts, January	RP
1401	Winslow, John	*Maunciple*	Moiety of one knight's fee in Hempstede held by John Wynselowe at 50s, February	CR

Edward Winslow's English Origins

Year	Individual	Suffix	Activity	Source
1401	Beauchamp, Thomas		Thomas Earl of Warwick reinstated in all possessions by Henry IV, and died 1401	BHO
1401	Winslow, Bro Will	Cellarer	William Wynslowe Prior of Hertford, AD 1401	Gesta p.480
1403	Winslow, William	Chaplain	William Wynselowe + Roger Poure Jurors Oxford February	CIPM new
1403	Winslow, William	Pavilioner	William Wyntelowe decd?? Pershore March	CR
1403	Winslow, William	Pavilioner	William Wyncelowe, Sandford Ferry tenancy extended, November	RP
1404	Winslow, John	Soton	Winslow, John Wynslawe, Inquest Bucks 1404 January	CIPM new
1404	Winslow, John	Maunciple	John and Mary Wyncelowe, deforciant, Essex property Ashdon etc., Michaelmas	Essex FF
1404	Winslow, William	Chaplain	William Wynslawe, chaplain, creditor, Wilts, February	RP
1404	Winslow, Thomas	Saddler	Thomas Wynselowe, London, of Cordwainer, surety November	CCP
1406	Winslow, John	Soton	John Wynselowe, London, mainprise, January	CR
1406	Winslow, John	Soton	John Wynselowe of London with Hemyng Leget, Escheator Essex & Herts	CR
1406	Winslow, Mary		Mary Crouchman, death of, 25 Feb. 1406, Inq PM Apr 1410	Inq PM
1406	Winslow, William	Armiger	Thomas Holgyll has taken profits since her death by king's grant [enrolment not found].	Inq PM 1410
1406	Winslow, William	Armiger	William Wyncelawe, her son by her former husband John Wyncelawe, is next heir.	Inq PM 1410
1406	Winslow, William	Chaplain	Winslow, William Wynslawe, rector of church near New Sarum, quitclaim 1406	Nat Arch
1407	Wynsle, William		William Wynsle of Herefordshire, mainpernor for debt, February	CR
1407	Winslow, Thomas	Saddler	Thomas Wyncelowe, mainpernor re "each of London Sadeler", May	CR
1407	Winslow, William	Chaplain	William Wynselowe wife Agnes aged 28+, sister of Thomas, next heir: Black Bourton etc. September	Inq PM 1407
1407	Winslow, William	Chaplain	William Wynselowe wife Agnes, seisin of Oxford and Berkshire, Chaucer Escheator, October	CR
1407	Winslow, William	Chaplain	William Wynselowe wife Agnes aged 28+, subsequent inquest, October	Inq PM 1407
1409	Winslow, William	Armiger	William Wynselow son of John & Mary of Hempstead, 21st Birthday November 1, 1409	Inq PM 1410
1409	Winslow, William	Pavilioner	William Wyncelowe, Sandford ferry rights transfer, November	RP

Edward Winslow's English Origins

Year	Individual	Suffix	Activity	Source
1410	Winslow, William	Chaplain	William Winslow, witness with John Blaket and Robert Andrews, Cricklade Wilts, February	CR
1410	Winslow, Mary		Mary Crouchman, death 1406 Feb 25 qv, Inq PM April 18	Inq PM
1410	Winslow, Mary	Armiger	William Winslow, confirmed as a Crouchman heir, April 18	Inq PM
1410	Winslow, William	Chaplain	Will. Wynslow clericus put in property possession, pay 200 marks. November	Tropenell
1410	Winslow, Mary	Mariota	Mary, Thomas Holgyll's wife, former wife of John Wyncelawe of Oxford, Dec 8	Inq PM
1410	Winslow, John	Maunciple	Mary Crocheman former wife of John Wyncelawe of Oxford, December	Inq PM
1411	Winslow, William	Armiger	William Wyncelawe proof of age, ward of Thomas Holgyll to be informed. January	Inq PM
1411	Winslow, Edmund	Kensington	Edmund Wynselowe, mainpernor Middx, July	CR
1411	Winslow, Edmund	Kensington	Winslow, Edmund Wynselowe, Juror, Wimbysshe, 1411 November	CIPM new
1411	Poure, Thomas		Poure, Thomas son and Heir of Thomas Poure, abducted, Oxford November	RP
1412	Holgyll, Thomas	Holgyll	Holgyll association with John Atte Wode, 1412	BHO
1412	Holgyll, Thomas	Holgyll	Holgyll has remarried Elizabeth by 1412	CR
1412	Bradmore, John	Pavilioner	Bradmore, death of former surgeon of Pavilioner, 1412	PhD
1412	Winslow, William	Chaplain	Winslow, William Wynselowe lands in Ramsbury, Wilts	Feudal V6
1412	Andrew, Robert	RobAndrew	Robert Andrew, sundry lands in Wilts and elsewhere, 1412	Feudal
1412	Tibbay, John de	Tibbay	John de Tibbay clerk to Queen Joan. Quitclaim Nun Eton co. Warrewyk. London, December	CR
1413	Winslow, John	Chesham	Winslow, John Wynselowe, creditor of Bruces, Bucks 1413, January	CR
1413	Winslow, Joan	Orphan	Winslow, William, birth date of Armiger's daughter Joan, June 11	Inq PM 1419
1413	Winslow, William	Chaplain	Winslow, William Wynslowe Tax Collecting for Wilts, July 13, alive	FR
1413	Winslow, William	Chaplain	William Wynslowe, messuage & shops in Salisbury, November	Tropenell
1413	Winslow, John	Chesham	John Winslow, debtor of Cornwall and Brewes, 1413-4	PRO
1414	Beaufeu, Thomas		Thomas Beaufitz, wife Katherine, property Moone Hall, Stambourne, 1414	FF Essex
1414	Winslow, William	Pavilioner	William Wyncelowe "deceased", re Meaux, February	CR

Edward Winslow's English Origins

Year	Individual	Suffix	Activity	Source
1414	Winslow, William	Pavilioner	William Wyncelowe, deceased, re-grant of ferry called Samfordhithe, March	RP
1414	Winslow, William	Pavilioner	William Wyncelowe deceased re abbot and convent of Colchestre, March	CR
1414	Winslow, William	Chaplain	William Wynselowe assumed death – no further record	none
1414	Tibbay, John	Tibbay	John Tibbay, father-in-law William Wynslowe, died 1414, probate July 28	Grey
1414	Tibbay, John	Tibbay	"died of a murderous attack" Archdeacon of Huntingdon, Chancellor of the Queen	Grey
1415	Winslow, John	Soton	John Wynslawe, clerk, to pay shipmasters & owners by indenture, April	RP
1415	Winslow, William	Armiger	William Wynslowe son of John and Mary, will July	PCC
1415	Winslow, William	Armiger	William Wynslowe son of John and Mary of Hempstead died 31 August 3 Henry V	Inq PM 1419
1415	Winslow, Richard	Clacton	William Wynslowe's will mentions Uncle Richard Winslow	Will
1416	Winslow, William	Armiger	William Wynslowe, Esq, Will mentioning London, Cambs, Essex property 1416	PCC
1416	Winslow, John	Soton	Sale of Hunsdon 1/3 property January	FF Herts
1416	Winslow, John	Soton	John Wynslawe, clerk, Southampton son of Pavilioner? May	RP
1416	Winslow, John	Soton	John Wynslowe, arrest commission Southampton 1416 July	RP
1416	Winslow, John	Soton	John Wynslawe mustering ships in Bristol and Dover, 1416 August	RP
1417	Winslow, Edmund	Kensington	Winslow, Edmund Wynslowe. Juror re Earl of Oxford, Kensington, 1417	IPM
1417	Oldcastle. John		Radwinter Landlord to William Winslow armiger, executed December	History
1418	Winslow, John	Soton	Johannis Wynslowe on campaign Rouen, Pont de L'Arche, Walter Beauchamp, 1418 June	Rymers
1418	Winslow, John	Maunciple	Homages and Services of John Wynselowe heirs re Essex property, September	FF Essex V3
1419	Winslow, John	Salop	Winslow, Joan wife John Wynslowe, property in Gloucs, Oxon, Berks, Hadley, Salop, May	Inq PM
1419	Winslow, William	Armiger	William Wynslowe died 31 Aug 1415. Daughter Joan heiress	Inq PM
1420	Winslow, Joan	Orphan	Winslow, Joan orphan and Sampford property plus maintenance, 1420 January	RP
1420	Winslow, William	Armiger	William Wyncelawe, armiger, tenant by knight service, inquest 1420, January	RP

Edward Winslow's English Origins

Year	Individual	Suffix	Activity	Source
1420	Winslow, William	Armiger	William Wyncelawe, armiger, tenant by knight service, inquest 1420, June	RP
1420	Winslow, William	Attorney	William Wynslowe of Wynslowe, Bucks, *gentilman*, failure to answer John Willicotes. July	RP
1421	Winslow, William	Armiger	William Wyncelawe, armiger, inquest re Joan succession December	RP
1422	Winslow, Thomas	Saddler	Thomas Wynselow citizen and 'sadeler' of London, debtors' prison, £40, 1422 March	CR
1422	Beauchamp, William	Powick	Died owning Powick near Pixham Ferry & opposite Kempsey	BHO
1423	Beauchamp, Richard		Manor of Elmley settles on Richard and wife Isabel Countess of Worcester	BHO
1423	Winslow, John	Chesham	John Winslow, willed Chesham Bois to wife Philippa, reversion to son John, died 1423	Hist Buck
1423	Winslow, John	Chesham	John Wynslowe or Wynselowe, Draper of London, Will 1423 November	PCC
1423	Winslow, John	Junior	John Wynslow, father of bastard daughter Agnes Wynslow, 1423 November	PCC
1424	Winslow, John	Yorks	John Wenslawe witness Yorkshire, February	Deeds
1424	Tibbay, John	Tibbay	Tibbay, John Tebeye, late rector of Wyncelogh, 1424, June	Deeds
1426	Winslow, Geoffrey	Galfrid2	Galfridus / Winslow, Geoffrey, reference to Earl's Croom, December	Fradd p. 162
1426	Winslow, Joan	Orphan	Joan Wynslowe, death 1426; inquest heard 1426 August 3	Inq PM
1426	Winslow, Joan	Orphan	Joan Wynslowe Inquest & settlement continues, 1426 October 24	FR
1426	Winslow, William	Armiger	William Wynslowe's mother in law JOAN died July 1426, Greyfriars wills, 12 July	Grey
1428	Beauchamp, Richard		Earl of Warwick admitted to Fraternity of St. Albans	Chronicon
1429	Winslow, William	Attorney	William Wynslow, witness to land transaction inc. Oxford and Berks, April	RP
1430	Winslow, John	Maunciple	John Winslow dec'd, reference former Hempstead land Feb 1430	Charter
1430	Throckmorton, John		John Throckmorton, Richard, earl of Warwick, property deals, April	Charter
1431	Andrew, Robert		Andrew criticised by Tropenell Cartulary, July	Tropenell
1432	Winslow, Agnes		Agnes Winslow, widow of William Wynslowe, Thriplow release claim, c.1432 undated	Early Chanc
1432	Winslow, Henry	KempHenry 1	Henry Winslow, acts as a Kempsey juror, October	Fradd p. 61

6.3   Bibliography

The standard abbreviations used in the footnotes are shown in the Preface, p. iii.

AUTHOR	WORK
ARNOLD, M. S.	*Select Cases of Trespass from the King's Courts 1307-99*, Selden Society, 1985
BEAUFOY, G.	*Leaves From a Beech Tree*, Basil Blackwell, Oxford, 1930
BLOMEFIELD, F.	*Collectanea Cantabrigiensa*, Norwich,1751
BRADMORE, J.	*Philomena*, British Library, MS. Sloane, 2272
BRAND, P. A.	*Origins of the English Legal Profession*. American Society for Legal History (1987), pp. 31-50.
CARTER, W. F. ED.	*Lay Subsidy roll for Warwickshire of 6 Edward III (1332)*, Dugdale Society, vol. 6, OUP, 1926
CLARK, J. W.	*Liber Memorandorum Ecclesie de Bernewelle*, CUP, 1907
CROWLEY, D. A., ED.	*Wiltshire Tax List of 1332*, Wiltshire Record Society, Trowbridge 1989
DAVIES, J. S., ED.	*Tropenell Cartulary*, 2 vols., Wiltshire Archaeological & Natural History Society, 1908
DELISLE, L. V., ED.	*Orderici Vitalis Historiae Ecclesiasticae*, ed. A. Le Prévost, Paris, 1838-55
DODD G., BIGGS D.	*The Reign of Henry IV: Rebellion and Survival, 1403-1413*, Boydell & Brewer, York Medieval Press, 2008
ESSEX AS	*Feet of Fines for Essex, Vol. 3*, Essex Archaeological Society, Colchester, 1929
FRADD, B.	*Winslow Families of Worcestershire 1400-1700*, Boston: Newbury Street Press, 2009.
FRASER, R.	*Mayflower Generation: Winslow Family and the Fight for the New World*, Rebecca Fraser, Chatto & Windus, London 2017
FREEMAN, J.	*Survey of English Place-Names, Herefordshire*, EPNS, University of Nottingham, John Freeman et al., 2017 and in progress
GILLESPIE, J. L.	*Richard II's Yeomen of the Chamber*. Albion, vol. 10, no. 4, 1978, pp. 319–329
GIVEN-WILSON, C.	*Illustrated History of Late Medieval England*, Manchester University Press, 1996.
GIVEN-WILSON, C.	*The Parliament Rolls of Medieval England, 1275-1504,* 16 vol. set, *Rotuli Parliamentorum,* Boydell Press 2005
HAGGER, M.	*Gesta Abbatum Monasterii Sancti Albani: Litigation and History at St. Albans*, Historical Research Volume 81, issue 213, 2008.
HAINES, R. M.	*Archbishop John Stratford, Political Revolutionary and Champion of the Liberties of the English Church, ca. 1275/80-1348,* Toronto Pontifical Institute of Medieval Studies, *1986*
HANAWALT, B.	*Wealth of Wives: Women, Law, and Economy in Late Medieval London*, OUP, 2007

Edward Winslow's English Origins

AUTHOR	WORK
HOLTON, D-P. & F	*Winslow Memorial: Family Records of the Winslows and their Descendants in America,* Self-published, New York, 1877
HUGHES M. W, ED.	*Calendar of the Feet of Fines for the county of Buckingham 7 Richard I to 44 Henry III,* BAS, vol. 4, 1942
KENT, WILLIAM	*Indulgences.* The Catholic Encyclopedia vol. 7, William Kent, New York, Robert Appleton Company, 1910
KINGSFORD, C. L., ED.	*History of the Grey Friars, Wills relating to Grey Friars, London: 1374-1430,* Manchester UP, 1915
LANG, S. J.	*Philomena of John Bradmore and its Middle English derivative: a perspective on surgery in late Medieval England,* PhD thesis, St. Andrews, 1998
LAPIDGE, GODDEN, KEYNES, EDS	*Anglo-Saxon England, vol. 22,* CUP, 1994
LEWIS, S., ED.	*Topographical Dictionary of England,* 4 vols. London, 1848
LIPSCOMB, J.,	*History and Antiquities of the county of Buckingham,* George Lipscomb, J. & W. Robins publ., London, 1847, 4 volumes
LYTE, H. C. MAXWELL, ETC	*Liber Fœdorum, the Book of Fees commonly called Testa de Nevill,* London, HMSO, 1920-31
MILLS, A.D.	*Dictionary of British Place Names,* OUP, 2011
MORIARTY, G. A.	*Wynslowe Family,* Miscellanea Genealogica et Heraldica, fifth series, 6, 1926-8
MORRIS, JOHN, ED.	*Domesday Book,* Essex, Phillimore, 1983
MUSSON, ANTHONY.	*Twelve Good Men and True? The Character of Early Fourteenth-Century Juries.* Anthony Musson, Law and History Review, Vol. 15, No. 1, Spring 1997 (1997), pp. 115-144.
NICHOLAS, N. H., TYRRELL, E., EDS	*Chronicle of London,* Longman, Rees, Orme, Brown and Green, 1827
NOY, DAVID	*Winslow in 1556, The Survey of the Manor,* BAS, 2013
NOY, DAVID	*Winslow Manor Court Books,* Vols. I and II, David Noy ed., Bucks Record Society, nos. 35-6, 2011
PAGE, WILLIAM, ED.	*Victoria County History of Buckingham:* Vol. 3, London, 1925
PAGE, WILLIAM, ED.	*City of St Albans: The Borough, History of County of Hertford:* vol. 2, London, 1908
PALMER, C. F. R., REV.	*Burials at the Priories of the Blackfriars,* The Antiquary, xxiv, Aug 1891, 76-79
GIVEN-WILSON, C. ETC.	*The Parliament Rolls of Medieval England, 1275-1504,* 16 vol. set, *Rotuli Parliamentorum,* Boydell Press 2005
POSTLES, D.	*Rutland Lay Subsidy, 1296/7,* David Postles, Leicester University, undated, found online

Edward Winslow's English Origins

AUTHOR	WORK
PUGH, R. B. ED.	*Abstracts of Feet of Fines relating to Wiltshire for the reigns of Edward I and Edward II,* Wiltshire Archaeological and Natural History Society, vol. 1; Devizes, 1939
RECORD COMMISSION	*Placitorum in domo capitulari Westmonasteriensi asservatorum Abbreviatio,* by command George III, 1811
RILEY, H. T. ED.	*Chronicon Rerum Gestarum in Monasterio Sancti Albani,* vol. 1, 1422-31, Longmans Green, 1870
RILEY, H. T. ED.	*Gesta Abbatum Monasterii Sancti Albani,* Thomas Walsingham and others, vols. 1-3, 1867-9
ROSKELL, J. S. ED.	*History of Parliament, 1386-1421,* 4 volumes, also available online
ROSKELL, J. S. ED.	*Three Wiltshire Speakers,* Wiltshire Archaeological & Natural History Magazine, Jun/Dec 1956, lvi. 342-58.
RYE, W	*Fines Relating to the County of Cambridgeshire,* CAS, 1891
RYMER, T.	*Rymer's Foedera,* 16 Volumes, Vol. 8, London, A. &J. Churchill, 1709
STAMP, A.E., ED.	*Register of Edward the Black Prince Pt. 4* England 1351-65, London, HMSO, 1932
STYLES, P. ED.	*History of the County of Warwick,* vol. 4, London, 1945
SUMPTION, J.	*Hundred Years War,* vols. 1-4, Faber and Faber, London, 1990 and ongoing
TOMKINS, S.	*Journey to the Mayflower,* Pegasus Books, New York, 2020
TRAVERS, A. ED.	*Buckinghamshire Feet of Fines 1259-1307,* Buckinghamshire Record Society, number 25; 1989
THOMAS A. H., ED.	*Calendar of the Plea and Memoranda Rolls of the City of London,* vol. 2, 1364-1381, London, 1929
WARD, J. C.	*Medieval Essex Community, The Lay Subsidy of 1327,* Essex Record Office Publication No. 88, 1983
WILLIAMS, G.	*Medieval London, From Commune to Capital,* London, Athlone Press, 1963.
WILLIAMS, R.	*History of the Abbey of St. Alban,* Rushbrook Williams, Longmans Green, London 1917,
WRIGHT, A P M, ED.	*Victoria County History,* Cambridge and the Isle of Ely: Vol. 8, ed. London, 1982
WRIGHT, THOMAS	*History and Topography of the County of Essex,* Geo. Virtue, 2 Vols., London 1831

6.4   The Winslows in Medieval London

This map of medieval London clearly shows Bow Church (5) located in Cordwainer Ward where John Winslow *Maunciple* resided. Watling Street, a Roman Road forming one of England's arterial highways, passes through Cordwainer from which it runs direct to St. Albans. After St Albans, Watling Street continues onward to Fenny Stratford, located only two miles away from the village of Winslow in Buckinghamshire (see top right of figure 2.2, page 41 above). The Winslows were ideally located for easy access to the medieval City.

Candlewick Street, home of William Winslow *Candlewick,* merged into Watling Street close to the Church of St. Swithin (18). The location of William's property development at the hospital of St. Katherine's Hospital appears in the bottom right corner below.

Kenelm Winslow was married in St Brides Church (2), shown located off Fleet Street on the left.

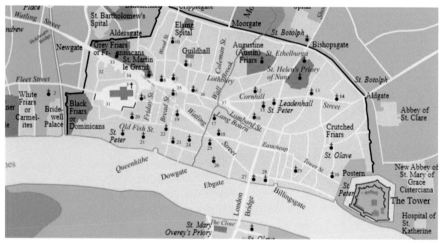

1 Temple Church	9 St. Michael le Querne	17 St. Stephen	25 St. Mary Bothaw	32 Old Deans Lane
2 St. Bride	10 St. Alban	18 St. Swithin	26 All Hallows	33 Warwick Lane
3 St. Pauls Cross	11 St. Lawrence	19 St. Mary Aldermary	27 St. Magnus	34 Meat Market
4 St. Augustine	12 St. Martin Outwich	20 St. Mary Magdalene	28 St. Botolph	35 Corn Market
5 Bow Church	13 St. Andrew	21 St. Mary Somerset	29 St. Dunstan	36 Cheap
6 St. Thomas of Acon	14 St. Katherine Cree	22 Holy Trinity the less	30 All Hallows	37 Poultry
7 St. Mary Magdalene	15 St. Michael	23 St. James	31 St. Paul's Bakehouse	38 Stocks Market
8 St. Peter	16 St. Edmund the King	24 St. Michael Paternoster		

Edward Winslow's English Origins

7   INDEX

Edward Winslow's English Origins

Edward Winslow's English Origins

Edward Winslow's English Origins

Edward Winslow's English Origins

Edward Winslow's English Origins

About the Author

Liam Donnelly has spent more than fifteen years working on the Winslows. His interest in the family was stimulated by living close by the original Winslow Hall where John Winslow *Maunciple* and Mariota Crouchman had set up home together in Hempstead in 1375.

The initial aim had been to uncover some background information about several local families, but the focus instead turned to the Winslows when it became apparent that much of their documented historical record contains so many anomalies. What started as a small project intended to last perhaps an evening or two grew into something bigger, a reflection of the family's remarkable story.

In his professional life Liam works internationally as a management consultant. He studied Classics and Theology at University and later qualified as an Accountant with Price Waterhouse in London. A lifelong interest in medieval history continues; and he has served as Treasurer of Cambridge Antiquarian Society, and because of the continuing Winslow research remains a member of Buckinghamshire Archaeological Society. Currently he is working for one of the UK's leading academic institutions.

Liam is always happy to help with any aspect of the Winslow project and can be contacted at:

winslowgov@icloud.com

Wincelow Hall, May 2022